POLITICAL TERRORISM

POLITICAL TERRORISM

Theory, tactics, and counter-measures

GRANT WARDLAW

Research Criminologist
Australian Institute of Criminology

CAMBRIDGE UNIVERSITY PRESS

Cambridge
London   New York   New Rochelle
Melbourne   Sydney

Published by the Press Syndicate of the University of Cambridge
The Pitt Building, Trumpington Street, Cambridge CB2 1RP
32 East 57th Street, New York, NY 10022, USA
296 Beaconsfield Parade, Middle Park, Melbourne 3206, Australia

First published 1982

Printed in Great Britain at the University Press, Cambridge

Library of Congress catalogue card number: 82-9431

British Library Cataloguing in Publication Data
Wardlaw, Grant
Political terrorism.
1. Terrorism
I. Title
322.4'2   HV6431
ISBN 0 521 25032 3 hard covers
ISBN 0 521 27147 9 paperback

BO

For Carole

Contents

Preface

In the past decade terrorism has become a household word, a spectacle played out before a worldwide audience as violent images are beamed into our homes by the mass media. But the advent of the 'terrorist phenomenon' has obscured both the real nature and the degree of threat of this form of political violence. An important factor is that we have lost sight of the historical continuity of terrorism. This defect of long-term analysis makes contemporary terrorism seem a particularly novel and dangerous threat. While it may be argued, as it will be in this book, that contemporary terrorism does indeed possess attributes which set it apart from its historical forebears the lack of appreciation of its continuity increases the probability of over-reaction.

Since some of the potential responses to terrorism pose an equal, if not a greater, threat to democratic freedoms than does terrorism itself, it is important that scholars and analysts in this field strive to provide a sense of perspective which can contribute to a balanced response to terrorist activity. This book has been written with the intention of providing such a balance. It is predicated on the belief that some potential forms of terrorism could pose a threat to democratic societies which would be inimical to their survival in their present form or which could contribute to a greatly destabilised political milieu in which danger and uncertainty (with their corresponding political and psychological costs) would come to characterise world affairs to a greater extent than is already the case.

Equally, however, it is stressed that we need to be able to evaluate the quality of the threat more accurately. Most forms of potential terrorism and all types to date pose no significant threat to the *existence* of democratic states. (They do, of course, endanger individual life and property, but they do not intrinsically undermine the state itself). However, in the long run, unnecessarily harsh counter-terrorist measures could pose a greater danger to democratic freedoms and institutions than does terrorism itself. To avoid this danger we need informed debate at many levels on certain policy issues relating to terrorism.

It is here that the serious student of terrorism must confront a potentially debilitating conundrum. On the one hand public debate requires issues to be opened out and sufficient information made available to allow informed discourse. On the other hand those in the security forces will argue that issues associated with terrorism should be closely guarded secrets, particularly those issues touching upon anti-terrorist operational methods and the detail of anti-terrorist policy. Sometimes these objections to open discussion are well founded and sometimes they merely reflect a siege mentality and the often self-perpetuating obsession with secrecy which characterises most law enforcement, security, and intelligence agencies. However, there have been a number of well-documented instances in which terrorists have changed specific details of their operations because of information published about previous tactics and the responses to them. The danger of providing this sort of assistance to terrorists emphasises the necessity of exercising restraint over the type of detailed information that is included in discussions on terrorism.

The policy adopted in this book has two aspects. Because of the dangers of over-reaction to terrorism – particularly the consequences for the sort of society in which we live which could be unnecessarily and adversely changed by some anti-terrorist measures – some major issues of counter-terrorist policy need informed public debate *in terms of general principles*. Balanced against this consideration is the need not to compromise legitimate and necessary counter-terrorist operations or preparations or to provide details of past actions and counter-measures which could be put to use by those planning a terrorist act. In this book no information on terrorist operations or counter-tactics will be divulged unless they have already been the subject of widespread reporting. Even then such references will be kept to a minimum.

The aim of this work is to outline the important considerations of policy which confront a democratic state in trying to combat terrorism and at the same time remain democratic. Before such an analysis can be undertaken it is necessary to gain a fundamental understanding of the nature of terrorism. Part One of the book attempts to provide the reader with a comprehensive introduction to the definition, history, theory, operation, and effects of terrorism as an essential background to policy analysis.

As Part One argues, the question of the definition of terrorism is central to an understanding of the phenomenon and to the success of any coherent and coordinated measures directed against it. To many, almost any act of violence may be included under the rubric of terrorism. On the other hand, others would not label as terrorism violent acts carried out within a revolutionary context which many would recognise as terroristic. The picture is further confused by a seeming similarity of behaviour when a violent act is carried out by a politically motivated individual, a criminal, or the mentally unbalanced. Is a member of the Black September organisation to be equated with a person who explodes bombs in a commercial location as part of an extortion attempt, or a deranged murderer or rapist who stalks terrified women on dark city streets? The behaviour of each surely contains significant elements of terror but does it contribute to understanding or the design of countermeasures to treat them all as instances of something called 'terrorism'? This book will argue that they can and should be treated as instances of quite separate phenomena. To include the activities of the criminal and the insane within the category of terrorism is to fail to distinguish some peculiar characteristics and consequences of politically motivated acts of terror and violence. Apart from any other consequences, lumping all of these types of terror-inducing acts together as 'terrorism' has the consequence of exaggerating the threat posed to society by those who espouse political violence and increasing the public perception of terror. Both reactions could well trigger a slide towards repression which is both unnecessary and potentially fatal to the type of society it is intended to preserve. Although it is never going to be possible to arrive at a definition of terrorism which suits all people it is nevertheless essential to attempt approximations which at least make policy makers think about and justify reactions to presumed acts of terrorism. Part One of the present work seeks to attempt such a definition and to place political terrorism into its historical, philosophical, and social context.

Part Two begins by outlining basic policy issues which should be the subject of public debate. Subsequent chapters address such topics as the role of intelligence agencies in counter-terrorist operations, relations between the police and the defence forces, the development of anti-terrorist legislation and international treaties, and the way in which media reporting of terrorist acts might be regulated. A chapter is devoted to a brief analysis of hostage incidents, since this form of terrorism exemplifies many of the policy issues facing the authorities. Another chapter assesses the way in which behavioural science research may feed into counter-terrorist operations and policy. Finally, a short assessment is made of likely developments in terrorist activity and the responses to it. It is hoped that this method of proceeding may contribute to informed and rational discussion on an issue of increasing salience which may eventually be vital to the continuation of a democratic form of government.

It is important also to point out what this book is *not* about. A number of interesting areas are not discussed because they are not as central as others to a work which essentially is devoted to analysis of policy options. The two most obvious omissions are analyses of the terrorist 'personality' and of the ethics of terrorism. The latter subject would be more at home in a work on the ethics of various strategies for political change. As far as counter-terrorist policy is concerned, it is presumed that political terrorists have solved for themselves the problem of whether or not their tactics are ethical and the only advantage to the authorities in exploiting the ethical issue is in persuading their citizens that terrorism is not a legitimate tactic even if, in some cases, the cause in which it is used may be a legitimate one.

As far as the terrorist 'personality' is concerned, we simply do not have sufficient empirical evidence of what makes an individual become a terrorist to make a useful contribution to counter-terrorist policy-making (although such information will eventually be necessary for any comprehensive general theory of terrorism). Some categorisations at the most general level (such as dividing those who employ terroristic-type tactics into political, ethnic, or religious crusaders, criminals, and the mentally disturbed) have some value in deciding how to handle a particular incident. But this book is concerned with only the first group and we cannot yet make enough distinctions between individual terrorist personalities within this group to offer useful guidance to policy-makers.

One final point should be borne in mind by the reader. It is that much of the discussion of policy issues may appear to be inconclusive in that often, no clear prescriptions emerge which could be immediately actioned by the authorities. This is partly deliberate and partly a consequence of the subject matter itself. It is deliberate insofar as the author has attempted to lay out the issues for debate without necessarily going into the detail of the operational consequences of certain policy decisions. For obvious reasons such detail should not be published. But more important, the way in which a particular policy will evolve would depend greatly on individual (often emergent) circumstances which cannot be usefully discussed in detail without making a number of assumptions and constructing alternative scenarios. The object of the present work is not to present such scenarios and the policies which may flow from them but rather to sketch the parameters which should determine the policy formation. However, it will be apparent throughout the discussion that the author is dedicated to analysing terrorism in such a way that the dangers of either over- or under-reaction to the threat are avoided. It is suggested that many discussions of terrorism do not avoid these pitfalls. Some argue that because of the relatively few people who are actually killed or injured by terrorist attacks they pose no significant threat to society. Others, particularly those who fear the occurrence of nuclear terrorism, contend that severe measures need to be instituted now in order to avoid or minimise calamitous effects which may destroy democratic forms of government. The thrust of the arguments presented in this book is informed by the opinion that neither of these extremes is the most functional response for a democratic society. It is argued that some form of middle course should be adopted which copes squarely with terrorism but does not undermine democratic traditions. The actual course to choose is very difficult to chart and subject to quite severe differences of opinion. Again, the object of this work is not to chart a specific course but to suggest the factors which need to be considered in doing so. The discussion is thus a stimulus to further investigation and debate rather than a prescription for policy (although a number of specific suggestions are indeed made by way of illustration). By so doing it is hoped that a need for analysis of policy issues concerned with terrorism will be met which is not usually addressed by current texts on terrorism.

This study owes much to the contributions of a large number of individuals and organisations. The Director and Board of Management of the Australian Institute of Criminology approved and supported this project and I express my gratitude to them. The analysis contained in the following pages benefited greatly from my discussions with academic colleagues and personnel in operational agencies. In particular I would like to thank the following people who critically commented on various drafts of the manuscript: Mr D. Biles, Dr J. Braithwaite, Chief Superintendent I. Broomby, Mr W. Clifford, Lt. Col. B. Dyer, Lt. Col. M. Eley, Chief Superintendent J. Fletcher, Dr P. Grabosky, Brigadier P.M. Jeffery, and Mr B. Swanton. I am particularly indebted to my wife Carole with whom many discussions have clarified much of my thought on terrorism. The section on the definition of terrorism in particular benefited from her insights. Needless to say, however, the opinions expressed are my own and do not reflect the official views of the agencies which the above individuals represent.

The transformation of my scribblings into a respectable manuscript was due to the excellent work of Janina Bunc, Evelyn Jacobsen and Marjorie Johnson and I extend my thanks to them.

GRANT WARDLAW
Canberra
November 1981

PART ONE

An introduction to political terrorism

1

The problem of defining terrorism

Groups with little or no direct political power have demonstrated repeatedly in recent years that by employing certain tactics, central to which is the use of directed terror, they can achieve effects on a target community which are out of all proportion to their numerical or political power. Such tactics attract worldwide publicity, create widespread panic or apprehension and cause national governments to concede to the demands of small subgroups within society. These effects in themselves create a demand for an understanding of the use of terror for political ends. In attempting such an undertaking it is desirable first to ascertain the substance of the threat – to separate the reality from the media image, to ascertain whether current terrorism is an outgrowth of past uses of terror or a unique phenomenon generated by new political forces. In addition to understanding its genesis and contemporary motivation there is a need to assess whether new developments such as transportation, communication, and weaponry give the use of terror more leverage than past forms of terror and therefore result in a greater threat than in the past.

The first analytical task facing commentators on terror is to define their subject matter. Because terrorism engenders such extreme emotions, partly as a reaction to the horrors associated with it and partly because of its ideological context, the search for a definition which is both precise enough to provide a meaningful analytical device yet general enough to obtain agreement from all participants in the debate is fraught with difficulty. Because of these problems, many analysts have tried to shrug them off with an obligatory reference to that famous phrase 'one man's terrorist is another man's freedom fighter'. This phrase, trite though it may be, does encapsulate the difficulties facing those who wish to delimit the boundaries of terrorism either for purposes of international action or academic research. Reference to it should not, though, persuade the reader of the futility of searching for the holy grail of a working definition of terrorism. Without a basic definition it is not possible to say whether the phenomenon we call terrorism is a threat at all, whether it is a phenomenon of a different nature to its predecessors, and whether there can be a theory of terrorism.

The definition of terrorism as a moral problem

A major stumbling block to the serious study of terrorism is that, at base, terrorism is a moral problem. This is one of the major reasons for the difficulty over the definition of terrorism. Attempts at definition often are predicated on the assumption that some classes of political violence are justifiable whereas others are not. Many would label the latter as terrorism whilst being loathe to condemn the former with a term that is usually used as an epithet. For a definition to be universally accepted it must transcend behavioural description to include individual motivation, social milieu, and political purpose. The same behaviour will or will not be viewed as terrorism by any particular observer according to differences in these other factors. However, if a definition is to be of use to a wider audience than the individual who constructs it, students of violence will have to try and divest themselves of the traditional ways of definition. Just as an increasing number of commentators seem to be able to even-handedly apply the term 'terrorist' to non-state and state actors they will have to apply it even-handedly to those groups with whose cause they agree and those with whose cause they conflict. The difficulty is that different groups of users of definitions find it more or less easy to utilise definitions which focus on behaviours and their effects as opposed to these factors tempered by considerations of motives and politics. Thus many academic students of terrorism seem to find little difficulty in labelling an event as 'terrorist' without making a moral judgement about the act. Many politicians, law enforcement and governmental officials, and citizens find themselves unable to take such a detached view. For this reason, it may not be too difficult to construct an acceptable definition within a given reference group. The problem arises when that group attempts to engage in dialogue with others.

This communication problem is of more than academic importance. It is one of the root causes of both the vacillations in policy which characterise the responses of most individual states to terrorism and of the complete failure of the international community to launch any effective multi-lateral initiatives to combat the problem. Within a given community those who study terrorism often cannot communicate with the policy-makers and law-enforcers because the latter groups often reject the analytical techniques of the former as being of insufficient relevance to the real world. Part, at least, of this lack of relevance is seen as an inability to distinguish between 'right' and 'wrong' acts. At the international level, the political support given to sectional interests militates against a universal definition that could form the basis for international law and action. Thus, for example, the Palestine Liberation Organisation (PLO) is seen by some nations as a terrorist group having no political legitimacy and using morally unjustifiable methods of violence to achieve unacceptable ends. On the other hand, other nations view the PLO as the legitimate representatives of an oppressed people using necessary and justifiable violence (not terrorism) to achieve just and inevitable ends. The definition rests, then, on moral justification. But, in fact, the proper study of terrorism should seek to explain a phenomenon, not justify it. And it must be realised by all that explanation does not entail justification.

The social meaning of terrorism

The slippery nature of the concept of terrorism (however it may finally be defined) is illustrated well by its selective use, particularly its selective pejorative use. Before turning to the task of constructing a working definition, it is instructive to consider how social meaning is assigned to the word 'terrorism'. One way to approach this problem is to utilise Berger and Luckman's analysis of the social construction of reality.[1] According to Berger and Luckman, social order is a totally human product and social reality is a process. People are continually making society and this society produces 'social' human beings. Accordingly, the moral meanings ascribed to people or events are situationally dependent. To those who try to view society in a disinterested manner it is obvious that change and process are characteristic of modern industrial societies. However, most people do not see society in this light because they have not been able to 'bracket' experience to arrive at this perspective. Thus Greisman notes: 'Frequently, people lend a concreteness and objectivity to social relations and institutions which, though purely conjectural in origin, become real in its consequences.'[2] Further, since powerful groups may benefit from such 'objectivity' they encourage such perceptions by the manipulation of information. Thus both institutions and roles become reified (that is, converted from the abstract to the material).

Greisman uses these concepts to analyse the way in which social meaning is assigned to terrorism. Most commentators on terrorism acknowledge the problem of value-neutrality in defining terrorism. What is described as terrorism by one group may be variously regarded as heroism, foreign policy, or justice by others. This has led a number of writers to contend that the term 'terrorism' cannot be used as a behavioural description because it will always carry the flavour of some moral judgement. However, its central place as a theme in violent struggle forces us to accord it some serious attention. Greisman argues that to make the term useful it is necessary to see how moral meanings are ascribed to terrorist acts so that we can see what variables make one act terrorist and another a mere function of foreign policy. Greisman borrows the concept of 'identification' from Kenneth Burke's *Rhetoric of Motives* to begin his analysis. Burke claimed that successful rhetorical persuasion results from creating in the observer an image of himself, which the observer can overlay with hopes of gain, be they monetary, emotional, or cosmic.[3] To the average observer *legitimacy* is the factor which draws them toward such identification. 'Legitimacy is a social product, and when it extends in a highly abstracted way to governments, these governments and these agents become reified.'[4]

While it is easier for governments than for terrorists to legitimate their activities, terrorists often strive for legitimacy. Often, though, such an endeavour is as much an attempt to legitimate their activities in their own eyes as it is to convince the public of their worthiness. In such cases the motivation for legitimation is more psychological than tactical. Nevertheless some broadly based non-government organisations employing terrorist tactics have succeeded in having a large degree of legitimacy ascribed to them. For example, the Palestine Liberation Organisation (PLO) is regarded as a legitimate government by many Palestinians – and non-Palestinians worldwide. Fletcher has described how many terrorists go about this legitimation process:

They regard themselves as the only possible remedy to the evils of the Establishment, and assert the "legality" of their actions. They solemnly claim sovereign rights for their organisations as they flaunt sovereignty's trappings and mannerisms. Thus, many call themselves soldiers, and adopt military designations for their organisations – for example, the IRA, JRA, Black Liberation Army, the Red Brigade, the Mohamed Boudia Commando, the Ulster Volunteer Forces and so on. They hold their victims in "people's prisons" and announce "trials", "sentences", and "executions" and they become a sovereign entity when they successfully force newspapers, radio, and television to publicise their manifestos and ultimatums word for word.[5]

It may be argued that this reified perception of government is one reason why terrorist acts by individuals or non-state actors and governments are ascribed different moral meanings, even though they may have the same net effect. Behavioural and stylistic variables which have come to characterise the two types of terrorism also contribute to this bifurcation in moral meanings. There are a number of obvious differences between the behavioural styles of governments and individual or non-state terrorists. The former draw on substantial resources and well-recognised claims to legitimacy, while individuals have little such claim and are typified by meagre resources and frugal modes of violence. Stylistic variables also contribute to the perceived differences. Foremost among these is the portrayal of the nation-state actors as *rational* beings whose actions serve a larger goal. The impression is fostered of persons of self-control, logic, and a sense of responsibility. These impressions are reinforced by lifestyles of

conservatism and attractiveness. The individual terrorist actor by cont.
is portrayed as irrational, driven by a deranged mind, and with aims of sei.
interest or illogical destructiveness. The difference is further reinforced by
the weapons which each may choose and the manner in which they carry
them. Often there are negative connotations to the weapons of the
individual terrorist – stolen firearms, bombs, rockets aimed at civilian
targets. The negative image of 'fighting dirty' is further impressed upon the
public by the fact that terrorist weapons are usually concealed from view
and frequently have the appearance of being less discriminating of targets
than weapons used by government forces. Of course this is not necessarily
true. It is just that government forces less often employ such weapons
against civilian targets. Many obvious examples come to mind. Consider
the image of a British soldier in Northern Ireland armed with a standard
infantry rifle. Consider by way of contrast a crudely made time bomb
planted in a pub or car. These images are replete with social meanings. The
soldier may be portrayed as a controlled individual legitimately carrying his
weapon, openly displayed. He must personally aim the rifle and will witness
its consequences. The person who plants a bomb carries no such stamp of
legitimacy. The bomb is placed in secret, will have unpredictable, and
undiscriminating (and more horrendous?) effects, and will explode after the
bomb-placer has decamped (and by implication does not take personal
responsibility for, nor even has to witness, the carnage that may have been
caused). Weapons disguised as everyday objects (such as letter-bombs)
may especially be open to interpretation as cowardly and illegitimate. Thus
the violence of official terrorism is reified and legitimised and that of the
individual is not.

Terrorism and 'identification'

One final factor deserves note in this process. If it is true that identification
is the key to rhetorical success, then an act will become to be seen as
terrorist if people identify with the victim of the act. (The role of the media
as instruments of legitimation is particularly noteworthy. A similar process
of identification occurs in other areas such as mugging, environmental
crimes, white collar crimes, etc.) If the identification is with the perpetrator,
the act is viewed in positive (or at worst neutral or ambivalent) terms. This
has implications for official regimes which practise terrorism. If such states
are industrialised societies then industries are active participants in official
terrorism (and so by extension are their employees). Further, state terror
usually involves a bureaucracy (police, armed services, intelligence agencies,
secret police, immigration control, information control, etc.) which, in
essence, is the administration of terror (either directly or indirectly) by large

numbers of citizens. (It could be argued that some terrorist groups, e.g. the Irish Republican Army, also have bureaucracies. But such a structure is more relevant to the organisation itself rather than society at large. It is largely a question of scale.) Because large numbers of the population participate to some degree in government-approved acts of violence, identification with the victim is problematic. Consequently, officially reified terror is not accorded the label 'terrorism' – the terrorist social meaning is absent. This reification and the legitimacy of official terrorism allows individual terrorism to be condemned as morally repugnant and official terrorism either not to be recognised at all or accepted as severe, but necessary. The serious student of terrorism must therefore make a deliberate decision about how to treat the term *terrorism* – banish it altogether since it may degenerate into little more than moralised name-calling, or acknowledge that some useful distinction between types of violence may be made if the concept is retained but apply the term even-handedly to governments, groups, and individuals. In this work the latter strategy will be adopted, although the focus will be primarily on individual or small-group terrorism.

Definitions of terrorism

In order to appreciate the nature of terrorism it is necessary to look at the definitions and concepts of terror and terrorism and to examine their often ambiguous relation to other forms of civil, military, and political violence and to criminal behaviour. Wilkinson notes that one of the central problems in defining terrorism lies with the subjective nature of terror.[6] We all have different thresholds of fear and our personal and cultural backgrounds make certain images, experiences, or fears more terrifying to each of us than to others. Because of the complex interplay of the subjective forces and of frequently irrational individual responses it is very difficult to accurately define terror and to study it scientifically. For this reason, and because of its inherently ideological nature, behavioural scientists have tended, until recently, to steer clear of the subject of terror and terrorism. Historians and social philosophers have not been so reluctant, however, and have provided valuable information which will be drawn upon in this discussion. In particular, they have studied those leaders, regimes and governments responsible for developing explicit theories and policies of terrorism, or have attempted to assess the socio-economic and political preconditions for and consequences of terrorism.

The first thing noted by these scholars is that the use of terror need not be politically motivated. It is obvious that criminals are more and more resorting to terrorist-type tactics for personal gain. Mentally unstable individuals may also terrorise others because of their condition. Finally, some members of society who are bored and/or sadistic may terrorise others to express their frustrations, vent their rage, or engage in symbolic acts of protest against society. The distinctions between various forms of terrorism are sometimes blurred by the fact that criminals or psychopaths who employ terror tactics may pretend to legitimate their actions by adopting political slogans (and who is to say where rationalisation ends and sincere political justification begins?), and because what we will term *terrorist* movements often recruit assistance from, and collaborate with, criminals. These confusions, together with the use of the word 'terrorism' almost entirely as a pejorative term to refer to the actions of some opposing organisation make problems of definition almost insoluble. As already noted, the problem is further complicated by the unwillingness of many to acknowledge that terrorism, whatever the definition may be, is as much a tool of states and governments as of revolutionaries and political extremists. It is all too easy to focus on the outlandish activities of small groups to the exclusion of the institutionalised, 'official' terrorism practised by a number of readily identifiable regimes. However, in order to discuss this topic meaningfully it is necessary to accept some basic definitions.

The first, and easiest, distinction to make is between terror and terrorism. The use of terror in itself does not constitute *terrorism*. As noted above, terror may be employed for criminal or personal ends. This area is not the subject of this book. Neither will we discuss the terror which is a by-product of wars. This work is concerned with the employment of terror as a weapon of psychological warfare for political ends. Consideration will also be given to terrorism used as a deliberate method of guerrilla warfare and therefore serving military ends.

Within this framework, many have tried to refine the definition of terrorism. For Thornton, terrorism is the use of terror as 'a symbolic act designed to influence political behaviour by extranormal means, entailing the use or threat of violence'.[7] Terrorism may achieve political ends by either mobilising forces sympathetic to the cause of the terrorists or by immobilising the forces of the incumbent authorities. The authorities have a certain initial advantage because of the inertia which characterises the normal political relationship between authority and citizenry. The terrorists are often viewed as a malignant growth which should be excised. According to Thornton one of the first and most vital tasks of an insurgent group is to disrupt this inertial relationship between the incumbents and the citizenry. Thus,

In order to do this, the insurgents must break the tie that binds the mass to the incumbents within the society, and they must remove the structural supports that give society its strength – or at least make those supports seem irrelevant to the critical problems that the mass must face. This process is one of disorientation, the most characteristic use of terror . . .[8]

An important emphasis in Thornton's definition of terrorism is on its *extranormal* quality. The use of terror may be placed in the upper levels of a continuum of political agitation, above political violence (such as riots). It is the extranormal nature of the use of terror that distinguishes it from other forms of political violence. Thornton is then faced with the difficulty, however, of defining 'extranormal' – a difficulty that he does not resolve. It would seem to be more productive to seek other ways by which terrorism might be distinguished from, for example, mugging – both of which have the effect of producing a state of terror in the victim. It seems on the surface that a distinguishing feature is that terrorism affects an audience wider than the primary victim. However, the same is true of mugging, although the audience may not be as large. If a number of muggings take place in certain locations, intense fear will be engendered in many other individuals who have cause to be in or near those places. The distinguishing feature, then, is the *design* to create anxiety rather than the 'extranormality' of the anxiety.

Terrorism is further characterised by its high symbolic content. Thornton contends that the symbolic nature of terrorism contributes significantly to its relatively high efficacy.

If the terrorist comprehends that he is seeking a demonstration effect, he will attack targets with a maximum symbolic value. The symbols of the state are particularly important, but perhaps even more are those referring to the normative structures and relationships that constitute the supporting framework of society. By showing the weakness of this framework, the insurgents demonstrate, not only their own strength and the weakness of the incumbents but also the inability of the society to provide support for its members in a time of crisis.[9]

Enforcement terror and agitational terror

Within this definition of terrorism, Thornton distinguishes two broad categories of the use of terror.[10] The first is *enforcement terror* which is used by those in power who wish to suppress challenges to their authority, and the second is *agitational terror* which describes the terroristic activities of those who wish to disrupt the existing order and ascend to political power themselves. His analysis thus meets the requirements of even-handed application of the concept of terrorism to the activities of both insurgents and incumbents. A similar distinction is observed by May who divides terrorism into two kinds: the regime of terror and the siege of terror.[11] The former refers to terrorism in the service of established order, while the latter refers to terrorism in the service of revolutionary movements. May acknowledges that the regime of terror is the more important of the two but notes how the siege of terror is what grips our attention: 'revolutionary terrorism, derivative and reflexive though it may be, exposes a level of perception into the universe of killing and being killed that may be even more revealing than state terrorism'.[12]

In fact it is one of the interesting puzzles of the study of terrorism as to why commentators and scholars tend to focus on the insurgent as opposed to the incumbent variety. There are a number of apparent explanations. As will be discussed in detail later, one of the hallmarks of terrorism is its dramatic, newsmaking nature. When terrorism becomes institutionalised as a form of government it makes the headlines less often. Government by terror simply has less news-value than the hijacking of an airliner. Another reason for the lack of attention paid to what May calls the 'reign of terror' may be traced back to the processes of constructing social realities discussed earlier. The portrayal of official terrorists as rational beings compared with the lunatic and out-of-control individual terrorist encourages the mass of society to see the threat to their physical and psychic integrity coming from the latter direction. Many adopt the attitude that while state terrorism may be undesirable and something eventually to be struggled against, the immediate threat comes from individual terrorists. It is the element of uncertainty that plays a large part here. State terrorism may be brutal and unjust but, in general, one knows what activities not to indulge in in order to escape its immediate and personal intrusion. Individual terrorism by contrast bears no necessary relation to one's own behaviour. It appears random and therefore more dangerous. Here again the impact of the media is an important factor. It must be remembered that many states currently experiencing terrorism are authoritarian ones or have some form of news control (some overt, some subtle). In such cases the media can hardly castigate authoritarian governments for their excesses – fearing reprisals such as licence cancellation – but they can, and do, bring terrorism by individuals or small groups into the homes of everyone. The view is therefore fostered of a society plagued by dangerous extremists damaging the fabric of everyday life and threatening the state while ignoring the often greater damage being perpetrated as a result of government policies and actions. Of course it is much easier to focus on a specific perpetrator than on an amorphous system. Finally, there are some sensible practical reasons for the reluctance of scholars to study state terrorism. Groom has noted that:

historians find it difficult to think themselves into the mores of a Robespierre's or a Stalin's reign of terror and it is dangerous to conduct field research in contemporary regimes of terror. It is far easier to conceptualize the use of terror as a weapon to achieve a specific goal rather than as a form of regular and normal government.[13]

Probably the only systematic effort to develop a general theory of terrorism based on an analysis of the use of official terror is Eugene

Walter's landmark work on successive rulers of the Zulu people in the nineteenth century.[14] Walter views terrorism as a *process of terror* having three elements: the act or threat of violence, the emotional reaction to extreme fear on the part of the victims or potential victims, and the social effects that follow the violence (or its threat) and the consequent fear.[15] This definition excludes restricted violence aimed at a clearly defined group of existing or past power holders in society. Episodes of terror do not constitute terrorism. A terrorist regime exercises a grip on the whole of society. Following an analysis of the use of official terror in traditional African societies Walter concludes that there are

five conditions necessary for the maintenance of a terroristic regime, which may also be understood as functional prerequisites: (1) A shared ideology that justifies violence . . . Legitimacy suppresses outrage. (2) The victims in the process of terror must be expendable . . . If the violence liquidates persons who are needed for essential tasks, or if replacements cannot be found for their roles, the system of co-operation breaks down. (3) Dissociation of the agents of violence and of the victims from ordinary social life. This double dissociation removes violence from social controls and separates the victims from sources of protection . . . (4) Terror must be balanced by working incentives that induce cooperation . . . (5) Cooperative relationships must survive the effect of the terror.[16]

This last point is an interesting one because it indicates that a society in which cooperation takes place in an environment devoid of friendship and trust would endure a system of terror better than a society in which cooperation is dependent on friendship and trust. 'Curiously, then, a society in which people are already isolated and atomised, divided by suspicions and mutually destructive rivalry, would support a system of terror better than a society without much chronic antagonism. If cooperative relations do not survive the deterioration of social ties under terror, the system will break down.'[17] It is a sobering thought when one considers how a modern industrialised society might be described!

While terrorism may be divided, without much argument, into gross categories such as siege of terror and state of terror, or enforcement terror and agitational terror, such categorisation is scarcely precise enough for more sophisticated conceptual analyses of the phenomenon under study. A priority in research in this field has been, therefore, an attempt to devise typologies which provide more precise definitions of subgroups of terrorism. Although there are many examples of such typologies,[18] that devised by Wilkinson is accepted by many (including the present author) as providing the clearest framework currently available for discussing terrorism.[19]

Wilkinson first draws a distinction between four types of terrorism – criminal, psychic, war, and political terrorism. Criminal terrorism is defined as the systematic use of terror for ends of material gain. Psychic terrorism has mystical, religious, or magical ends. War terrorism to quote

Walter's definition aims 'to paralyze the enemy, diminish his resistance, and reduce his ability to fight, with the ultimate purpose of destroying him'.[20] Wilkinson's main distinction between military and civil terrorism is that the former aims, generally, at annihilation and the latter at control. (However, this is a somewhat dubious distinction because military terrorism is as much involved with political/social consequences as it is with pure destruction for tactical ends.) Political terrorism is very generally defined as the systematic use or threat of violence to secure political goals.

Wilkinson's analysis begins by distinguishing between political terror and political terrorism. Political terror occurs 'in isolated acts and also in the form of extreme, indiscriminate and arbitrary mass violence'.[21] Such terror is neither systematic nor organised and is often difficult to control. 'Therefore neither one isolated act, nor a series of random acts is terrorism.'[22] By way of contrast, political terrorism 'is a sustained policy involving the waging of organised terror either on the part of the state, a movement or faction, or by a small group of individuals. Systematic terrorism invariably entails some organisational structure, however rudimentary, and some kind of theory or ideology of terror.'[23]

The difficulty with excluding an isolated act from the compass of terrorism, however, is that it is not possible to know how to classify any particular act until it is seen that it is or is not part of a series. Thus, a bombing that occurs today might be classified as an act of terror (not terrorism) initially, but be reclassified to an act of terrorism some days hence when further bombings establish a pattern (presuming also that the bombings meet the other criteria of political terrorism). The fact that acts can be so easily reclassified makes the distinction a rather arbitrary one. The more serious the initial act the greater the problem too. Imagine that a political group possesses a nuclear device and threatens to detonate it unless certain demands are acceded to by the government. Imagine further that this is the first act on the part of the group. Surely one would not have to wait until the group perpetrated another act for the first to be an instance of terrorism; particularly since it is theoretically possible for one such act (with a nuclear device, for example) to lead to acquiescence to the demands of the perpetrators. It seems then, that Wilkinson's exclusion of isolated acts from the ambit of terrorism and his focus on 'systematic' acts of terror makes the definition too limited to include some important (although extreme) instances of terrorism. Insofar as we are interested in analysing the degree of threat posed by particular acts, however, the concept of looking for systematic uses of terror has some utility.

Political terrorism

Wilkinson divides political terrorism into three types: revolutionary terrorism, sub-revolutionary terrorism, and repressive terrorism. Revolutionary terrorism is defined as the use of 'systematic tactics of terroristic violence with the objective of bringing about political revolution'.[24] It is characterised by four major attributes: (1) it is always a group, not an individual phenomenon, even though the groups may be very small; (2) both the revolution and the use of terror in its furtherance are always justified by some revolutionary ideology or programme; (3) there exist leaders capable of mobilising people for terrorism (Wilkinson attributes more importance to the availability of leaders as stressed by collective behaviour theorists[25] than he does the role of personality factors stressed by some other theorists [26]); (4) alternative institutional structures are created because the revolutionary movement must partake action in the political system and therefore must develop its own policy-making bodies and codification of behaviour. To give an even more precise picture of revolutionary terrorism we should add Hutchinson's list of essential properties: '(1) it is part of a revolutionary strategy; (2) it is manifested in acts of socially and politically unacceptable violence; (3) there is a pattern of symbolic or representative selection of the victims or objects of acts of terrorism; (4) the revolutionary movement deliberately intends these actions to create a psychological effect on specific groups and thereby to change their political behaviour and attitudes.'[27]

Having defined revolutionary terrorism, Wilkinson then divides it into various subtypes. These are:

(i) Organisations of pure terror (in which terrorism is the exclusive weapon), (ii) revolutionary and national/liberationist parties and movements in which terror is employed as an auxiliary weapon, (iii) guerrilla terrorism – rural and urban, (iv) insurrectionary terrorism – normally short-term terror in the course of a revolutionary rising, (v) the revolutionary Reign of Terror – often directed at classes and racial and religious minorities, (vi) propaganda of the deed, when this form of terror is motivated by long-term revolutionary objectives and (vii) international terrorism (that is terrorism committed outside the borders of one or all of the parties to the political conflict), where it is motivated by revolutionary objectives.[28]

The second category in Wilkinson's typology is Sub-Revolutionary Terrorism which is defined as terror used 'for political motives other than revolution or governmental repression'.[29] Whereas revolutionary terrorism seeks total change, sub-revolutionary terrorism is aimed at more limited goals such as forcing the government to change its policy on some issue, warning or punishing specific public officials, or retaliating against government actions seen as reprehensible by the terrorists.

Wilkinson's third category, Repressive Terrorism, is defined as 'the systematic use of terroristic acts of violence for the purposes of suppressing, putting down, quelling, or restraining certain groups, individuals or forms of behaviour deemed to be undesirable by the oppressor'.[30] Repressive terrorism relies heavily on the services of specialised agencies (the secret security *apparat*) whose members are trained to torture, murder, deceive, etc. Walter notes the importance of having this group set apart from the rest of society (in Walter's African communities such men were called the 'king's knives') and they are also always above appeals to the law.[31] Recent examples of separateness of the 'terror staff' are Hitler's SS with their isolated system of values, unique uniforms and hierarchies and 'Papa Doc' Duvalier's Tonton Macoutes with the famous sunglasses which provide a striking visual representation of the psychological distance which terror staffs try to establish to separate themselves from the populace. Wilkinson notes that initially the terror *apparat* is deployed against specific opposition groups. However, it frequently is later directed against much wider groups (ethnic or religious minorities, for example) and finally turns upon certain of the primary group itself. Such a change is not exclusive to repressive terrorism, of course.

An excellent example of this change in the targets of terror is given by the *régime de la terreur* which evolved in the revolutionary period in France between 1793 and 1794 (from which time our terms 'terrorism' and 'terrorist' emerged). Starting with attacks against relatively well-defined 'enemies of the revolution' the Terror under Robespierre reached terrible heights of savagery with the passing of the Law of Suspects on 17 September 1793. This law enabled the Committee of General Security and the Revolutionary Tribunal to arrest and, often, execute almost anyone remotely suspected of treachery. Thus while aristocrats had been a prime focus early in the Terror, an analysis of the backgrounds of 12,000 persons guillotined during the Terror as a whole and whose social status could be ascertained, revealed that only 37 per cent were aristrocrats.[32] (In all, it is estimated that on the eve of the end of the Terror there were nearly 400,000 'suspects', men, women, and children, imprisoned under the Law of Suspects.[33] Greer estimates that 40,000 people were executed during the period 1793–94).[34] Furthermore, as the Terror progressed it soon turned upon sections of the revolutionary movement itself. Thus in the summer of 1793 Robespierre ordered the hunting and execution of the Girondins (a more moderate revolutionary faction than Robespierre's Jacobins) and in April 1794 the Cordeliers (another faction) shared the same fate. Eventually, of course, the Terror ended when Robespierre's system was used against him. In the summer of 1794 several of the Committee of Public Safety, in particular Joseph Fouche (the 'butcher of Lyons', often referred to as the father of the modern police state), realised that they were Robespierre's next victims. On 8 Thermidor (26 July 1794) when Robespierre told the Convention that he had drawn up a list of traitors in their midst, but would not reveal their names, he signed his own death warrant. 'When Robespierre entered the National Convention late in the stormy summer morning of 9 Thermidor, he found a mob of delegates united by the determination to murder him before he could murder them; and that was the end of him.'[35] Robespierre and his inner cabal were executed and the Terror came to an end.

In summary, for Wilkinson, political terrorism is 'the systematic use of murder and destruction, and the threat of murder and destruction in order to terrorise individuals, groups, communities or governments into conceding to the terrorists' political demands'.[36] Political terrorism may take many different forms which may be reasonably clearly distinguished for analytical purposes. In this book the emphasis will be almost exclusively on revolutionary and sub-revolutionary terrorism. A number of definitions of terrorism have been considered in this chapter. It is immediately apparent that they all refer to a common quality – that is the abnormal quality of terrorism as perceived by the victim, the target or the audience. What differentiates terrorism from other forms of violence is its unexpected nature, its element of surprise and shock. It is this quality which makes terrorism frightening, rather than the actual physical impact of any incident. The definitions further point to the political context within which terror is employed and which again makes it different from some other violent acts.

Definitional problems and a new definition of terrorism

Many definitions, including Wilkinson's, emphasise the necessity to perceive a systematic use of terror tactics before individual acts within the series can be accurately labelled as 'terrorist'. The difficulties inherent in such an insistence have been mentioned. Further, most definitions do not spell out clearly that terrorism may be used by both insurgents and incumbent regimes. In order to try to meet these objections and also to include the essential criteria common to existing definitions, the following working definition of political terrorism has been constructed for the purposes of this book: *political terrorism is the use, or threat of use, of violence by an individual or a group, whether acting for or in opposition to established authority, when such action is designed to create extreme anxiety and/or fear-inducing effects in a target group larger than the immediate victims with the purpose of coercing that group into acceding to the political demands of the perpetrators.*

One final feature of definitions such as that given above is that such terms as mindless, senseless, or wanton violence are not evident. Although these are the terms which are most widely associated with terrorism in media reports (and, thereby, in the minds of the public) Jenkins has pointed out that it is important to emphasise that scholarly treatments of terrorism do not suggest that terrorism as a tactic is irrational or psychopathic (although some individual terrorists may be).[37] However one may personally feel about terrorist acts or how abhorrent they may be, they are not, in the frame of reference of the terrorist, either wanton or irrational. Terrorism is not mindless. It is a deliberate means to an end. Terrorism has objectives, a point which is often obscured by the fact that, to the observer, terrorist acts are random and directed at killing those whose deaths can be of no value to the terrorist cause. In order to understand this seeming paradox it will be necessary to examine the historical genesis of modern terrorism, to outline its theoretical rationale, and to analyse the ways in which contemporary terrorism is both a continuation of a historical trend and a unique phenomenon of our times.

2

Terrorism: a historical perspective

Part of the solution to the question of whether or not contemporary terrorism poses a unique threat to social order lies in an appraisal of its degree of continuity with previous manifestations of political terrorism. The history of terrorism is a full-scale investigation in its own right and it is not intended to pursue such a history here. Nevertheless it is important that some of the landmarks should be pointed out in order to view current terrorist movements in a proper perspective.

As noted earlier, the terms 'terrorism' and 'terrorist' have their roots in the French Revolution. Terrorism was defined in the 1798 supplement of the Dictionnaire of the Academie Francaise as 'système, régime de la terreur'.[1] Laqueur notes that a French dictionary published in 1796 referred to the fact that the Jacobins used the term in a positive sense when referring to their activities, 'but after the 9th of Thermidor, "terrorist" became a term of abuse with criminal implications'.[2] Since that time *terrorism* has been used to denote almost every imaginable form of violence, many forms not in accordance with the broad definitions discussed earlier.

Of course, even if the term *terrorism* itself is relatively new, the phenomenon to which it refers is not. The *sicarii*, a religious sect active in the Zealot struggle in Palestine (AD 66–73) seem to have undertaken activities which would qualify them as terrorists. Better known are the Assassins, a sect of the larger Ismaili sect of Muslims whose activities between the eleventh and thirteenth centuries have long stimulated the curiosities of historians and the imaginations of fable-builders. This sect which was finally suppressed by the Mongols, developed a specific religious doctrine justifying the murder of their religious and political opponents (the Seljuqs) who they saw as the unrighteous ones.

However, although there have always existed these and other isolated examples of terrorism, its systematic manifestations did not emerge until the French Revolution and found particular expression in the later part of the nineteenth century. Terrorism was extensively used by the Russian revolutionaries in 1878–81 and again in the twentieth century, by radical national groups in Ireland, Macedonia, Serbia, and Armenia, and by anarchists in France, Italy, Spain, and the United States, particularly in the 1890s.

Terrorism in nineteenth-century Russia

Historically, it is probable that the most important of all the terrorist movements was the *Narodnaya Volya* which operated in Russia between January 1878 and March 1881. This organisation evolved a specific policy of terrorism and was responsible for a concerted terrorist campaign against the Tsarist authorities. According to Morozov, one of Narodnaya Volya's leading theoreticians, terrorism was a new cost-effective form of struggle which would overthrow the Tsarist tyranny.[3] Many of the central figures in Narodnaya Volya emphasised, like Morozov, that terrorism was ethically a better choice than allowing the carnage that would result from a mass insurrection. If innocent people died as a result of terroristic activity it had to be accepted as an inevitable consequence of war. It was, however, preferable to the slaughter which would accompany a mass struggle.

Narodnaya Volya's terrorist campaign differed from the co-existing anarchist activities taking place elsewhere in Europe. Anarchist terror was characteristically an individual activity whereas Russian terrorism was a directed campaign. 'Russian terrorism was both one aspect of the formation of a revolutionary socialist party and a symptom of a general crisis in Russian society.'[4] However, the Narodnaya Volya faded as a potent force and with it terrorism which was not widely apparent again as a programme in Russia until two decades later with the formation of the Social Revolutionary Party. The new wave of terror opened in 1902 with the assassination of Sipyagin, the Minister of the Interior. This time, however, terrorism was not seen as a solitary weapon which could replace mass struggle, but rather as a tool to supplement and strengthen the revolutionary potential of the masses. In this development there are increasing parallels with modern philosophers of terror. The parallels extend also to organisational detail. One characteristic of modern terrorist groups is to set apart in a semi-autonomous unit the terrorist activities of the revolutionary movement. Similarly in early twentieth-century Russia the terrorist 'Fighting Organisation' (*Boevaya Organisatsia* – BO) was established and given autonomy within the Social Revolutionary Party.

Laqueur argues that the terrorist activities of the Social Revolutionaries had a marked effect on Russian public opinion.[5] Whereas the activities of the Narodnaya Volya had attracted support mostly from the intelligentsia, the terrorism of the early twentieth century was much more widely applauded. Even so, discussion and argument about the usefulness, place, ethics, and tactics of terrorism continued to divide the revolutionary parties and factions and with the emergence of the class struggle its use petered out. (Not only that, but a great disaster befell the BO in that one Azev, who rose to the head of the organisation turned out to be a double agent of the Okhrana, the Tsarist secret police.) Thus after the first decade of the century terrorism was characterised by sporadic actions and systematic terrorism was no longer a feature of pre-revolutionary Russian political life.

In trying to understand the influences important in the formation of terrorist policy in late nineteenth and early twentieth century Russia it is important to separate out several trends. The most prominent theoretical influences were anarchism and nihilism. These philosophies found their most famous expression in the writings of Bakunin and Nechayev, particularly the *Revolutionary Catechism* published in 1869. The Catechism is often quoted by contemporary revolutionary groups as a guide to parts of their thinking. It is essentially a handbook of terrorist organisation and tactics, and a description of the ideal terrorist. According to the Catechism the revolutionary has no feelings or interests outside of the revolution. He will cut himself off from all normal social intercourse and hates and despises the existing social ethic with a devastating malevolence. His aim is the total annihilation of the existing order, but no vision of the order to replace it was ever articulated by these apostles of destruction. In the event their influence was more intellectual than concrete. Nechayev claimed to have started a network of revolutionary cells which never in fact existed and it seems that his only real organisation was a secret society with only a handful of members. His only act of terror was committed against one of his own co-conspirators when with the help of five other members, he murdered Ivan Ivanov in late 1869. In 1872 Nechayev was arrested in Switzerland, handed over to the Tsarist police, and tried in 1873 for Ivanov's murder. He was sentenced to 20 years' imprisonment and died in 1882 in a prison in St Petersburg.

The anarchist tradition

Mikhail Bakunin was a particularly important figure in the development of anarchist terrorism. A brilliant revolutionary orator who had little in the way of concrete ideas for a future society, Bakunin travelled all over Europe fomenting and assisting revolutionary endeavours. His major concern was the destruction of the prevailing social order. In fact, Bakunin believed that *any* state was eventually exploitative and regarded violence and bloodshed as the only purgative to cleanse society. He fought bitterly with Marx who argued that it was capitalism, not the state as a concept, that was inherently unjust, and who viewed Bakunin's views as fanatical and dangerous because they led to no systematic thought for the future. (Although Marx believed that the state would – and should – eventually wither away.)

Bakunin also disagreed sharply with Marx over the revolutionary value of the proletariat. Whereas Marx assigned them the primary historic mission of overthrowing capitalism, Bakunin placed his faith in the revolutionary potential of peasants and thieves. The idea of an army of thieves came from Wilhelm Weitling, a disciple of the French revolutionary Louis Blanqui and an early German communist, who in 1848 advocated forming a savage army of murderers and thieves as the vanguard of the revolution. Bakunin's ideas are reflected today in some of the writings of the philosopher Herbert Marcuse and in the composition and actions of West Germany's Baader-Meinhof group. However, following his death in 1876 Bakunin's disciples chose, for the most part, to ignore these ideas and focused instead upon the concept of 'propaganda of the deed' with which, for many, Bakunin's name is now synonymous. Simply stated, this concept advocates the necessity for members of the revolutionary vanguard to undertake acts of violence as individual revolutionary statements.

According to Woodcock,[6] a well-known historian of anarchism, the concept of 'propaganda by deed' can be traced back to an Italian, Carlo Pisacane, who had written that ideas emanate from deeds and that intellectual propaganda was an empty gesture. However, it was a leading French anti-parliamentarian, Paul Brousse, who coined the phrase 'propaganda by deed'.[7] He argued that the propaganda disseminated by way of newspapers, public meetings, and pamphlets was of limited value. It could be countered by the 'lies' of the bourgeois press and distorted by bourgeois orators. And as the hard-working masses had little time or inclination to attend to intellectual debate or literature it was doubtful whether the message would ever permeate its intended audience. What was necessary was a practical demonstration which could not be ignored and would awaken the consciousness of the masses. Kropotkin, a leading ideologist of the anarchist movement in the 1870s, took up this theme and formulated anarchist action as constant agitation by any means possible – including the gun and the bomb. Laqueur claims that 'when he [Kropotkin] took over the leadership of the Anarchist movement in the late 1870s he was one of the main protagonists of individual terror as a means to arouse the spirit of revolt among the masses'.[8] Since that time, violent political activists of many persuasions have turned to the theory of 'propaganda by deed' to justify their employment of terrorist tactics.

The anarchist views of Nechayev, Bakunin, and later Kropotkin, exercised particular influence in Russia, especially between 1905 and 1914. In Western Europe, too, although, somewhat earlier, the anarchist philosophers influenced the tide of events. In 1881 an anarchist International was established in London and sponsored the anarchist terrorism of the 1890s, particularly the incidents in France. In 1893, houses were dynamited in Paris by François-Claudius Ravachol, a common criminal who attempted to give a veneer of justification to his acts by adopting anarchist philosophies. In 1894, Auguste Vaillant threw a bomb into the Chamber of Deputies, an action which led to his execution. He was avenged later that year when an Italian anarchist named Caserio, assassinated the French President Sadi Carnot. Also in 1894, one week after Vaillant's execution, another avenger, Emile Henry, exploded a bomb in a Paris cafe, wounding twenty people, one of whom later died. When it was drawn to his attention that his victims were ordinary citizens guilty of no capitalist crimes, Henry replied: 'There are no innocents'. This attitude is often reflected today in the justifications of contemporary terrorists (although it was by no means characteristic of all anarchists).

Such anarchist attacks generated considerable attention, coinciding as they did with widespread anarchist propaganda proclaiming the positive virtues of violence, and created an impression of an international conspiracy which in fact did not exist.[9] However, the export of ideas ensured that anarchism became at least a temporary feature of life in many countries. In Ireland, the United States, Macedonia, Turkey, and India (to name some major examples) the ideas took hold and stimulated various, not necessarily anarchist, organisations to take up a terrorist programme. Such tactics were not the exclusive domain of left-wing revolutionaries either, as is attested by the terrorist activities of the Hungarian 'Arrow Cross', the Macedonian IMRO, and the Romanian 'Iron Guard'.

The acts of the anarchists and the Russian terrorists indicate some of the major conflicts and contradictions within terrorism. Foremost amongst these is the indefinite nature of the boundaries between political violence and ordinary criminal acts. Often terrorism has, in fact, degenerated into pure robbery and criminal violence. Thus 'propaganda of the deed' melted into the robbery and murder of the *Illegalistes* group in France, the Spanish *pistoleros*, and the *bezmotivnyi terror* (terror without motivation) during the 1905–07 revolution in Russia.

Terrorism and morality

The problem of the definition of legitimate victims also plagues terrorism. When a corrupt society is the target it is often difficult to deal meaningful blows at the symbols of that society. The most accessible targets are human beings and it is all too easy to expand the concept of enemy to encompass anyone who is not actively involved in overthrowing the society. Again the distinction between revolutionary action and violent crime becomes blurred, with a programme of terrorism degenerating into indiscriminate and arbitrary terror and sheer gangsterism. Thus it has been said that: 'The indiscriminate murders at Lod, Avivim, M'alot, Rome, Munich and

Athens, London, Birmingham and Belfast are today's manifestations of that degeneration.'[10]

By way of contrast, what characterised the Russian terrorism of the late nineteenth-century was its specific concern for the ethics and legitimacy of the use of terrorist tactics. In a document entitled *Podgotavitelnaja Rabota Partii*[11] by Andrey Zhelyabov, a member of Narodnaya Volya who was executed for his part in the assassination of Tsar Alexander II, terrorism is endorsed, but only as a poor alternative in the worst possible historical conditions. In another pamphlet entitled *Terrorism and Routine*,[12] published in 1880, Tarnovsky defended terrorism on the grounds that it avoided the massive toll of death and suffering which could only come from revolution. In 1881 when James Garfield, the President of the United States, was assassinated the Executive Committee of the Narodnaya Volya issued a statement condemning the use of terrorist tactics in a democratic society such as the United States. They believed that terrorism could only be justified in extreme circumstances and denounced all such actions in countries which permitted normal political activity.

It is interesting also to examine the Marxist position on this issue since many contemporary terrorist groups claim that they are guided by some form of Marxist ideology. As with many aspects of Marxist theory, turning to the writings of Marx provides justification for a number of contradictory positions. In their early communist years both Marx and Engels were committed to the view that violence was the engine of social change. They argued that violence was primarily necessary to transform the nature of the working class (comparable to the anarchist's 'propaganda of the deed' perhaps?) or, in other words 'that it was therapeutic in character, and that it alone would psychologically renovate the working class so that it would be fit to rule'[13] (a notion resurrected in the twentieth century by such figures as Sartre and Fanon). E. S. Beesly, Marx's English positivist friend, reported on the basis of many conversations with him that Marx 'had no expectation that his scheme of society could be realised other than by violent insurrection'.[14] However, later in life Marx tended to downplay his earlier advocacy of therapeutic violence and held that in some countries (notably England) it might be possible to bring about the social revolution by peaceful and legal means. But as Feuer comments:

Marx no longer extolled the therapy of violence; its use he justified only in the setting of absolutist regimes, where democratic processes were non-existent for the workers. Nonetheless a strain existed in the Marxist tradition of an unconscious compulsion to choose that alternative among those available for presumable action towards socialist goals, which would involve a maximum of violence. Destructivism became then an end-in-itself even more real that the professed socialism.[15]

From these beginnings, then, sprang the ideology that powered the terrorist movements that have emerged since the Second World War. From the terrorist activities of the Irgun and Stern gangs in Palestine, to the colonial terrorist movements such as the Algerian FLN, to the Vietnamese NLF, to the contemporary terrorist organisations of the Middle East, Africa, South America, and Europe can be traced a philosophical and intellectual (and in some cases an operational) debt to the Russian terrorists and the anarchists of the late nineteenth/early twentieth century. Although the use of terror is not in itself a novel phenomenon, the programme of terror really has its solid origins in those times. Although the lineage is obvious, the question to be asked is whether the modern heirs represent a different order of things than did their immediate forebears. It is to this question that we turn now.

3

The changing nature of terrorism

A major question which both scholars of terrorism and those charged with its control seek to answer is whether contemporary terrorism is fundamentally different in any ways from its historical forebears. The answers to this question will be vital in both assessing the threat posed by terrorism and in tailoring a response to it. A consensus is emerging that there are indeed significant differences both in the philosophy and tactics of terror and in the social and political environment in which it operates. These differences will be examined here. The consequences of these changes for threat assessment and responses to terrorism will be addressed in later chapters.

Terrorism and technological change

Many of the differences that may be observed are directly or indirectly a consequence of technological change. The most obvious relevant developments have been in the fields of transport, communications (particularly as applied to news gathering and distribution), and weaponry.

The advent of the jet airliner and the fact that it is readily accessible to large numbers of people has brought with it mobility and a significant increase in the range of possible targets within the reach of any particular group or individual. The emergence of transnational terrorism involving terrorists of different nationalities planning, training for, and executing acts of political terrorism has been greatly facilitated by air travel.

The organisation, orientation, and technical sophistication (particularly in the field of satellite technology) of the news media have significant implications for the style and range of terrorist activities to which modern society may be prey. Media coverage of a terrorist operation is often the major objective of the perpetrators. The insistence of many news directors that they have a social obligation to present the news 'as it happens', without restriction or censorship, while ignoring its potential consequences makes it very easy for the terrorists to stage events with assured worldwide audiences. As will be discussed in a later chapter, there is an urgent need for governments, law enforcement leaders, and news organisations to meet to discuss their various duties and responsibilities in such a manner that a coherent policy can be agreed to which attempts to deprive terrorists of their stranglehold on the media (not that the media are exactly unwilling victims) without unnecessarily restricting the freedom of the press to report the news.

The increasing reliance of our society on technology has also changed the nature of the threat posed by terrorists. Much of the functioning of heavily industrialised societies is concentrated on a decreasing number of critical locations or processes. As Robert Kupperman, the Chief Scientist of the US Arms Control and Disarmament Agency, has commented:

Commercial aircraft, natural gas pipelines, the electric power grid, offshore oil rigs, and computers storing government and corporate records are examples of sabotage-prone targets whose destruction would have derivative effects of far higher intensity than their primary losses would suggest ... Thirty years ago terrorists could not have obtained extraordinary leverage. Today, however, the foci of communications, production and distribution are relatively small in number and highly vulnerable.[1]

In other words, one of the possible social consequences of mass populations and technological innovations is that 'the small bands of extremists and irreconcilables that have always existed may become an increasingly potent force'.[2]

Because of technological advances society now also faces threats of a different order to those that have existed in the past. The most obvious example is the possibility that a terrorist group may gain access to nuclear, biological, or biochemical materials. The possession, for example, of even a very crude nuclear device would give such a group unheard of publicity and negotiating power, with unknown effects on public confidence. If only for its dramatic publicity value it is likely that a terrorist group in the future will attempt to penetrate a nuclear facility or divert radioactive material.

The consideration which weighs against the ultimate execution of a threat to detonate a nuclear device or release a biological agent is that it is realised that such an action would almost certainly harm the terrorists' cause. Particularly with biological and biochemical materials, the possibility has existed for some time that they could be used in a blackmail situation. But they have not been used, probably because, as one commentator has said, terrorists want a lot of frightened people watching rather than a lot of people dead.[3] However, scenarios involving such agents are not altogether improbable. For example, in April 1975 German terrorists stole 54 litre bottles of mustard gas from a military store and threatened to release it in several cities. There may be future situations in which a terrorist group, perhaps needing to escalate violence to be taken notice of in a world used to killing and maiming, feels compelled to employ extreme measures. Another possibility is that the so-called 'lunatic fringe' of the terrorist movement, such as the Japanese United Red Army, will employ these special weapons. Whatever the case, it is clear that the potential for the use of special weapons is present and needs to be considered in national and international policy planning.

Probably the greatest threats posed by technological advances, however, are in the field of conventional weaponry. Until recently, most of the significant advances in military technology have involved relatively large weapons and weapons guidance systems. In the last few years, however, considerably more attention has been paid to improving the impact of the individual infantryman and consequently much of the research and development effort has gone into the refinement of personal weapons. This trend has significant implications for terrorist groups. Because of the ability to miniaturise weapons and guidance systems a completely new range of small, portable, cheap, highly accurate, and relatively easy to operate weapons has been created. Because they are to be used by the average infantryman they are being mass-produced. Because they are mass-produced they stand a much greater chance of falling into the hands of terrorists. Further, since advances in weaponry are so rapid, large numbers of these new weapons will quickly become obsolete and be disposed of through arms dealers and other avenues, thus increasing the chances of distribution outside the armed forces even further. Already earlier generation weapons of this type have found their way into terrorist hands. There are numerous examples. Arab terrorists with Soviet SA-7, hand-held, heat-seeking surface-to-air missiles have been arrested outside Rome airport. In January 1975 the Black September Organisation used a Soviet 40-mm RPG-7 grenade launcher to attack an El Al Boeing at Orly Airport, Paris. They missed, and hit a Yugoslav Airlines DC-9 instead. The IRA have also used the RPG-7 in Belfast. But these weapons are primitive in terms of range, accuracy, and destructive power when compared with the latest weapons. Examples can be found in any defence journal. A number of man-portable anti-tank weapons employing sophisticated guidance systems are now available. The Soviet AT-3 'Sagger' wire-guided missile was used effectively in the Yom Kippur War, weighs only 12 kg and is believed to have a range of 3000 m. There are numerous Western counterparts or improvements to the 'Sagger' including the US 'Dragon' and 'TOW' missiles, the Franco/German 'HOT' and 'Milan' systems and the British 'Swingfire', all of which are being mass-produced.

In addition to delivery systems, there have also been significant advances in propellants and explosives. Non-military developments such as digital clocks, day-date watches, and long-lasting power cells have further increased the flexibility available to amateur bomb makers. When added together these factors point to greater scope for terrorist activities in terms of increased accuracy, destructive power, distance from target (and hence a greater chance of escape), and most of all – dramatic impact. This suggests that there should be more concern for the side-effects of such things as military technology policy, and certainly steps should be taken to increase security precautions with respect to weaponry. Of course, technology has also advanced in the countervailing area of surveillance and detection and this will go some way to helping us deal with potential problems. But as Brian Jenkins points out 'the full application of such technology implies great social control. We have accepted such controls for brief periods to deter certain crimes like hijacking. But we do not live in airports, nor do I think we would like to. Thus, though a countervailing technology may be there, its application could be costly in terms of human liberty.'[4] Its application in sufficient quantity to significantly solve the problems of weapons security is, therefore, highly improbable under current social conditions.

Societal attitudes and terrorism

Other contributions to the changing nature of terrorism may be found in the context in which it occurs. Radical changes are occurring in the attitudes of different groups in society towards each other, particularly in regard to attitudes to authority. Authority is more and more viewed as something to be earned, not something which is either an intrinsic quality of a prescribed group or a bureaucratic ordinance. The situation and its consequences are summarised by Groom[5] in the following terms:

Structural violence[6] is being laid bare and increasingly those who have benefited from it are being challenged and forced to cede or to defend their privileges by overt violence. Role differentiation has nothing inherently unstable about it. It only gives rise to relative deprivation,[7] status disequilibrium, multiple dysfunction and perhaps terrorism when it is based on criteria which are not acceptable to all the relevant actors and when the role is not being fulfilled to the general satisfaction in the circumstances of the day. Authority without coercion can only be sustained on the basis of a continuously renewed consensus. In short, the exercise of authority requires the participation of all: not the active participation of everyone, but sufficient to satisfy those who are interested.

When such participation is denied, authority may be challenged. With both the increasing levels of participation required by a myriad of groups who feel they have no means other than coercion to make their voices heard and the democratisation of access to the tools of violence, terrorism is increasingly seen as a viable option. With the leverage occasioned by the technological factors outlined above, it is increasingly an option which must be taken seriously by those in authority.

Related to the challenge to authority is the rate of change in society.

Change is now a greater feature of life than at any previous time in history and, if they are to survive, authority structures must be able to change correspondingly in order to accommodate these changes. However, there are always incumbent authorities who will try to deny this reality and not accommodate change. Such behaviour can only lead, in the extreme, to continuous use of coercion and repression which eventually, in combination with the forces generated by the imperatives of change, lead to social collapse. However, it is also true that stability is desirable. In modern social organisation it provides psychological benefits to the members of society and facilitates many important functions. Stability is not the hallmark of a stagnant society as long as it has relatively fluid boundaries. A stable society should be able to adapt to change and to forecast major shifts in social organisation thereby enabling society to plan to accommodate them and also give the citizenry dependable expectations for the future.

However, as rates of change increase it becomes increasingly difficult for both authorities and the populace to adapt. There are two major types of change involved. First, individuals are changing roles more frequently than they ever have in the past. With the changing levels of education and new social attitudes many people change both occupational, and personal roles over a lifetime. No longer, for example, do many people find themselves in the same job, or even occupation, when they retire as that which they entered upon leaving school. At the same time, the roles themselves are undergoing change. Frequently, what is expected of individuals fulfilling the requirements of the role changes and, often, so does the social status attaching to the role. For some individuals or groups these changes may be too difficult to cope with or may have derivative effects which are severely disadvantageous. Sometimes resort to political violence, and in the extreme political terrorism, is an option which presents itself as offering solutions to the problems caused by the changes. Indeed terrorism may be aimed at reversing the process to undo the changes themselves. Thus:

If institutions do not change sufficiently rapidly there will be a gap between institutional values and practices, their actual and erstwhile constituencies and the environment generally. This can give rise to structural violence, to challenges to authority, to the growth of perceptions of relative deprivation and status disequilibrium and, ultimately, to revolutionary activity to change structures using terrorism as a weapon.[8]

It could well be, then, that there are now more conditions conducive to terrorism, that more people may see terrorism as the only way to remedy their problems, that more people have access to the means to effect terrorist intentions, and that technological changes have produced circumstances greatly increasing the leverage and power which may be exercised by terrorist methods. Another question of importance now is: are the contemporary terrorists themselves (as opposed to the weapons, the power they may exercise, or the environment in which they operate) significantly different from their predecessors?

While not claiming that the Russian terrorists of the Narodnaya Volya (and similar organisations) were saints, they do appear to have viewed terrorism in a different light to present-day terrorists. In the first place, ethical concerns seem to have weighed much more heavily upon them. Questioning of the right to kill was central to many of the tactical and philosophical debates, a feature which seems to be peripheral today. Kalyayev, who in 1905 assassinated the Grand Duke Serge Aleksandrovich, gave up his first attempt to do so because the Duke's children were riding in the carriage with him and the bomb would have killed them too. Similar incidents were not uncommon at the time. Such concern for moral niceties is rarely observed today. (Although it should be noted that such debate has resulted in splits over tactics within a number of contemporary terrorist organisations, e.g. the IRA, the Palestinian resistance movement, and the Basque ETA.)

Standards and modes of behaviour have changed. The Narodnaya Volya, the French Anarchists or the Irish dynamiters would not have abducted children and threatened to kill them unless ransom was paid, they would not have hired agents to do their own work, nor would they have given parcels of explosives to unsuspecting tourists . . . When all allowances have been made for the primitive character and the violent traditions of certain societies, there is no escaping the fact that nineteenth-century terrorists acted according to standards very different from those prevailing at present.[9]

However care must be taken not to suggest a distinct cut-off line between the past and the present. While hostage-taking, for example, was not a hallmark of early Russian terrorism there were, in fact, those who advocated it. Vladimir Burtsev, the man who unmasked the police agent Azev (who had become head of the Social Revolutionary Party's Terror Brigade) frequently exhorted his co-conspirators to ignore moral considerations when conducting terrorist activities. In a pamphlet called *To Arms*, published in London in 1903, Burtsev advocated the taking of hostages as a necessary terrorist tactic. No doubt specific instances both in the Russian terrorist movement and in modern terrorist activities can be found to counter the general line being advanced here. The point, however, is that as a rule these historical differences in attitudes and tactics *were* observed.

The shaping of terrorist philosophies

Certainly all the societal and technological changes which have had an impact on authority structures and social organisation have also affected terrorists – both as individuals and as groups. With the opportunities offered by technology, new philosophies (or self-justifications) have been shaped to accommodate them. Thus the possibilities of accurate time bombs which can be left in specific places to detonate at predetermined times has meant a radical change in many aspects of that small tactical area. It means that escape is much more possible for the terrorist, which in turn eliminates much of the personal heroism required of the anarchist bomb thrower. It means a less discriminating and more anonymous attack which in turn requires a change of philosophy which can be used both as self-justification and as justification to the world. Social, and more important, political changes mean a greater involvement by third parties in terrorist struggles. In the nineteenth century the cross-fertilisation was largely of ideas. The philosophy and tactics of the Narodnaya Volya were a significant influence on other European groups but each terrorist struggle was, in essence, a self-contained one. Terrorism is now an export industry. Not only is one group 'inspired' by the activities or ideas of another, there is a complex interrelationship of training, logistic support, personnel, and operations between them. The fact that these relationships, exemplified by modern transnational terrorism, have so little in common with the terrorists of yesteryear, has prompted a number of commentators[10] to see such activities as a form of surrogate warfare between nation-states rather than as individual political struggles.

By examining the various forms of inter-relations between terrorist groups, ideologies, and tactics a very plausible case can be made that the most important differences between past and present terrorism may be traced to the modern, transnational flow of information.[11] The complex worldwide structure of information channels which has been generated by developments in transportation and communications and increasing levels of education has had far-reaching consequences for the development of perceptions and attitudes, fears and aspirations, and awareness of other peoples and other problems. All of these changes have complex interactions with the level of violence in society. Such violence is only poorly understood but a number of models provide a starting point for analysing the destabilising forces which may create political violence, and some of these will be discussed later.

One factor common to many theories, though, is the role assigned to catalysts. Often a particular catalyst is necessary for a group to become mobilised to political violence and changes wrought by information flows could well prove to be such a catalyst, especially in destabilised, divided societies. It can be argued that although ideas such as those that preach revolution, have always spread throughout the international community the spread is now of an extent, degree, and speed such as has never before been achieved. Particularly important is the fact that such a spread of ideas has led to the wide acceptance, as ethical or justifiable, of tactics that would in the past have received little or no support. Thus the flow of information may either stimulate dissent and/or play a major part in determining its form. Redlick makes the following comments about the effects of information about other terrorist activities on the behaviour of the Quebec Liberation Front in Canada:

> the transnational flow of information may provide dissidents with the inspirational and material spark that will cause them to resort to terrorism. For example, a variety of external factors, such as the writings of Frantz Fanon, had subtle and extensive influence on the Quebec and Palestinian terrorist movements. The information obtained from external sources provides the terrorist with tactical, strategic, and ideological knowledge about the art of bomb-making, hostage-taking, and kidnapping. Moreover, information concerning the Algerians, Palestinians, and Tupamaros permeated the intellectual milieu of Quebec and contributed to the creation of a climate in which the use of violence appeared justifiable and necessary to a small group of Quebecois. Inspired by militant anticolonial rhetoric, this radical fringe of the separatist movement quickly became committed to terrorism as utilized elsewhere in its pursuit of Quebec's independence. Thus, when some radicals resorted to terrorism, they were taking into account not only their limited capabilities, but also the successful examples of the Algerians, Cubans, and later the Palestinians and Tupamaros.[12]

Perhaps the final, and for the security authorities amongst the most difficult, change in the nature of terrorism is the way in which the dividing line between terrorism and criminality has become less and less distinct with time. With the defeat of the autocratic governments of nineteenth- and early twentieth-century Europe and the disintegration, often under terrorist pressure, of colonial governments the targets of terrorism have become less concrete. In a society which allows the people no part in government and no freedom of expression, the targets of terrorism (both in terms of goals and the specific objects of physical attack) are able to be clearly stated and clearly understood by the populace. Where such systems have been replaced by liberal democracies, the philosophies of terror have come to be stated in more abstract terms. (This is not necessarily true of the many totalitarian or dictatorial states. But in such states the level of repression is such that terrorism is not a major problem within the boundaries of the state.) Thus the targets are 'symbols' of 'systems', the definitions of which are not rigid and the undesirability of which is not universally agreed (or its undesirability is undisputed but there is disagreement about the extent of its undesirability). Because the targets have ill-defined boundaries they tend to become wider and wider. As has already been noted, this inevitably leads to a choice of human targets, the consequences of which have been described by Iviansky in the following terms:

When one wants to deal a blow at the corrupt and criminal bourgeois regime, at 'the bourgeoisie in the abstract', at the class as a whole, it is not long before one starts hitting at any bourgeois – because every bourgeois is a criminal. In the end, this becomes no more than a modern variation of an ancient malady: the need for a scapegoat, the desire to strike at an invisible enemy who afflicts and distorts our lives. The abstract targets – the state, the government and its representatives – are usually well guarded and inaccessible. Terrorism in all its manifestations is thus forced to deal its blows at the accessible targets, i.e., at human beings. The fine line between revolutionary struggle and crime is obliterated.[13]

Summary

In summary, while there is a clear historical lineage which may be traced between contemporary terrorism and its forebears in the French Revolution and the political movements of the late nineteenth and early twentieth centuries, there are now evident significant departures from the tradition. Social and technological changes have wrought their own direct effects on terrorist operations and their potential utility on effectiveness. Corresponding to these changes have been significant evolutions in terrorist philosophy and tactics. All of these factors have resulted in a different threat to stability than that posed by previous terrorist movements.[14] In order to appreciate the nature of this threat and be able to meet it, it is necessary to understand how a modern theory of terrorism has developed and what are the objectives and purposes of contemporary terrorism. It is to these matters that Chapter 4 is devoted.

4

The purpose of terrorism

The use of terror to instil and manipulate fear may serve a number of purposes. Depending on the situation, terrorism may be aimed simultaneously at several objectives, both tactical and strategic.

It was stated earlier that one of the principle aims of terrorism is to divide the mass of society from the incumbent authorities. According to Thornton this process of disorientation is one of the most characteristic uses of terror.[1] However, he warns that 'terror is only appropriate if the insurgents (or incumbents) enjoy a low level of actual political support but have a high potential for such support. If their potential is low, terrorism is likely to be counter-productive.' In the latter case, those who use it may discover that terrorism leads to a wave of outrage and revulsion against them, sweeping aside any latent or actual base of public support and sympathy for their political cause. Or, in other conditions, it may lead to spontaneous (and unanticipated) counter-violence and terror with the emergence of vigilante groups or rival terrorist units. The original terrorists may then find themselves sucked into a kind of inter-communal or inter-movement struggle which acts to neutralise their potential effectiveness in influencing long-term policy or constitutional changes.

The psychology of fear

Because of these dangers it is vital to their success that the terrorists have a firm understanding of the effects of disorientation and of the nature of the society in which they try to induce it. (Obviously, it will be equally necessary for the incumbent government's security forces to have a similar understanding.) At one level the terrorist must try to disorient the population by showing that the government is unable to fulfil primary security functions for its subjects – that is the provision of safety and order. On a deeper level, however, the aim is, to isolate the citizen from his or her social context. The ultimate of the terrorisation process occurs when the individual is so isolated as to be unable to draw strength from usual social supports and is cast entirely upon his or her own resources. Thornton

34

believes that 'disorientation occurs when the victim does not know what he fears, when the source of his fear lies outside his field of experience'.[2] If the victim cannot obtain an understanding of the source of danger within a framework which he or she is able to construct from his or her own resources it is likely he or she will turn to a leader who gives the appearance of wisdom, thereby deriving the strength to interpret and control events. If the incumbent forces have been shown to be unable to provide this framework and the associated security, the time is ripe for the terrorists to show that they have a viable political alternative which is able to offer the required stability. 'The role of agitational terror is now over; it now remains for the insurgents to demonstrate that they are capable of infusing meaning into the unstructured environment.'[3]

The proper use of terror to enable the terrorists to arrive at this point requires a solid understanding of the psychology of fear and the potential ways in which people may respond. It requires (preferably by design, but probably more often by accident) a fine balance if one is to predict when to apply terror, to whom, and for how long in order to achieve the desired result. The crux of the matter is the response to fear and anxiety. While fear may be a response to actual instances of terrorism, for the most part a well-engineered campaign will engender a continuous, high level of anxiety because the threat is vague, unpredictable, and incomprehensible. A feeling of impotence in changing the course of events contributes significantly to anxiety. Studies of the victims of air raids during the Second World War illustrate the importance of a feeling of extreme helplessness as a major cause of anxiety and the consequent shaking of the belief that 'it won't happen to me'.[4] The most psychologically damaging factor is the unpredictability of danger,[5] a factor which is particularly amenable to manipulation by terrorists.

The aim of instilling fear to produce personal disorientation is, of course, to upset the social structure so that no one any longer knows what to expect from anyone else. This divides society into frightened groups of individuals concerned only with personal survival. 'Terrorism destroys the solidarity, cooperation, and interdependence on which social functioning is based, and substitutes insecurity and distrust.'[6]

The results of this process, however, are somewhat unpredictable. First, political action, the aim of the terrorists, may not be provoked by fear. Instead, the targets may become numbed by the violence, and evidence a psychological tolerance which is often a precursor of hostility. This hostility is as likely to be directed against the terrorists as against the government and is a constant danger when terrorism is used to foster a collapse of confidence in the regime. It is possible, though, to begin to unravel some of the factors that contribute to the development of a tolerance to violence. The duration and magnitude of the terrorist threat is one major determinant. Again the studies of World War Two air raid victims provide instructive data. Vernon reported that people found a regular succession of raids less disturbing than those which occurred at irregular intervals.[7] The only exception to this general rule seemed to be those who had experienced a narrow escape or direct personal loss during a series of air raids.[8] In these cases 'near escapes' were more disturbing when they occurred in rapid succession; recuperation was possible when raids were more widely spaced. Thus in a terrorist campaign 'Sustained intense relentless terrorism is more likely to numb the target than is sporadic terrorism.'[9] Terrorist movements must always, then, guard against the overuse of violence.

A second factor which may determine reaction to terrorism involves the sort of messages delivered to the populace by the terrorists. There is some evidence that if the terrorists make positive recommendations to the populace on how to relieve the stress they are experiencing then action is more likely to follow. However, even here there is a problem having to do with the inherent nature of terrorism. As Hutchinson comments:

But even complying with revolutionary demands does not provide complete relief, for there is a boundary line in terrorism between too much clarification and too much obscurity; overstepping the line in the first direction makes terrorism lose its unpredictability and thus its power to terrify. Going too far in the second direction may cause the target to revolt.[10]

However, terrorist propaganda may be an important element in deciding whether the hostility engendered by terrorism will be directed against the incumbents or insurgents. A significant finding of the air raid studies was that it was often not the countries responsible for the bombing that were blamed by the victims. Rather the victims blamed their own governments for failing to protect them.[11] The aim of terrorist propaganda must be to tip the balance so that it is the government that becomes the target for popular aggression. This is a critical and difficult task, the failure of which has led to the elimination of many revolutionary groups. Often the balance is heavily influenced by the past record and present response of the government. If the anger of the populace is directed at the terrorists it is sometimes possible for them to turn the tide by denying responsibility because the credibility of the government is not sufficient to eliminate doubt as to the truth of the terrorists' claims. An excellent example of this is the way in which the Algerian FLN (Front de Libération Nationale) terrorists managed to avoid responsibility for the Melouza massacre in 1957. In this incident the male inhabitants of the village of Melouza were executed by the FLN for rebelling against FLN terrorism, supporting a rival nationalist group and also cooperating with the French army. Although international opinion was not reversed, the FLN managed to persuade most Muslims in Algeria that it was the French who had committed the murders in order to discredit the FLN. In large part this success was due to the fact that the French had no reputation for honesty in Algeria and the Muslims did not believe their protestations of innocence.

There is disagreement among theorists over the extent to which the success of terrorism depends on polarisation of the community. Gurr argues that terrorism, whatever its short-term merits, will not result in long-term ideological support. 'Support given under coercion is unlikely to develop into a more enduring allegiance unless it can be systematically maintained over a long period.'[12] Leites and Wolf, on the other hand, argue that whole-hearted mass support is not necessary. They claim that 'the only "act" R [rebellion] needs desperately from a large proportion of the populace is *nondenunciation* (that is, eschewing the act of informing against R and noncombat against it)'.[13] Equally as powerful as sympathy prompting support for the terrorists are lack of enthusiasm for the authorities, fear, and economic motives. Thus terrorism to be successful needs a judicious combination of public sympathy for the terrorist cause, coercion, and accurate calculations by the terrorists of their chances of success. An aim of terrorist tactics which is related to the creation of community disorientation is that of provoking repressive measures of an illegal or unconstitutional nature by the incumbent rulers or of forcing the intervention of a third party. If the government uses extra-legal methods or methods which restrict or deprive ordinary citizens of their human rights in order to suppress terrorists they lose both their legitimacy and public confidence and support. Thornton points out that such use of terror is 'most effective when it is indiscriminate in appearance but highly discriminate in fact'.[14]

Probably the best-known theorist on methods of provoking the security forces into heavy-handed over-reaction or illegal behaviour is Carlos Marighela. In his *Minimanual of the Urban Guerilla*, Marighela is quite specific about the aim of terrorist tactics:

From the moment a large proportion of the population begin to take his activities seriously, his success is assured. The Government can only intensify its repression, thus making the life of its citizens harder than ever: homes will be broken into, police searches organised, innocent people arrested, and communications broken; police terror will become the order of the day, and there will be more and more political murders – in short a massive political persecution . . . the political situation of the country will become a military situation.[15]

The Tupamaros in Uruguay explicitly followed Marighela's teachings in attempting to force the government to become repressive to such an extent that a climate of collapse would be engendered which would allow the political arm of the guerrilla movement to pose as the viable alternative and accede to power. In that case, however, only the first part of the scenario came true. It is true that repression increased to such an extent that the only liberal democracy in South America disappeared. But what replaced it in 1972 was not the neo-Marxist regime of the terrorists' dreams, but a ruthless, right-wing, authoritarian government which still exists today.

Terrorism and publicity

Another major aim of terrorism, in some instances the foremost aim, is that of publicity. By staging acts which gain the world's attention, terrorists are able to gain recognition of their cause and project themselves as a group that must be listened to and taken account of. Frightening acts of violence and the ensuing atmosphere of alarm and fear cause people to exaggerate the importance, size, and strength of some terrorist organisations. However, because of their numerical inferiority it is important that terrorist groups indulge in dramatic and shocking violence if they are to be noticed. The importance of the media as a vehicle for the expression of terrorist messages cannot be overstated. Terrorism and media coverage enjoy something of a symbiotic relationship. Television in particular is no longer a medium which simply responds to terrorist events, it is an integral part of them. Because of the vast, instant audience that can be conjured up by television, terrorists have learned to stage-manage their spectaculars for maximum audience impact. This is at least partly the reason for the dramatic increase in the occurrence of hostage and siege situations in the past few years. The drama of the situation can be increased by taking hostages. If certain demands are not met, hostages may be killed, thereby escalating the suspense and forcing the authorities to take the terrorists even more seriously. Such increasing tension also serves to intensify outside pressure on the authorities to give in to all or some of the terrorists' demands. The hostages may well have no real or symbolic value as individuals as far as the hostage-takers are concerned. They may be, and often are, anonymous individuals occupying no positions of power and belonging to no particular nation. Thus, for example, on 30 May 1972 when three members of the Japanese Red Army attacked passengers at Israel's Lod Airport they were not planning to kill anyone in *particular*, but rather *anyone at all* who happened to be there. When the shooting and explosions had stopped there were 27 dead and 76 wounded, a large number of whom were Puerto Rican Christian pilgrims. Hardly important pawns in international power politics. For the most part, then, terrorism is aimed at the audience, not the victims (except where an assassination is designed to remove a particular individual from power, for example). Indeed, as has been claimed often, terrorism is primarily theatre.

That the use of terror as a vehicle for attention-getting is successful can be illustrated by many contemporary examples. Thus, as Jenkins says, 'Insurgents fought in Angola, Mozambique, and Portuguese Guinea for fourteen years using the standard tactics of rural guerrilla warfare. The world hardly noticed their struggle, while an approximately equal number of Palestinian commandos employing terrorist tactics have in a few years become a primary concern to the world.'[16] In terms of generating worldwide public awareness of a cause, the most spectacular success was the Black September raid on the Munich Olympics in 1972. Millions of people were instantly appraised of the plight of the Palestinians by the carnage at Munich. However, awareness has not led to a resolution of the 'Palestinian question'.

Other purposes

Terrorism may be aimed at causing or hastening a general breakdown in social order, demoralising the citizens and causing them to lose faith in the ability of the incumbent government to maintain order and stability or to guarantee their safety. Particularly when a revolutionary group becomes impatient with the people – on whose behalf they claim to act – because they fail to appreciate and act upon the revolutionary message, they may well turn to terrorism as part of a campaign to politicise and mobilise the populace. In theory, if terrorism can be used to show that a government is powerless to protect its people or to keep vital functions operating and forces the government to waste resources in massive security operations and indulge in repressive measures which affect the lives of ordinary people, there will come a time when the people will revolt against the government. In practice, however, such a strategy often backfires and the use of terrorism may well turn the people, even sympathisers, against the terrorist violence and its perpetrators, and lead to support for the government's efforts to wipe out the terrorists.

There is ample historical evidence that terror alone is not generally an effective weapon for bringing about the overthrow of incumbent governments. The few cases in which terrorism played a major part in bringing sweeping political changes have arisen in certain colonial independence struggles against foreign rule, as in the case of the ending of the Palestine Mandate after the terrorist campaigns of Irgun and Stern, and the EOKA campaign in Cyprus. However, as Wilkinson has shown in his analysis of these situations, even in these rare cases special conditions prevailed that made terrorism a more potent weapon.[17] First, for various reasons of political expediency and international pressure the occupying power was unwilling to carry through draconian measures to wipe out the terrorist organisations. In each case there were also inter-communal power struggles within the colony which rendered a peaceful diplomatic settlement and withdrawal difficult if not impossible. Finally, where terrorists were successful (for example, in Aden) they already enjoyed considerable support within their own ethnic groups which created great difficulties for the intelligence services in penetrating groups for information and also provided much active and tacit collaboration and support for the terrorist operatives.

A further major aim of specific terrorist operations is to wring concessions from the controlling power. This may take the form of a demand for policy changes (for example, the Austrian government agreed to stop allowing Jewish refugees transit through Austria on their way to Israel in return for the safe release of hostages held by Palestinian terrorists in September 1973), ransom (particularly used by South American terrorist groups), the release of prisoners, or the publication of a terrorist manifesto. The use of hostages as a bargaining lever creates a dramatic situation which ensures that the terrorists' demands are taken notice of.

Terrorism may serve a number of purposes internal to the terrorist movement itself. Groom notes that 'terror may serve as a blooding device for once a recruit has incriminated himself with an act of terror it is harder for him to defect and he can be controlled by the threat of being revealed by his associates to the authorities'.[18]

This is borne out by Frantz Fanon who speaking of the terrorists in the Algerian FLN said that their leaders' trust in them was 'proportional to the hopelessness of each case. You could be sure of a new recruit when he could no longer go back into the colonial service.'[19]

Terrorism may be used to enforce obedience. This is the aim of 'institutional' terror as practised by secret security organisations who attempt to create an atmosphere of fear which ensures that opposition to the regime is difficult to organise. However, individual terrorist organisations also use terror to ensure the loyalty of their members. In February 1972, a hideout of the Japanese United Red Army was discovered in Karuizawa, a mountain spa some eighty miles from Tokyo. 'There fourteen mangled and tortured bodies were found; one half of the group had liquidated the others for antirevolutionary failings, a few had apparently been buried alive.'[20]

Another internal function served by terrorism is that of building morale amongst members of the movement and their supporters. If terrorists can penetrate a security ring and explode a bomb, kill a highly protected target, or force concessions out of a target organisation their power and credibility will be enhanced.

Finally, reference must be made to what might be termed the psychological purposes for which terrorism is utilised. Some leading philosophers and advocates of terror, foremost amongst them Frantz Fanon and Jean-Paul Sartre, have sought to show that violence is a phenomenon which is personally positive and liberative. Particularly in his major philosophical work *Critique de la Raison Dialectique*[21] Sartre elevates terror to the highest position in human affairs. It is the driving force of social organisation and the key to freedom. For Sartre, the exercise of terror is one of the conditions of freedom.[22] It is a condition in a different sense than that implied by Marxist philosophers, however.[23] Marx saw that violence would be necessary in the revolutionary struggle because the bourgeoisie will not relinquish power without a fight. But violence is only a tool, a means to an end.[24] Sartre's philosophy goes considerably beyond this functional approach. Sartre glorified terror and violence as ends in themselves, as cleansing and purifying forces.

Sartre's philosophy was mirrored by Fanon when he considered the case of his adopted country, Algeria. He too saw violence as a cleansing force which unified the people and advocated terrorism as a tool for freeing the native from his feelings of inferiority, and from despair and inaction. Violence directed against the oppressors, Fanon claims, 'makes him [the native] fearless and restores his self-respect... When the people have taken violent part in the national liberation they will allow no one to set themselves up as 'liberators'... Illuminated by violence, the consciousness of the people rebels against pacification.'[25] Curiously, Fanon, who was a psychiatrist, himself provided evidence against the 'violence as psychological therapy' theory in the form of case studies of Algerians traumatised by French violence and of FLN terrorists suffering immense psychological pain as a result of their violence. Of course, this paradox can be resolved. One has to admit that emotional guilt caused by terrorism is highly individual. As Hutchinson notes 'the majority of FLN terrorists did not feel so guilty that they refused to commit acts of terrorism'.[26] As for case studies of the traumatic effects of French violence one can merely (and perhaps reasonably) make a distinction between the violence that one inflicts and that which is inflicted upon one. Thus Amar Ouzegane, an FLN leader, claimed that 'One must differentiate between "violence which liberates and violence which oppresses".'[27] Ouzegane also suggests that terrorism fulfils other internal functions, namely relieving the tension caused by inaction and controlling militant impatience.

Urban terrorism, our liberating terrorism, functioned as a safety valve. It permitted patriots ulcerated by the unequal struggle, revolted by French injustice . . . , to liberate themselves from an unconscious psychological complex, to keep cool heads, to respect revolutionary discipline.[28]

Summary

Thus terrorist activities may have many aims. Whilst the primary effect is to create fear and alarm the objectives may be to gain concessions, obtain maximum publicity for a cause, provoke repression, break down social order, build morale in the movement or enforce obedience to it. Several of the objectives may be accomplished simultaneously by a single incident.

Whether or not terrorism will meet these aims is critically dependent upon the accuracy of the terrorists' calculations concerning the timing, degree, and type of terrorist activities.[29]

5

The development of terrorism as a strategy

It has been shown that the use of terror has a long history and is not, as many seem to believe, a novel phenomenon of the twentieth century. It can certainly be argued, however, that terrorism as a coherent philosophy and the *kind* of terrorism society faces today are unique, and certain modern variants trace their immediate antecedents to theories of revolutionary warfare developed primarily in this century. Perhaps the greatest guerrilla theorist was Mao Tse-tung who developed a coherent theory which integrated what were essentially a set of military tactics used by those who lacked armies. Mao deviated significantly from both the existing Marxist revolutionary theories and existing military strategy. In his famous slogan 'political power grows out of the barrel of a gun', Mao acknowledged the military basis of political power. However, he also knew that at the beginning of the struggle his forces would be numerically and technologically inferior and so emphasised the importance of political power as a substitute for military power. Thus, it was considered vital that the guerrillas be highly motivated politically so that, strengthened by the political support of the peasantry, they could survive early military reverses and have the determination to carry on a protracted campaign which would eventually wear down the less committed and dedicated opposition.

This concept of a people's war avoided thinking only in terms of quantities of arms and resources, and showed how a revolutionary group could eventually defeat militarily superior forces. Jenkins argues that:

In saying that guerrillas aimed for and depended upon the political mobilization of people who would be mere bystanders in a conventional military conflict, Mao introduced a relationship between military action and the attitude and response of the audience. This added a new dimension to conflict, which until then had measured achievement primarily in terms of the physical effect that any military action had on the enemy. Now it was being said that the effect that any violent action has on the people watching may be independent of, and may equal or even exceed in importance the actual physical damage inflicted on the foe. Terrorism is that proposition pursued to its most violent extreme.[1]

As we have seen, terrorism is violence for effect. The actual physical damage it causes is often not all important – the aim is to have a *dramatic* impact on the audience. However, while the foundation for a theory of terrorism was laid by Mao, its expression is not found in his writings, which still emphasised the importance of military power. Russian Marxist theories of revolution, while approving of wholesale terror in the name of protecting the revolution, tend to downplay total reliance on military means, and particularly terrorism, in the actual making of the revolution. In fact, it is in the Jewish struggle to force the British to leave Palestine and in the colonial independence guerrilla campaigns that programmes of deliberate terrorism first emerge.

The colonial struggles

The justification for the use of extreme violence by colonial independence movements was that colonialism itself is 'violence in its natural state, and it will only yield when confronted with greater violence'.[2] (Similar views have been expressed by various Palestinian groups.) In pursuing this violence, legitimate targets were considerably wider than in previous movements of violence, and included obvious figures such as colonial administrators and high-ranking security forces officers and gradually diffused to take in ordinary soldiers and police personnel, small-scale business people, civilian employees of the colonial government and anyone remotely connected with the administration. In the extreme, the definition of legitimate target included anyone not actively participating in the anti-colonial struggle. It is this narrowing of the category of innocent bystanders which is a hallmark of modern terrorism.

The emergence of terrorism in colonial struggles may partly be explained by the political situation which followed World War Two and in which context the independence movements flourished. Colonialism was beginning to be viewed as immoral and a hang-over from bygone times by many citizens of the colonial powers and by influential non-colonial governments. Consequently public opinion at home and abroad inhibited the colonial powers from displaying the military might they were capable of and which in the past they would have employed to put down the insurrections. This was of major significance because it hinted at the possibility of the success of independence movements without their having to indulge in protracted military campaigns or build up, bit by bit, a party organisation which could orchestrate political mobilisation. Thus:

In the wake of the First Indochina War and the bitter struggles in Indonesia and Algeria, colonial governments were anxious to avoid the military costs, the potential military disasters, the inevitable domestic political divisiveness, and condemnation by the international community that a protracted and debilitating military campaign against guerrillas in a distant colony could bring. The mere threat of such a struggle could often persuade colonial governments to retire gracefully. Colonial insurgents found terrorism to be an effective means of broadcasting their opposition to continued colonial rule, of embarrassing the colonial government, or gaining instantaneous worldwide attention, sympathy, and support, which in turn could be translated into international pressure on the colonial government, and of forewarning the colonial government of the kind of struggle it would face if it chose to resist.[3]

It is doubtful that the anti-colonial guerrillas fully understood the results of their actions (or, more accurately, predicted their effects) but the nexus they formed between violent action and an audience (be it the colonial government, its citizens, or world opinion) succeeded in effectively neutralising the military muscle of the colonial powers. Their acts of violence, insignificant in terms of military capability, were able to achieve domestic and international political pressure on the colonial government far in excess of the pressure they could have exerted militarily – in some cases sufficient to bring about withdrawal of the colonial army.

It is interesting that, with the exception of Cuba, few guerrillas have been able to achieve the success of colonial freedom fighters. There are a number of obvious explanations for this. First, despite their military superiority, colonial governments must exist under the psychological and political disadvantages discussed above, which indigenous governments do not. Further indigenous governments are much more unwilling to give up power, that power being all they have (as opposed to a colonial government which can give up power in a colony without losing power at home). The failure of conventional guerrilla tactics against indigenous governments has been particularly obvious in South America where rural guerrillas have not managed to advance beyond the remote areas in which they first started fighting. This in turn has led to the development of urban guerrilla tactics which aim to take the struggle directly to the government. It is in urban guerrilla theory that the tactics of terrorism become most apparent and this theory provides the link between earlier revolutionary theories and modern terrorism. Urban guerrillas first seek to gain international attention by dramatic acts of violence. Assassinations, bombings, kidnappings, bank robberies, and hijacking have all become common weapons for urban political activists. Other groups have adopted these tactics and carried them further by extending the conflict to individuals and countries not directly involved in the struggle. This is international terrorism, a new departure in the tactics of terror.

International terrorism is thus an offshoot, the newest branch in the evolution of modern revolutionary and guerrilla warfare theories. It elevates individual acts of violence to the level of strategy (and therefore is denounced by orthodox Marxists as adventurism). It denigrates conventional military power by substituting dramatic violence played for the people watching. It violates the conventional rules of engagement: it reduces the category of innocent bystanders. It makes the world its battlefield: it recognizes no boundaries to the conflict, no neutral nations.[4]

Terrorism and revolutionary warfare

To understand the place of terrorism in revolutionary warfare it is necessary to delve more deeply into the theory of revolutionary warfare itself. First it helps to distinguish between a multitude of terms which create confusion in such a discussion, particularly the terms 'irregular', 'guerrilla', and 'revolutionary' warfare. For the present purposes the term 'irregular' warfare will be used to connote the broad span of unconventional warfare under which all the other types are subsumed. 'Guerrilla' warfare is a form of irregular military operation in which hit and disappear tactics are employed to attack (usually) conventional military forces and often to operate in support of regular military forces engaged in conventional warfare. The important point to note is that both the targets and the operations are essentially military ones. In contrast, 'revolutionary' warfare may employ both guerrilla and conventional methods (either separately or together) but also uses psychological-political methods in order to establish an alternative political system. This conceptual distinction is made by Colonel Georges Bonnet, a French military analyst, who proposes the following equation:

$$RW \text{ (revolutionary war)} = G \text{ (guerrilla tactics)} + P \text{ (political activity)}[5]$$

Thus, the central objective in revolutionary warfare is not only (or even at all) military victory but the support of the people. Guerrilla tactics are therefore secondary to political tactics. Of course politics is also integral to other forms of unconventional warfare and eventually any form of warfare. Rather than having limited political goals, revolutionary warfare seeks nothing less than total political change. Since the people are the target, psychological/political methods must be paramount.

As noted earlier, Mao Tse-tung may be credited with first developing a systematic theory of revolutionary warfare. Since his early writings, the theory has been developed in different directions by General Vo Nguyen Giap, the famous North Vietnamese strategist, Che Guevara, Regis Debray and others. In each variant, terrorism has been assigned a role and these theories have had considerable influence on the justification for and practice of political terrorism generally. It will therefore be useful to briefly summarise the salient features of the theory of revolutionary warfare advanced by these leading thinkers.

In his famous essay, 'On Protracted Conflict',[6] Mao divided revolutionary warfare into three phases. Phase one involves the incumbent forces' strategic offensive and the insurgents' strategic defensive, during which guerrilla tactics are secondary to conventional mobile warfare. The second phase 'will be the period of the enemy's strategic consolidation and our preparation for the counter-offensive'.[7] This is the longest phase, and the one during which guerrilla warfare rises to a position of primacy. Following this equilibrium period, the third phase is entered during which the insurgents mount a counter-offensive and force the incumbents into a strategic retreat. Again guerrilla warfare assumes a secondary role and conventional methods become most important. However, according to Mao, these military considerations are overshadowed by the importance of psycho-political tactics. Shultz emphasises this when he writes:

Thus, ideological thrust, organizational form, and programmatic content are essential, for the insurgents must demonstrate to the populace that there are alternative structures to satisfy their needs. Only in this way will the insurgents be able to socialize and mobilize the populace into backing their cause.[8]

Thus revolutionary warfare is both constructive and destructive. With this in mind, it is possible to examine the role of terrorism in revolutionary warfare.

Mao, and subsequent developers of aspects of his theories, assigns a specific role to terrorism. While recognising that terrorism may backfire and increase support for the incumbents rather than the insurgents, Mao nevertheless states that:

It is necessary to create terror for a while in every rural area, or otherwise it would be impossible to suppress the activities of the counter-revolutionaries in the countryside or overthrow the authority of the gentry.[9]

General Giap, in his essay 'The South Vietnamese People Will Win' also directly advocates the use of terrorism:

At the price of their hard won experiences, our compatriots in the South realized that . . . the most correct path to be followed . . . is revolutionary violence and revolutionary war . . . Only by revolutionary violence can the masses . . . take power.[10]

As implemented by the National Liberation Front (NLF or Vietcong) in South Vietnam 'revolutionary violence' included all of the major terroristic acts (assassination, bombings, hostage-taking, etc).

Other theorists are more restrained in their advocacy of terrorism. Che Guevara, for example, warns that terrorism is:

a measure that is generally ineffective and indiscriminate in its results, since it often makes victims of innocent people and destroys a large number of lives that would be valuable to the revolution.[11]

However, Guevara does accord terrorism a limited role:

Terrorism should be considered a valuable tactic when it is used to put to death some noted leader of the oppressing forces well known for his cruelty, his efficiency in repression, or other quality that makes his elimination useful. But the killing of persons of small importance is never advisable, since it brings on an increase of reprisals, including deaths.[12]

Debray, in his book *Revolution in the Revolution*, also directly limits the usefulness of terrorism:

Terrorism cannot assume any decisive role, and it entails certain dangers . . . But if it is subordinate to the fundamental struggle, it has from the military point of view a strategic value.[13]

This brief survey shows that the most prominent revolutionary warfare theorists argue that terrorism has a limited and secondary role only in revolutionary warfare, and that it must be employed selectively and cautiously lest the tactic backfire. It could be noted that all of these theorists were strong advocates of rural guerrilla warfare and wrote little about the urban variant which is now becoming more prevalent. However, even the best-known guerrilla theorist, the Brazilian Carlos Marighela, believed urban operations to be secondary to rural ones. According to Marighela the function of urban guerrilla warfare is to

wear out, demoralize, and distract the enemy forces, permitting the emergence and survival of rural guerrilla warfare which is destined to play the decisive role in the revolutionary war.[14]

And though Marighela's advocacy of terrorism as a tactic to provoke repression is well known, he also warned against the use of terrorism as an end in itself.[15]

The reason for the relegation of terrorism to secondary status was obvious for the revolutionary theorists. Revolutionary warfare, if it is to be successful, requires the commitment, or at least the cooperation, of the populace. It is not possible to obtain such commitment in the long term (although it may be in the short term) if the populace suffers under a campaign of terror. In fact, there are recent historical examples of insurgencies collapsing because of a policy of terror being misused. Paret and Shy claim that towards the end of the communist insurgency in Greece in the late 1940s, over half a million of what should have been the insurgents' strongest supporters were driven into the cities by the widespread and indiscriminate use of terror.[16] According to these analysts, this exodus significantly contributed to the defeat of the communists. They also claim that the collapse of the Malayan communist insurgency (1948–54) can be partially attributed to the insurgents' excessive use of terrorism.[17] It seems almost inevitable that such a collapse will follow the indiscriminate use of terrorism against the general population. As Shulz comments:

Terror may . . . be used effectively against the populace but only under very selective and controlled conditions. Second degree terror – Kidnapping and Indoctrination – may be used against certain class elements to induce them to support the insurgency . . . However, terror tactics, as the various revolutionary warfare theorists have noted, may backfire over the long run and therefore they warn against the abusive use of such tactics, especially when directed at elements of the general populace.[18]

It can been seen, then, that insurgents who adhere to the 'classical' theories of revolutionary warfare assign a specific, subsidiary, and controlled role to terrorism. Thus, for example, Shultz has analysed the terroristic activities of the NLF in South Vietnam and concludes that they follow, in all major respects, the pattern laid down by the 'classical' precepts of revolutionary warfare.[19] However, as well as groups adhering to the theoretical propositions of revolutionary warfare, there is increasing evidence of a trend towards nihilistic tendencies in some terrorist groups.[20] Such groups pose a particular threat because they have no theoretical or tactical limits to their behaviour. They are not concerned to win the 'hearts and minds' of the people, but rather seek only to destroy. With the possibilities for mass destruction or mass disruption which exist in modern society, such groups present a danger and challenge such as has never existed in the history of terrorism to date. It is against these groups that society will have to pit its best skills in the future.

6

Trends in terrorism

One of the consequences of the difficulty of defining terrorism is that it makes the phenomenon very hard to measure accurately. Without a comprehensive and well-accepted definition it is obvious that different measurement attempts will enumerate different incidents or classify them in different ways. In order to attempt to judge the comprehensiveness and validity of any quantitative analysis of terrorism it is, therefore, necessary to study and to accept the definitional premises upon which it is based. Judging the accuracy of the analysis also poses problems because of the difficulty of knowing whether or not all relevant incidents have come to the notice of the analysts. These problems are less critical in the area of international terrorism because the incidents are usually well publicised (and thus easily counted and cross-checked) and fall within widely accepted definitional bounds. However instances of national or domestic terrorism are very hard to measure with an accuracy which would allow great confidence to be placed in trend analyses based upon them.

A recent report by the United States Central Intelligence Agency (CIA) illustrates that even compilation of statistics of international terrorism are fraught with danger. Since 1968, the CIA has kept computerised records on international terrorism. In this context international terrorism is defined as:

The threat or use of violence for political purposes when such action is intended to influence the attitude and behaviour of a target group other than its immediate victims and its ramifications transcend national boundaries.[1]

These records are used to compile an annual report on international terrorism. The 1980 report was interesting in that it completely revised many of the figures published in previous years. 'The agency said that its previous data had been too dependent on "US sources" and that it is now satisfied that its records are "complete and current".'[2] The report also listed several new categories, including 'threats' and 'hoaxes' which had not been listed in previous reports. Thus, whereas the 1979 report said that there had been 3,336 incidents of international terrorism between 1968 and 1979, with a peak of 413 in 1976, the 1980 report claimed that there were 6,714 incidents between 1968 and 1980, with 760 in 1979. According to the CIA,

50

there were 587 deaths due to international terrorism in 1979 and 642 in 1980. The fact that an agency with the resources of the CIA can conclude at a particular point in time that many of its previously published statistics were underestimates makes it difficult to have confidence in the accuracy of their figures. How do they know they have obtained all the relevant data now – or, more particularly, how can we be assured that they have? It is because of these uncertainties that many students of terrorism are wary of making precise quantitative analyses of trends in terrorism.

Nevertheless, accepting the cautions and limitations implied by these uncertainties, it can be useful to examine some of the chronologies produced by various intelligence and research organisations in order to ascertain general trends in terrorism. An example of such an organisation is the United States-based RAND Corporation which for some years has been closely monitoring terrorist events and which has produced a number of useful chronologies and trend analyses which made some attempt at quantifying terrorism and evaluating the success of terrorist tactics.[3] One such analysis examined incidents of international terrorism by year for the years 1968–77.[4] Data analysed included the total number of incidents of international terrorism involving fatalities or injuries by year; the total number of fatalities in incidents of international terrorism by year; and the number of 'major' incidents of international terrorism by year. The data showed that, generally, although there are increases and decreases from year to year, there is an increasing use over time of the tactics of international terrorism.

One particularly noteworthy feature of the data produced by the RAND study is that the picture they convey is not the same as that which one would have obtained by sampling public or governmental reaction to the events during the individual years in question. For example, although in overall terms there was less international terrorism in 1972 than in 1970 (84 *versus* 101 incidents, according to the RAND survey), 1972 marked the turning point in many governments' determination to undertake serious measures to combat terrorism. The probable reason was that two particularly shocking events, the Lod Airport massacre and the Munich Olympics incident, had special impact.

Similarly, 1975 was frequently referred to in the news as the 'year of the terrorist'. In fact there were some spectacular events, such as two attempts to shoot down airliners at Orly Airport in Paris, the seizure of embassies in Stockholm, Kuala Lumpur, and Madrid, the IRA's bombing campaign in London, the hijacking of a train in the Netherlands, the seizure of the OPEC oil ministers in Vienna, and more. However, on all the measures recorded in the RAND study, international terrorism had in fact declined. What this illustrates is that mere counting of events does not measure the things that

Table 1. *A comparison between RAND Corporation and US Central Intelligence Agency estimates of incidents of international terrorism and deaths in international terrorist incidents for the years 1968 to 1977*

Number of international terrorist incidents per year			Number of deaths in international terrorist incidents per year		
YEAR	RAND[a]	CIA[b]	YEAR	RAND[a]	CIA[b]
1968	35	111	1968	21	34
1969	51	166	1969	7[c]	29
1970	101	282	1970	74	110
1971	52	216	1971	7	36
1972	84	269	1972	130	145
1973	163	275	1973	92	124
1974	153	382	1974	247	315
1975	89	297	1975	92	240
1976	151[c]	413	1976	200	402
1977	143[c]	279	1977	145	235

[a] *Source*: B.M. Jenkins. International terrorism: trends and potentialities. *Journal of International Affairs*, 1978, *32*(1), 114–23.
[b] *Source*: Central Intelligence Agency. *International Terrorism in 1979*. April 1980.
[c] Data estimated from graphs in Jenkins article cited in (a).

matter. What we count does not necessarily reflect people's perceptions of terrorism, and in many ways it is perception which is at the core of the phenomenon of terrorism. After all, it should be remembered that 'terrorism is not simply what terrorists do, but the effect – the publicity, the alarm – they create by their actions'.[5]

A comparison of the RAND figures with those produced by the CIA provides further evidence of the problem of knowing how accurate quantification of terrorist data may be. Table 1 shows the RAND data on total number of incidents of international terrorism and numbers of fatalities in international terrorist incidents for the years 1968 to 1977, compared with the CIA data for the same headings over the same period. As may be seen, the data are substantially different for all years, thus leaving the student of terrorism with the problem of deciding which, if either, is an accurate set of data. It is suggested that this comparison along with many others which could be made,should alert us to the dangers of making absolute quantitative statements about terrorism. Further, any quantitatively based trend analyses should be approached with some caution.

However, if hard statements about numbers of events are difficult to make, there are sufficient data available on qualitative changes in terrorism to make it meaningful to analyse the manner in which terrorism is being employed, how the nature of terrorism is changing, and what implications these changes have for counter-terrorist policy and operations. In the following pages we will examine some of these trends.

The move to urban operations.

However, even if simple counting exercises do not necessarily reveal meaningful trends in contemporary terrorism other analyses do uncover such trends. For example, a trend of great importance is that over the last two decades the urban drift evident in most societies has led to urban terrorism more and more supplanting rural guerrilla tactics as the major force in revolutionary warfare. Particularly following the failure of the rural-based, Castro-inspired revolutionary attempts in South America, the emphasis has increasingly been placed on urban operations. Often such operations are termed 'urban guerrilla warfare', but such a term is really a misnomer for simple urban-based terrorism.

Accompanying the move to the cities has been a significant shift in the ideological underpinnings of many terrorist groups. In particular there appears to be a growing element of nihilism entering the equation, with a growing number of terrorist groups appealing to no specific constituency on whose behalf they claim to act. This trend has important consequences for terrorist tactics and targets:

As motivation tends away from a positive ideology toward a nihilistic attitude, certain constraints normally characteristic of popularly oriented and ideologically based movements also will fade in importance. The concern of the nonideologically motivated focuses on the requirement for immediate action to alter existing conditions and not upon the creation of an ultimate utopia or the form it should take. While one previously fought for a constituency, the tendency is now basically just to fight. The successors to the Baader-Meinhof gang exhibit this trend more and more.[6]

The clear danger is that much terrorism could degenerate into motiveless acts. As Laqueur notes:

The less clear the political purposes in terrorism, the greater its appeal to unbalanced persons. The motives of men fighting a cruel tyranny are quite different from those of rebels against a democratically elected government. Idealism, a social conscience or hatred of foreign oppression are powerful impulses, but so are free-floating aggression, boredom and mental confusion. Activism can give meaning to otherwise empty lives.[7]

The 'ecstasy factor'

Along with this shift in emphasis on the justification for the use of terrorism has gone an increase in what might be called the 'ecstasy factor' in terrorism. In a thought-provoking essay on the nature of terrorism, William May has argued that most analysts have looked at terrorism only as a type of political strategy – and further, as a strategy which is often found wanting because of its frequently counterproductive nature.[8] May suggests that our puzzlement as to why terrorists continue to employ a potentially (and often actually) self-destructive tactic reflects our failure to appreciate that terrorism carries an important dimension outside the realm of political discourse, namely, an ecstatic element. To the extent that the ecstatic element predominates, the exercise of terror may become an almost religious experience for the terrorists with the production of emotional concomitants becoming a primary motivating force. This element of ecstasy is akin, but not identical, to (and probably overlaps) the 'cleansing' aspects of terrorism eulogised by Fanon and Sartre. The latter see the use of terror as an important part of personal development. May claims the ecstatic element to be essentially 'just for thrills'. The ecstatic element, when dominant, goes hand in hand with nihilism and sets apart terrorists of this ilk from those who believe in some order or justice which is attainable by the rational and calculated use of terrorism as a political weapon. When justice is less specific and the terrorists motivated more by the emotional consequences of terrorism, violence escalates.

> The perceived injustice puts one literally *beside oneself* with rage. In a state of outrage, one moves quickly from selective terrorism to the justification of indiscriminate and random violence so that the whole world might attend to injustice done.[9]

It is difficult to say whether or not there has been an increase in the ecstatic element in terrorism in recent years. Certainly it is not a novel phenomenon. There were clear elements of ecstasis in some of the acts of terrorism in Russia and Europe in the late nineteenth and early twentieth centuries. But on the whole the political, strategic element was dominant. Today there exist examples in which it is not at all clear that terrorism as strategem is the primary factor. The later activities of the Baader-Meinhof remnants are a case in point. Perhaps the best example is the massacre at Lod Airport by the Japanese Red Army. A reading of the transcript of the trial of Kozo Okamoto, one of the terrorists involved in that event, reveals a significant ecstatic element. However, the terrorism of ecstasy need not increase the frequency in comparison with past times in order to pose a new threat. The combination of any group primarily (or even significantly) motivated by non-strategic factors and the existence of new vulnerabilities and new weapons presents frightening possibilities which have not hitherto existed.

International links

Another trend which has revealed itself in recent years is the emergence of working relations between terrorist groups from divergent political, ethnic, and geographical backgrounds. There is now substantial evidence of cooperative efforts in the fields of training, procurement of weapons and documentation (passports, visas, identity cards, etc.), reconnaissance of airline routes and targets, and actual terrorist operations. Such links are substantially different from the mostly abstract or supportive relations between previous terrorist organisations (although there are a number of examples of past terrorist groups having concrete assistance from outside forces).[10] Many terrorist operations are now complex international efforts, although they may nominally be conducted on behalf of one particular organisation. Apart from these links between terrorist organisations themselves, a number of nations give either sanctuary or financial support (or both) to the terrorists. Often this cooperation between so-called individual and nation-state actors is quite open.

The debate about the extent of the international terrorist network and the question of who, if anybody, directs it became an important political issue with the assumption of Ronald Reagan to the Presidency of the United States and the open accusation by his Administration in 1981 that the Soviet Union was the puppet master of international terrorism. The debate has centered in particular on a book entitled *The Terror Network* by Claire Sterling,[11] who also gave evidence to a new Senate Subcommittee on Terrorism and Security which, among other issues, began to probe international links between terrorist organisations in a series of hearings which started in April 1981.

Sterling's work has been widely interpreted as providing extensive evidence of Soviet *control and direction* of international terrorism. However, in the book itself Sterling does not assert that the Soviet Union is the mastermind behind some international terrorist plot. Rather, she details a long list of incidents in which the Soviets have had a hand in terms of provision of finance, arms, training, and other assistance, either directly or through proxies such as Libya, North Korea, Cuba and a host of other intermediaries. The difficulty with her work is that Sterling has left a number of ambiguities on the question of Soviet direction unresolved and, as Brian Jenkins has pointed out,[12] these ambiguities are easily used to reinforce prejudices held by supporters of the Reagan Administration's 'tough' approach to terrorism and international security issues generally.

This,in its turn, has produced a passionate rejection of Sterling's thesis (or presumed thesis, since she nowhere actually claims Soviet direction) in some quarters. As Rubin notes:

On one level, this attitude springs from concern that U.S. policy is single-mindedly defining all threats and all problems in the world as coming from Moscow. On another, there is the view that human rights policy – aimed at protecting people from terrorism from above – is being abandoned in favour of a concentration on terrorism as more narrowly defined. Both points are well taken and reflect real problems.[13]

What then *is* the situation regarding Soviet involvement in international terrorism? In the United States, the State Department, the CIA and the Defense Intelligence Agency all initially denied that evidence existed of extensive Soviet involvement (in spite of the fact that one of the first public references to its presumed existence was in the 1976 CIA report on terrorism). All three agencies were asked to review their data on this issue and, in their 1981 report on international terrorism, the CIA claimed that the Soviet Union is deeply involved in support of revolutionary violence 'which frequently entails acts of international terrorism'.[14] However, nobody has yet provided unequivocal evidence that supports a simple-minded Soviet-culprit theory of terrorist control and neither are there any serious analyses of Soviet strategic objectives and the manner in which these ends would be served by support for terrorism. The evidence of Soviet support for destabilising influences in the Western-aligned world is over-whelming but it indicates a capacity of opportunistic exploitation of situations rather than their specific creation and direction. As one review of Sterling's work points out the evidence to hand at present provides

a convincing indictment of Soviet *involvement* in a wide assortment of terrorist movements, including such apparently diverse causes as those of the Irish Republican Army Provisionals, Italy's Red Brigades, and the Turkish Peoples' Liberation Army, to name just a few. But this Soviet involvement is generally (and accurately) depicted more as a case of fishing in troubled waters than one of being the driving force. The Soviets, Sterling seems to say, operate on the principle that what is bad for one's enemy is good for one's self. If, therefore, this movement or that cause could embarrass and "destabilise" (her word) the West, why not lend a hand?[15]

The development of international terrorist links and their support by foreign governments raises another possibility which has been discussed by Brian Jenkins.[16] This is the possibility that governments, rather than political groups, may turn more frequently to sponsoring terrorist activities as an arm of foreign policy, thus engaging in terrorism as surrogate warfare. Jenkins suggests that with the development of weapons of mass destruction it is becoming increasingly impractical and undesirable for nations to become involved in conventional war. The alternative of protracted, low-level war is also debilitating and unattractive. Jenkins, however, suggests that there is a third alternative – that of 'surrogate war'.

Terrorism, though now rejected as a legitimate mode of warfare by most conventional military establishments, could become an accepted form of warfare in the future. Terrorists could be employed to provoke international incidents, create alarm in an adversary's country, compel it to divert valuable resources to protect itself, destroy its morale, and carry out specific forms of sabotage. Governments could employ existing terrorist groups to attack their opponents, or they could create their own terrorists. Terrorism only requires a small investment, certainly far less than what it costs to wage conventional war.[17]

Taken as a whole these trends indicate the necessity for a serious, but measured, response to terrorism. Contemporary terrorism potentially is able to exert more leverage than ever before and there are indications that some groups who resort to terrorism will not in the future show the restraint that (whatever their atrocities) has characterised them in the past. Nevertheless, whilst emphasising the need for better preparation, it must also be borne in mind that the actual physical damage caused by terrorists to date has not been great. Jenkins estimates that between 1968 and 1977 there were 1,019 incidents of international terrorism.[18] In fact, casualties occurred in only 303 incidents, with most lives being lost in a small number of plane crashes and major assaults (such as that at Lod Airport). Many commentators have noted that the number of deaths and injuries due to terrorism is only a fraction of the number due in the same period to murder or road accidents. This of course misses the point about the psychic effects of terror but, nevertheless, it does put the actual destruction into perspective.

7

The effects of terrorism

The incidence and changing significance of terrorism has had some obvious effects. The most evident is the diversion of resources into internal security functions. Protecting political leaders, guarding vital locations, screening people at airports, and hardening targets all require increasing amounts of money, labour, and time. The most publically visible security precaution is the screening of passengers at airports. Apart from the time and inconvenience costs to the public, the financial costs of screening precautions have been enormous. One study estimated the costs of mandatory screening in the United States at $194.2 million for the period 1973–76,[1] An analysis of the deterrent effects of screening showed that this was a cost of $3.24 million to $9.25 million expenditure to deter a single hijacking.

There has been a rapid increase in internal security budgets, which shows no sign of abating, and the private security industry is increasingly involving itself in internal security-type operations. This latter trend is particularly worrying in view of the competitive nature of the private security industry and its lack of public accountability. Jenkins sees this as part of

a major shift in society from viewing security in terms of secure national frontiers, clearly a national responsibility, to the defense of "inner perimeters" – guarded facilities, privately patrolled communities, security buildings, alarmed homes – where the burden of defense is increasingly placed upon local government, the private sector, and the individual citizen.[2]

In the legal sphere terrorism has also had effects. There have been many attempts to agree upon some form of international law to regulate political crimes of violence and a number of international conventions on such things as air piracy and protection of diplomatic persons have been signed. However, for several reasons, these agreements are either of little utility or apply to only small areas of the problem. The first difficulty is that of definition. The United Nations, for example, has been trying for years to arrive at a satisfactory definition of terrorism, without success. The deliberations of the special UN ad hoc committee on terrorism[3] illustrated nicely the divisions, political differences, and sectional interests which prevent agreement on this topic. (This debate is considered in detail in Chapter 11.)

At the domestic level, legal changes have also followed the increased incidence of terrorism. In some countries police powers have been broadened (for example, in the United Kingdom the Prevention of Terrorism (Temporary Provisions) Act 1974 and 1976, increases the time the police may hold for questioning persons suspected of terrorist activities, gives them greater powers of entry and search, and allows them to summarily deport suspects). Such legislation must be carefully used and monitored or it may easily be used to suppress legitimate political dissent. Serious concern has already been expressed that this is the case in Britain. Figures released by the authorities show that of a total of 5,875 persons detained under the Act to the end of October 1977, only 247 were charged with any offence. Of these, only 129 were charged with offences specifically included in the Act or with offences connected with terrorist activities.[4] More recent figures issued by the Home Office show that over the complete period of operation of the Acts (9 November 1974 to 30 June 1980) 4,834 persons had been detained but almost 90 per cent were released without being charged or having an exclusion order made against them.[5] These figures give some credence to the view expressed by bodies such as the National Council for Civil Liberties that the police are using the powers invested in them under the Act to justify 'fishing expeditions' for intelligence gathering and to harass those whose views they find objectionable.

Equally disturbing to some commentators is that some nations have chosen not to enforce their laws against terrorists for fear of provoking an incident aimed at themselves. Many European governments have released or avoided bringing to trial terrorists belonging to groups with international connections. They would rather abdicate their legal responsibility in order to avoid the responsibilities inherent in being the target of a future terrorist attack. For example, in September 1970 the veteran hijacker Leila Khaled and an associate took over an El Al Boeing 707 soon after take-off from Amsterdam. In a struggle on board, Israeli security agents shot and killed the accomplice, and wounded and arrested Khaled, who was subsequently legally detained in London by the British Authorities. However, in contravention of their own legal principles, the British released Khaled some days later in exchange for the release of passengers held by the Popular Front for the Liberation of Palestine (PFLP) following a spectacular trio of aircraft hijackings. Another example occurred in 1977 when French authorities allowed Abu Daoud to leave France for Algiers, knowing that he was wanted by the Israeli and West German governments for his alleged participation in the massacre at the Munich Olympics in 1972. In fairness, it should be added that there has been a swing away from such acquiescence in the recent past. In 1977 the British government volunteered expert assistance to the West Germans to effect the resolution of the Mogadishu incident. Two members of the Special Air Service assisted the GSG-9 assault on a hijacked airliner. This act was not clearly in the narrow British interest in that it could have provoked retaliation on British personnel or installations when Britain need not have become involved in the incident at all. But the offer exemplifies a new cooperative spirit which is becoming evident in combating terrorism, especially in Western Europe.

The final set of effects of terrorism has been the rapid increase in attention to anti-terrorist response capabilities. Many countries have set up special coordinating bodies to handle any terrorist crisis. There is increasing debate about the potential role of the military in internal security functions and a number of specialist military or quasi-military precision strike forces have been established to counter terrorist threats. The use of such forces in practice has had mixed results. In July 1976 the Israelis mounted a bold and successful commando rescue operation at Entebbe Airport in Uganda to release the hostages taken during the hijacking of an Air France plane by Palestinian terrorists. In October 1977 a similar rescue was carried out by members of the West German Federal Border Police to release hostages on a Lufthansa plane hijacked by the Popular Front for the Liberation of Palestine on behalf of the West German Baader-Meinhof group. The most recent successful military-style rescue was the assault on the Iranian Embassy in London by a unit of the British Special Air Service Regiment in May 1980. Two similar rescue attempts have proved equally spectacular failures. The first was an assault in February 1978 by Egyptian commandos on a Cyprus Airways jet forced to land at Larnaca Airport, Cyprus by two Palestinian gunmen who had shot and killed Yusuf Sebai, an Egyptian editor and personal friend of President Sadat. Because they did not arrange proper clearance with the Cypriot authorities, the Cypriot National Guard attacked the forces as they attempted to storm the airliner. The Egyptians lost 15 dead and failed to get into the aircraft, the terrorists eventually surrendering to and being tried by the Cypriot authorities. More recently the failure of the United States in their attempt in April 1980 to rescue hostages held in the American Embassy in Tehran illustrated many of the difficulties involved in orchestrating a long-range military intervention in a terrorist/ hostage incident. A full discussion of the role of such units is given in Chapter 10.

Summary

The perception of terrorism as a threat to contemporary liberal democracies has already had significant effects on those societies. Large amounts of money and physical and personnel resources are being diverted into internal security functions on the justification that more protection is needed against terrorism. In some states laws have been passed limiting personal freedom and increasing police powers, again allegedly because such measures are necessary to counter the terrorist threat. In the absence of such a threat these measures would be regarded as unacceptable to a free society. (In fact, of course, the measures are so considered by many who believe either that the threat is not real or, if real, that the measures are a dangerous over-reaction.) These changes and their derivative effects require careful monitoring. While it is obvious that a democratic society needs to seriously consider aspects which render it vulnerable to terrorist pressure it must, at all costs, resist the temptation to over-react to the threat of terrorism. The result could well be an oppressive society. In order to avoid this happening, societies will have to try to understand more about the nature of terrorism so that they can respond at the minimum effective level with maximum effect. The aim of the remainder of this book will be to lay out for discussion some of the major policy issues which will need to be resolved in order for democratic societies to tailor the most appropriate response to terrorism.

PART TWO

Some selected problems in the response to terrorism

8

Counter-terrorist policies: fundamental choices

In Part One of this book it was argued that contemporary terrorism constitutes a potential threat to the stability and, in the extreme, the existence of democratic states. While it is true that the existence of injustice or inequality within such states provides a fertile ground for the development of social movements which view terrorism as a legitimate tool for change it is not the case that the elimination of these evils (to the extent that such is possible) would necessarily eliminate the threat of terrorism. While such social improvements would reduce the incidence of terrorism, the increasing evidence of nihilistic philosophies and idiosyncratic motivations among terrorist groups combined with the disruptive/destructive potential inherent in nuclear, biological, and biochemical materials implies that we will always have to face policy choices other than prescriptions for social change.

This does not imply that governments can ignore or downgrade acknowledgement of social problems and policies designed to remedy them. Social injustice, unresponsive government, etc. may be objective causes of political violence, including terrorism. In reality, anyway, the future holds problems of a structural nature (for all types of political systems) which indicate that a truly just and equal society is little short of fanciful. Democratic states which strive for, but do not meet, just goals will be challenged in the future by those who demand change (where change may also include a return to a pre-existing order as opposed to a bold new future). It is the duty of these states to evolve policies aimed specifically at countering such demands if the tactic chosen to advance them is terrorism. In this section of the book policy options in a number of important areas will be examined in detail. Policies to be examined include those relating to intelligence gathering, the news media, the use of the armed forces in a counter-terrorist role, domestic anti-terrorist legislation and international treaties, and the handling of hostage situations. There are decisions to be taken in all of these areas which have important consequences for the type of society in which we will live and they ought properly to be the subject of informed public debate. A separate chapter on the role of behavioural science research will outline the methods by which some of the questions raised by policy analysis might be answered. The purpose of the present chapter, then, is not to analyse specific policies in depth, but rather to raise general matters of principle which will guide the discussion of issues in the following chapters.

Policy options

In general, the attitudes taken toward terrorism and appropriate policies to be used in dealing with it have become polarised into a soft, compromising view on the one hand, and a tough, no-concessions, authoritarian view on the other. Extensive media coverage of terrorist incidents and subsequent decisions taken by governments to resolve them have resulted in a hardening of public and official attitudes in many cases. Often this has been a consequence of biased and ill-informed media comment (particularly during the course of an incident when public feelings stirred up by media coverage have effectively limited the options open to the authorities). The result has been that much debate, both by the public and by involved officials, has tended to reflect as much prejudice and stereotype as logically reasoned responses to delicately balanced situations.

What is necessary for an effective guide to anti-terrorist policy formation is a set of principles based on an analysis of successful tactics used in the past contained within the bounds of some basic assumptions about the sorts of actions acceptable to a democratic society and capable of absorbing change as a result of research and new data flowing from more contemporary operational experience. The broad policy guidelines should be capable of informing decisions on a wide range of disparate policy issues. The following list contains some examples of the sorts of actions which might be suggested as part of an anti-terrorist campaign. Its length indicates the complex and widely varied nature of the options facing policy makers. But the list itself only touches on a few of the potential options. Its coverage is by no means exhaustive. The following options might be suggested as parts of an anti-terrorist campaign.

1. Attempt to find long-term solutions to the underlying causes of terrorism. This approach involves a decision to acknowledge that there are remediable inequities in society which may provide objective causes of terrorism. Such an approach probably is the most significant because of the widespread policy changes with extensive effects on other aspects of the social milieu which might be occasioned by it.
2. Increase the size and powers of the security forces (for example, increase manpower, search and entry powers, power to detain without

trial, etc.). This would involve major policy decisions about the nature of policing our society, civil rights, etc.

3. Introduce capital punishment for terrorist activities. Such a move involves policy decisions about the role of capital punishment, whether terrorists are to be treated as a separate class of offenders (as opposed to reintroducing capital punishment generally), which types of terrorist acts are to be made capital offences.

4. Enact legislation limiting rights of assembly and increasing controls over the members of society by way of identification cards, registration of residence and extensive use of computerised files. This has implications for the type of society we have, police powers, civil rights, etc.

5. Establish a 'third force' or special military units to cope with terrorist attacks. The decision to employ new types of force involves policy decisions about how early to commit military forces, the role of police in anti-terrorist operations, and civil-military relations.

6. Announce a policy of 'no negotiations' with terrorists. Such a policy implies a wide range of decisions about such issues as the value of individual life, the authority and prestige of the state, and how far in reality such a policy would be pursued (for example, would the government refuse to negotiate in the face of a credible nuclear threat?).

7. Increase physical and procedural security. Such an increase revolves around related issues of the economics of such measures, powers given to security officers (particularly those employed by private security organisations), and civil rights.

8. Introduce internment without trial or special legal procedures designed to limit intimidation of witnesses (such as the so-called Diplock courts in Northern Ireland). The introduction of measures outside of the normal legal process requires major policy decisions about the legal system, civil rights, and the political consequences of such changes.

9. Place legal limits on the ability of the media to report terrorist acts. This may involve suggestions as to the timing, duration, or content of news reports. Such restrictions involve some of the most controversial policy decisions about freedom of the press, free speech, and the nature of government.

10. Introduce special anti-terrorist legislation which may mandate a combination of the above or other measures. Such legislation implies that a decision has been taken that terrorists cannot be dealt with by normal legal processes and leads to consequential policy changes in the law, police powers, civil rights, and governmental intrusion into everyday life.

11. Make it illegal for individuals or private organisations to pay ransom to terrorists or to take out ransom insurance and place a legal duty on

people to report hostage takings to the police. Such measures involve decisions about the rights of individuals to take whatever action they consider necessary to safeguard the lives of those for whom they are responsible when a conflict exists with what the authorities see as undesirable consequences for society in general.

12. Promote and become a signatory to international treaties providing for extradition or trial of captured terrorists, suspension of air services to countries providing safe haven for hijackers, etc. This involves decisions about the effectiveness of international measures, the definition of terrorism and whether or not to allow 'political exception' clauses.

13. Research and develop alternatives to hostage negotiations. This implies a recognition that hostage-taking is likely to decrease in frequency or take on new forms as negotiation techniques appear more successful. Consequently important policy decisions would have to be made about research directions and issues such as attitudes towards more aggressive incident resolution techniques.

14. Suggest that terrorist groups be encouraged to adhere to the norms articulated by the customary laws of war, the Geneva Conventions, and the Nuremberg Principles (a suggestion which has been characterised as 'patently valueless, representing the *reductio ad absurdum* of legalistic naivete').[1] To support such a suggestion would require a policy decision to recognise terrorist groups as political entities and to accord them special prisoner-of-war status if captured.

15. Develop and deploy highly intrusive technologies as pre-emptive moves (for example, technologies for monitoring and surveillance). Such deployment requires major policy decisions about civil rights, police powers, and the nature of society.

The foregoing list illustrates the complexity of the decisions facing authorities in the field of counter-terrorist policy. Again it is emphasised that the list is not exhaustive. Many other equally important issues face the policy makers. What is evident though is that the major decisions focus around a relatively small number of major issues, namely the general nature of the society in which we live and, specifically, police powers, civil rights, and the rule of law. Many of the specific issues enumerated above will be examined in detail in the following chapters. However, specific policies need to be formulated in the context of a general understanding of how a society views itself and its legitimate responses to violence and subversion. The question which first needs answering is: What are the major principles around which we should build our counter-terrorist strategy?

The rule of law

The foremost principle must be the objective of the maintenance of democratic processes of government and the rule of law. This principle has been stressed by Wilkinson who writes:

> It cannot be sufficiently stressed that this aim overrides in importance even the objective of eliminating terrorism and political violence as such. Any bloody tyrant can 'solve' the problem of political violence if he is prepared to sacrifice all considerations of humanity, and to trample down all constitutional and judicial rights.[2]

It is quite obvious that terrorism can be minimised, if not entirely eliminated, within a State if the government is fully determined to use all its potential powers of coercion, ranging from large secret security organisations and systems of imprisonment without trial, to persecution and torture, be it obvious as in Idi Amin's Uganda, or more 'subtle', as in the Soviet Union's use of psychiatric facilities for its opponents. Terrorism has little chance in a totalitarian regime, an old-fashioned autocracy, or a right-wing militarist state. However, what is left is merely another form of terrorism – institutionalised, bureaucratised terror, or as Hacker terms it 'terror from above' rather than 'terror from below'.[3] To believe that depriving citizens of their individual rights and suspending the democratic process is necessary to maintain 'order' is to put oneself on the same moral plane as the terrorists, who believe that 'the end justifies the means'.

However serious the threat of terrorism, we must not be tempted to use repressive methods to combat it. To believe that we can 'protect' liberal democracy by suspending our normal rights and methods of government is to ignore the numerous examples in contemporary history of countries where 'temporary', 'emergency' rule has subsided quickly and irrevocably into permanent dictatorial forms of government. While we must avoid the easy move to repression as a counter to terrorism, it is equally vital that we do not allow ourselves to be so overcome by our democratic sensibilities that our response is weak and vacillating, and characterised by inaction. It is as much a betrayal of our beliefs and responsibilities to do not enough as to do too much. We must uphold constitutional authority and law and order, and we must do so with firmness and determination. To do so requires political will; but most importantly it requires citizen support. To gain such support the political will must be translated into effective action. First, the government must be open and honest about its policies and objectives. As will be stressed when we come to examine the role of the army in counter-terrorism, it is particularly important in a society such as ours to spell out clearly the circumstances under which military aid to the civil power would be invoked, the rights and responsibilities of military personnel operating in an internal security role, and the lines of control and command.

Second, the government must accord full and proper support to its civil and security force personnel who are involved in counter-terrorist operations. In particular, it is necessary to avoid sudden changes in security policy which could undermine both official and public confidence in the government's ability to handle difficult situations. Policy vacillations also expose weaknesses and differences within the government ranks which can be exploited by terrorists.

Third, any anti-terrorist measures must be, and be seen to be, directed only at terrorists. The response must be limited, well-defined, and controlled. It must also, wherever at all possible, be publicly explained. To quote Wilkinson again:

A slide into general repression generally indicates that the government is exploiting the crisis situation for the enhancement of its own political powers, or to destroy legitimate political opposition. Moreover, repressive over-reaction plays into the hands of terrorists by giving credence to the claim that liberal democracy is a sham or a chimera, and encouraging terrorists to pose as the defenders of the people.[4]

It is most important that executive control of anti-terrorist and security policy rest with the civil authorities (the elected government) who are accountable to the people for their actions. Further, it should be both policy and practice for the government and its security forces to act within the law. Not only does failure to do so place the government in a morally difficult position (if it does not obey the law, why should anyone?) but also such action is likely to undermine their support and provide valuable ammunition for a terrorist cause. Propaganda capital can very easily be made out of violations of the law by government servants, and such propaganda can be used as additional justification for a terrorist campaign. While the law can be a refuge for the law-breaker and a hinderance to the law enforcement official, the law is the basis of our system of government and must be upheld. Otherwise are we any better than the terrorist who also argues on the grounds of expediency?

Arguments about legal behaviour are particularly important in the field of intelligence gathering. As will be argued in a later chapter, intelligence is the central pivot around which an effective counter-terrorist operation revolves. It is also potentially dangerous to the democratic form of government itself, particularly when a large and ill-controlled intelligence and subversion apparatus is established or grows and begins to consider itself the defender of all things 'good' and assumes executive functions. Recent investigations by the Church Committee of the United States Congress concerning domestic intelligence gathering should alert us to the dangers.[5] It is possible to tighten democratic control and accountability of intelligence agencies without damaging their effectiveness.[6]

The problem of concessions

It is apparent from the foregoing that governments should adopt a consistent firm approach to the handling of terrorist situations which avoids extremes of policy (either hard- or soft-line). Part of this approach must be, a policy of no deals or concessions to terrorists' *political* demands. This is perhaps the most difficult question of all to resolve. Critics, particularly the relatives and friends of those involved, consider it callous and inhumane to refuse to accede to terrorist demands if the alternative is the killing of innocent hostages. Of course, anyone who is placed in the decision-making role in such a situation finds himself in a terrible position. Not only must he or she agonise over the possibility of consigning innocent people, very often women and children, to a violent death, but he or she will often be under intense public pressure to avert such a happening by whatever means necessary – including giving in. Even the Israeli government whose 'no deals' policy is publicly stated and well known (although not as rigid in practice as most people believe), was forced to consider a deal with the terrorists who held over 100 Israeli hostages in an Air France airbus at Entebbe in 1976. As is well known, the situation changed dramatically with the bold and successful Israeli commando attack on Entebbe on 3 July 1976. So we don't know whether or not the Israeli government would or could eventually have been able to negotiate a peaceful conclusion to the affair.

Yet suppose that in such a situation a rescue mission could not be mounted. Faced with the death of so many hostages, the political pressures to make concessions to save lives may well be overwhelming. But even conceding the inevitability of the occasional surrender, the long-term costs of capitulation must be assessed as very high. Wherever possible a hard line against significant bargaining must be maintained. Wilkinson has written that:

The great disadvantage involved in any concession or bargain, which will have to deliver some tangible gain to the terrorists if it is to be effected, is that the terrorists will have set a precedent and established a model for emulation by other groups. Moreover if the terrorist weapon is seen to pay off against a particular government, the authority and credibility of that government is thereby gradually diminished, terrorist groups are tempted into increasingly brazen attempts at blackmail, and there is a dramatic inflation in the ransom price demanded by the terrorists.[7]

There is now ample evidence to show how terrorist groups escalate their demands if governments make concessions to them. The kidnapping by Brazilian terrorists of Western diplomats is a case in point. On 4 September 1969, the US Ambassador to Brazil was kidnapped and then released following the release of 15 terrorist prisoners. On 11 June 1970, the German Ambassador was kidnapped. This time the price paid was 40 prisoners. When the Swiss Ambassador was kidnapped on 7 December 1970, the price paid for his release rose to 70 prisoners. Admittedly Brazil has succeeded to a large degree in controlling this particular form of terrorism but the price has been very high. In large measure terror from above has replaced terror from below.

In Argentina, the ERP (Ejertico Revolucionario de Pueblo or People's Revolutionary Army) have extracted some huge sums of money as ransom because international corporations have met their demands. On 23 May 1971, an executive of the Swift Meat Packing Company was kidnapped, to be released a week later when the company paid the ERP $62,500 for food and clothing for the poor. In March 1972 Fiat were prepared to pay $1 million for the release of one of their executives, but the police discovered and attacked the terrorists resulting in the deaths of the hostage and four members of the ERP. 1973 was a financial boom year for the ERP. The following companies paid huge ransoms in return for kidnapped executives: Ford Motor Company, $1 million (protection money against further kidnap attempts); Acrow Steel, $2 million; Firestone Tire and Rubber, $3 million; and most important of all, Exxon Oil, the staggering sum of $14.2 million.[8] The record, however, is currently held by another Argentinian terrorist group, the Montoneros, who extorted $60 million in cash and $1.2 million in food and clothing distributed to the poor in exchange for two Argentinian millionaire businessmen. It is not hard to image what sums of money as large as these do for the potential of terrorism.[9]

An extreme hardline policy of 'no concessions' is exemplified by the US government's approach. They have faced a large number of kidnappings of diplomats, military personnel, businessmen, and tourists. Whenever the government has been directly responsible for negotiations they have refused to give in to terrorist demands. The individual price for such a policy has been high. A number of diplomats have been murdered because of their government's determination to stick to its policy. It is suggested that the general approach taken by the US government is in its own, and others', long-term interests if terrorism is to be successfully combatted.

Contrary to the view expressed above that the United States policy has been the correct choice, Jenkins, Johnson, and Ronfeldt argue that the policy has been irrelevant to the outcome of terrorist events.[10] In a study on international hostage episodes they specifically analysed events involving American hostages. They showed that between August 1968 and June 1975 attempts to make hostages of American officials occurred with an average frequency of once every three months. From September 1969 to June 1975 successful seizures of American hostages coupled with ransom demands occurred at an average rate of one every five months. Analysing these figures in the context of world trends, Jenkins *et al.* concluded that:

Given the correspondence we noted between the number of kidnappings and the overall level of terrorist activity in the world, given that in most cases the demands were *not* on the United States government, and finally given the lack of any conclusive evidence of a relationship between government policies and the occurrence or absence of subsequent hostage incidents, we are inclined to argue that the influence of American policy on the frequency of kidnappings of American officials has been marginal. The crackdowns on urban guerrilla movements in countries where American officials had been targets of kidnapping attempts – Brazil, Uruguay, Guatemala, Turkey – appear to be a more decisive factor in deterring or preventing future incidents.[11]

In fact, more recent figures show a continuing assault on American officials. In the last ten years (1971–80) the US State Department lists 254 significant terrorist attacks against US diplomatic installations or individuals. Five US ambassadors were killed in terrorist incidents during the years 1970–80. Although many of these incidents did not involve hostage taking or did not involve demands directly against the US government one can only speculate on what encouragement might have been given to other groups if it had become apparent that the US government would grant significant concessions in return for the safety of its diplomats. It seems that a reasonable case can be made for the deterrent value of a no-concessions policy. It will not stop terrorist attacks but it may conceivably lessen their future occurrence.

However, it can be argued that the US has gone too far because it refuses even to negotiate with terrorists. This extreme determination to adopt the hardline approach is only likely to reduce their options since under some circumstances even political terrorists may be induced to release hostages, for example, in return for only minor concessions. It seems pointless to risk human lives in these situations for the presumed benefits of maintaining a 'tough' approach. The move toward hostage-taking emphasises this point. Whereas past terrorist tactics have virtually left governments having a 'no deals' policy with only two options – either to let the terrorists carry out whatever threats they have made or try an assault on their base, if known, thereby possibly risking innocent lives – the upsurge of hostage/siege situations has allowed the development of more sophisticated negotiating techniques. While the issues about concessions are still real, experience has shown that the dynamics of a siege situation are such that, given careful and skilful handling, terrorists may be persuaded to surrender their hostages without significant gains to themselves. For this reason, a 'no concessions' policy should not imply a 'no negotiations' one.

This point is underlined by the case of Israel which, as previously discussed, maintains the most rigid no-negotiations policy. Israel has always maintained a clearly and widely articulated policy of neither negotiating with nor making concessions to terrorists attempting to bargain with the Israeli government. In addition, they have consistently followed terrorist attacks against Israeli targets with swift and destructive reprisal raids or with assassinations of terrorist leaders (the latter carried out by the so-called 'Wrath of God' units). Although these actions could be argued to have deterred an even greater number of incidents of terrorism, they certainly have not made Israel immune from terrorist attack. It is at least as plausible to argue that the no-negotiation policy has not deterred the terrorists. In fact it is possible that the policy has led the Palestinians to the belief that escalation in the nature of their attacks is necessary to force Israel's hand. It has been suggested that the attack on the children at Maalot in May 1974 was such an escalation. In fact, the Israelis have not yielded but it may be argued that the response could lead to even more horrendous actions designed to force the Israeli government to negotiate. (It should be borne in mind when assessing the relevance of this line of argument, however, that the Palestinian raids are military operations and not traditional terrorist attacks. Since there is a confusing overlap between terrorism and guerrilla warfare it is difficult to tease out the appropriate lessons to be learnt from specific incidents which fall within the grey area between the two.) It is submitted, then, that a fine line can be drawn (not without great difficulty and ambiguity) between no-negotiations and no-concessions. In many cases it seems possible to negotiate without conceding to political demands and this seems to be a practical policy to adopt wherever possible.

What this implies for governments is that they will have to intensively study different ways in which international terrorist incidents have been handled and attempt to analyse relationships between government conduct of a crisis, the immediate outcome of the crisis, and any broader, long-term political consequences. For governments it is the broader consequences that are important and would include such things as:

1. Loss of confidence in the government and its ability to guarantee the safety of its citizens and uphold the law.
2. Changes in civil liberties.
3. Evidence of subsequent terrorism as an escalation of a present campaign or as contagion.
4. Any attainment of terrorists' political goals.

If such an analysis shows that certain responses in certain circumstances produce politically superior outcomes, then a government can devote policy and planning resources to the job of attempting to maximise these outcomes. At the same time the analysis might reveal the sorts of incidents that tend to push governments into self-defeating responses, and the government can then introduce safeguards and preventive measures designed to minimise the occurrence of such incidents.

Policy models

To give an idea of some of the options facing governments, Bobrow has
listed four basic models of terrorist crisis resolution.[12] These models are:

(1) *The domination model.* This model involves no bargaining, with the
government's aim being to surround, isolate, and annihilate the terrorists.
The terrorists' options are to surrender and take the consequences, or resist
and be killed. The fate of the hostages is of secondary importance in this
model.

(2) *The contingent concession model.* Here attempts are made to isolate
the terrorists, but limited bargaining then occurs. If the hostages are
released the government might undertake to hear the terrorists' grievances
(which may be considered as mitigating circumstances). However, the
government still insists on some form of retribution (e.g. a trial) and makes it
clear that the alternative to accepting the limited concessions is still
annihilation. According to this model, the fate of the hostages is a
consideration, but in the final analysis is still subordinate to actions that
maintain the superiority of the state.

(3) *The ransom with entrapment model.* This model implies that
bargaining takes place as if the government is going to comply with the
terrorists' demands. The aim is to deceive the terrorists into releasing their
hostages so that they may then be overcome without in fact delivering the
ransom.

(4) *The ransom with eventual retribution model.* This model recognises
that the terrorists control the immediate situation and that the safety of the
hostages is of prime importance. In the government's view their only option
is to accede to the terrorists' demands but they still have it in mind to
somehow punish them at some future time.

Of course these models are very simplified versions of reality and do not
embrace all possibilities, but they do encapsulate most responses to date. It
is necessary to develop such models and analyse the outcomes which have
occurred when a particular model has been employed. We may then be in a
better position to face the future. Some of the more important issues which
will determine the face of that future will be considered in the following
chapters. Within the context of the general principles discussed above,
specific policies will be evolved to cope with circumstances pertinent to
these specific areas. The following chapters will analyse these problems
and suggest appropriate directions for relevant, workable and democratically
acceptable counter-terrorist policies.

9

Terrorism and the media: a symbiotic relationship?

(or 'Don't shoot. We're not on prime time')

If the freedom to publish rests, as indeed it must, upon a general public interest expressed in terms of 'need to know,' is this not most sensibly limited by that other public interest of denying to those who would damage the common weal the use of this potent, near irresistible force of the media? There is a real competition of interests here which must be resolved on a philosophical plane before the practical issues can be tackled. The terrorist is an urgent suitor; if he cannot get what he wants by seductive means, he will not hesitate to attempt rape. The real problem seems to be uncertainty on the part of the media whether to play coy handmaiden or harlot.[1]

It is well recognised that some form of symbiotic relationship exists between the news media and perpetrators of spectacular terrorist incidents. One of the most important aims of a terrorist attack is to gain publicity for a particular cause. In some cases, publicity is the sole aim. The presumed primary aim of the news media is to inform. However, it is at least as important in practice to entertain, shock, amuse or otherwise affect the emotions of the audience. This is particularly true of the medium of television. Competition between media organisations seems to heighten the necessity to focus on the emotion-generating as opposed to the purely informational aspects of news reporting. Terrorists are well aware of this phenomenon and consciously script what has been termed 'live-action spectaculars' – news events which cannot be ignored by the media. A leading American researcher has summed up the situation in the following terms:

There is simply no way that the Western media can ignore an event that has been fashioned specifically for their needs. Television terrorists can no more do without the media than the media can resist the terror-event. The two are in a symbiotic relationship, so that any restriction of one narrows the bounds of the other. To be free means that the media are open to capture by spectacular events. And the media have been captured, have proven totally defenseless, absolutely vulnerable. Of all the foundations of a free democratic society, that most basic – the freedom to know, to be informed – has guaranteed that such knowledge and such information can be fashioned by the fanatic through the conduit of the media eye. To close that eye would erode a fundamental right, would close an open society. Yet not to do so assures future massacres, further terrorist-events with little hope of audience saturation.[2]

76

The effects of media coverage

The dilemma that seems to face liberal democracies, then, is that media reporting of terrorist events has very damaging effects, but that significant restrictions on such reporting would have different, but no less important negative consequences. Specifically, it is alleged that media coverage of terrorist events has some or all of the following effects:

1. It provides a platform for the expression of extremist views which provoke violence and undermine the authority of the state.
2. The reporting of spectacular terrorist incidents has a contagion effect which increases the probability that other groups or individuals will emulate the violence being reported.[3]
3. Coverage of an ongoing incident hinders effective police operations and may place the lives of hostages and police in jeopardy.
4. Coverage of an ongoing incident puts inappropriate pressure on the authorities which limits their powers of decision-making.
5. The large number of reporters at and extent of coverage of a terrorist incident reinforces the terrorists' sense of power and, particularly in the case of deranged terrorists, may contribute significantly to the prolonging of the incident or to an increase in its serious consequences.
6. Related to the contagion effect is the claim that excessive detail of both terrorist and counter-terrorist operations supplies disaffected groups with tactical and strategic information and technical knowledge which make the resolution of future terrorist incidents more difficult.
7. The competitive nature of news gathering places an undue emphasis on the sensational aspects of terrorist events and makes entertainment of public violence rather than performing a public duty to inform.
8. The instantaneous reporting of terrorist incidents and the existence of some newsgathering practices (such as telephone contact with terrorists in the course of an incident) make reporters participants in, rather than observers at, a terrorist event and diminish the ability of the media to report objectively.

The response of many governmental and law enforcement officials to these charges is to suggest various forms of restrictions that should be placed on media reporting of terrorist incidents. These suggestions run from self-imposed industry guidelines to governmental regulation amounting to strict censorship. The spectre of censorship casts long and dark shadows in democratic states and it is therefore necessary to examine both the evidence for the charges which could lead to censorship being imposed and any alternative measures short of censorship which could meet any well-founded objections to current media presentation of terrorist events. In pursuing these questions we must not indulge a facile belief that only the media and the terrorists seek to exploit terrorism for their own ends (one for increased audiences and profits and the other for publicity for their cause). Governments, too, are sometimes eager to over-emphasise the seriousness of the 'terrorist problem' to justify increases in the public security apparatus and incursions upon civil liberties.[4] It is an old and well-tried trick to divert attention from economic and social problems to focus attention on an ill-defined and frightening 'enemy'. In many parts of the world today, terrorism is such a diversion. In fact it is possible to imagine governmental officials doing more to destroy democracy in the name of counter-terrorism than is presently likely to be achieved by terrorists themselves.

The foregoing comments should be borne in mind while examining specific objections to current media practices in covering terrorism and in discussing what, if any, steps should be taken to limit or control these practices. In most countries which have experienced significant acts of terrorism it is the police who are the most vociferous critics of media behaviour. They have two primary concerns. The first is that reporting of terrorist violence is excessive, sensational, and sometimes unbalanced and that these factors produce a contagion effect. If contagion is used to imply fashions or fads in terrorist tactics the police can point to plenty of relevant examples. The publicity surrounding the early aircraft hijacking incidents in the 1960s is a case in the point. Not only did this become a familiar act by political terrorists, but became extremely popular amongst criminals and the mentally disturbed. When D.B. Cooper parachuted from a hijacked airliner with $200,000 in ransom in 1971 the media reporting of the event was sensationalised and given a prominence out of all proportion to the act. Within a week, five other individuals imitated Cooper; many more did so subsequently. If one looks at chronologies of events of political terrorism it is apparent that during particular periods bombing, or assassinations, or hostage-takings enjoy a particular popularity. Frequently it is possible to identify early in each series a highly publicised event of that class.

However, if contagion is equated with an absolute increase in political violence, the evidence is not as compelling. There is no clear evidence that publicity is responsible for significantly affecting the occurrence of terrorism. It is much more likely to affect the form than the frequency of political terrorism. In the case of the deranged we might expect that a certain percentage of individuals will see publicised a method of securing power which would stimulate them to action. But in the case of the highly volatile terrorist acts that cause widespread fear, such contagion is as yet unproven.

The second, and more easily substantiated charge of the police is that some newsgathering practices hinder the effective management of terrorist incidents, particularly those involving the taking of hostages. The media have on some occasions provided terrorists with direct intelligence by broadcasting information about police movements, possible tactical approaches, and so forth. In one case, that of the hijacking of the Lufthansa jet to Mogadishu in October 1977 (which was eventually concluded by the spectacularly successful assault by the West German GSG-9), the action of the media contributed directly to the death of a hostage. (The terrorists heard radio broadcasts revealing that the German Captain of the airliner was secretly passing information to the authorities during routine transmissions to the ground. The Captain was subsequently executed.) In another highly publicised incident, that of the Hanafi Muslim takeover of three buildings in Washington, DC in March 1977, the media were strongly criticised for a number of potentially dangerous actions. Charles Fenyvesi, a reporter who was held hostage in the B'nai B'rith building relates these actions as follows:

The most damaging case concerned the TV reporter who caught sight of a basket, lifted up by rope, to the fifth floor, where, the world later learned, some people evaded the round-up and barricaded themselves in a room. Their presence apparently was not known to the gunmen, who held their prisoners on the eighth floor but patrolled the lower floors until late Wednesday afternoon. The gunmen were probably informed of the TV reporter's scoop by their fellow Hanafis who monitored the news media outside the captured buildings. Fortunately the gunmen did not break through the door.

Another case of a reporter endangering lives occurred when Khaalis was asked, during a live telephone interview with a leading local radio station, 'Have you set a deadline?' The police and all the other experts had thought that the absence of a deadline was one encouraging sign. Fortunately, Khaalis was too engrossed in his rhetoric to pay any attention to the question.

A third example; One prominent Washington newscaster called Khaalis a Black Muslim. Khaalis, whose family was murdered by Black Muslims, flew into a rage and stormed into the room where the hostages were held. He declared that he would kill one of us in retaliation for the newsman's words. The police, meanwhile, advised the newscaster to promptly issue an apology, and Khaalis was eventually mollified.[5]

There are numerous other similar incidents reported in the literature on terrorism. The most potentially disruptive media tactic is that of direct contact with terrorists during a hostage-taking incident. Such action ties up lines of communication at crucial times and obviously may have a detrimental effect on careful hostage negotiations. It is difficult to think of any legitimate reason for the media to try to establish direct contact with terrorists when hostage lives are at stake. It is significant that during the first night of the Hanafi seige in Washington, DC, no less than 15 calls came from radio and television stations and newspapers in *Australia* to the hostage-takers. It is difficult to see what justification there could be in terms of the Australian peoples' 'right to know' or informational needs for such an intrusive technique in a domestic situation in another country.

Other accompaniments to modern newsgathering techniques also pose problems. For example, the large scale use of portable lighting by TV cameramen (especially with large numbers of competing crews) can create dangers. At a famous seige situation in a Brooklyn sporting goods store the New York City Police Department tried to create a news blackout and shut off electric power to the surrounding area. The media set up portable generators and floodlights which had the undesired effect of plunging the hostage-takers into shadow but silhouetting the police sharpshooters. In this case, the NYPD learned the folly of trying to exclude the media and now go to considerable lengths to aid the media in such situations (including having media representatives attend hostage negotiator training sessions so that they understand what is involved).

The advent of modern television technology has also brought its own dangers. A revolution involving three crucial developments which became widely available in the early 1970s challenges many aspects of TV ethics and practices. The three vital pieces of equipment involved are the portable, lightweight video camera ('minicam'), the battery-powered, portable video recorder, and the time-base corrector (which converts the output of the video recorder into a picture with sufficient stability to be broadcast). With these pieces of equipment live transmissions can be made from almost anywhere. The most important consequence of instantaneous broadcasting is that it largely eliminates the function of the editor, which in some circumstances might be expected to prevent journalistic excesses. Particularly with competition for 'scoops', live reporting can lead to situations in which unnecessary violence is broadcast, the terrorists have an unedited platform, or information is conveyed which directly changes the situation. An example of the latter is given by the case of a hostage situation in Cleveland, Ohio. A TV reporter contacted the news producer and told him the situation was about to end. Wanting to get an on-the-spot exclusive the producer authorised live coverage which showed police snipers moving into position. The hostage-taker saw the transmission, thought he was about to be assaulted, and terminated negotiations. It took many hours to re-open negotiations and the local police chief later said that the incident would have been concluded a day earlier had the live transmission not taken place.[6]

It is undeniable, then, that some specific instances of media coverage of terrorism have jeopardised the safety of hostages (in some cases to the extent of being a contributory factor in their deaths), made police operations more difficult, produced situations in which pressure has been put on decision-makers which has severely limited their options, and unnecessarily prolonged hostage situations. Large-scale reporting of terrorism has probably encouraged more individuals to engage in terrorism, but this is difficult to prove. Almost certainly it has influenced the form of subsequent terrorist activity. Finally, and not infrequently, the media have been, at the least, remarkably insensitive to the feelings of hostages and their families and have displayed a marked lack of taste in the way they have presented personal suffering as entertainment for a voyeuristic public. All these instances are highly undesirable and should be significantly reduced. It does not seem justified, however, to regard them as dangerous, or serious enough to warrant significant control of media practices. But they are of sufficient concern to warrant media attention to ways in which offensive practices may be limited.

Media self-regulation

Now even when one suggests some form of self-regulation or self-editing of reporting of specific events, many journalists believe that a vital freedom is in danger. They believe that the freedom to report news is an absolute value which must always prevail when in conflict with other values such as privacy, respect for the law or individual safety. They argue that it is not part of the media's responsibility to prevent violence or to determine the validity of grievances. The media are there to report information, thus ensuring the public's right to know, and allowing them the opportunity to make their own minds up about the truth or falsity of the claims. Thus Richard Salant, president of CBS News, concedes that while terrorism may possibly be encouraged by broadcast coverage he sees that the news industry is merely

in the business of giving ideas. We present facts from which people draw their own conclusions on, whether it's politics or terrorists or anything else – people draw ideas from them. If we start playing God and say that fact or this viewpoint . . . might give people ideas, we would have to stop covering politics, covering practically anything but volcano eruptions and natural disasters . . . I'm not about to play the idea of God and decide which ideas are good and which ideas are bad.[7]

These may be noble sentiments but they do not reflect the reality of any reporting. There exist forces in the news industry which undeniably affect the presentation of 'facts' so that subtly or obviously, ideas are presented as being good or bad. The idea of a 'free market' of ideas seems a rather romantic notion in these days of monopolistic, group-ownership and cross-media control of news outlets. Further, sociological studies of the production of news leave little doubt that material is selectively chosen and presented in accordance with institutional pressures.[8] It is absurd in the face of the evidence to argue that the media are merely passive observers passing on all the information they receive in order to let the public reach their own informed decisions. Thus, while one may sympathise with journalists who see any form of control as being the thin end of the censorship wedge, they ignore the reality of their own situation. Surely the question is one of proportionality, not of absolutes. As one American professor of journalism has written:

The problem lies in journalism's moral neutrality posture, which prohibits the development of an ethic oriented toward the maintenance of the community, its standards, values and culture. Traditions that prescribe an inflexible 'watchdog' role for the press, or emphasize the publication of terrorist rhetoric when the community itself feels intimidated, appear self-defeating. Clearly judgements must be made by journalists that differentiate between the wars of ideas fought within the legitimated institutions of the community, and struggles fought outside these institutions and which rely on violence rather than verbiage, intimidation instead of intellect.[9]

It is submitted that the media will have to exercise some self-regulation of reporting of terrorism to in fact avoid the sort of explicit regulation which the critics of self-regulation fear. It may reasonably be argued that the media are in large part responsible for the hysteria which surrounds terrorism and that it is the consequences of this hysteria which are more dangerous than the actual specific objections to media activities in covering terrorism. If the media exploit terrorism for competitive reasons they will play into the hands both of the terrorists and of those who wish to use terrorism as an issue to bury other problems and as an excuse to control the news. What must be faced is that the problem is neither one of 'easy answers nor complex solutions but rather complex choices. The exercise of any one of these choices will leave some constituency dissatisfied.'[10] The choices involve a number of competing interests which include the following:

1. The need for a free press to provide information to the public.
2. The need to ensure the safety of the victims of terrorism.
3. The need not to unnecessarily prolong or make more difficult the tasks facing police in a terrorist situation.
4. The need to maintain the human rights of freedom of speech, criticism, and publication.
5. The need to avoid encouraging future imitation of terrorist acts.
6. The need to respect the privacy of hostages and their families.

Since these interests will rarely coincide the media must make decisions about whether their actions will be guided primarily by the interests of the hostages, the police, the larger community or by the financial and organisational interests of their own companies. It is simply dishonest of the media to deny that such choices are made and influence their dissemination of news. It is therefore important that gatherings such as police/media seminars and interaction with the community should take place to help the media reach their decisions about how they are going to respond to critical situations. The media must be able to respond to such questions as

By what standards – other than fear of losing out to the competition and the inherent excitement of live pictures of, say, a man in imminent danger of having his head blown off – do such events qualify as significant in terms of the values supposedly cherished by serious journalists?[11]

The fundamental question is 'Is the public's right to know superior to all other rights: the hostages' right to life, the hostages' right to privacy, the terrorists' right to a fair trial, society's right to protect itself?' If 'right to know' means 'right to know *everything*' the answer is clearly no. How then should we approach the question of regulation? As stated earlier, the evidence does not support the belief that media coverage of terrorism constitutes anything like a serious enough danger to justify governmental restrictions on reporting of such events. Media practices frequently are lacking in taste, make resolution of terrorist incidents more difficult, and place individual lives in jeopardy. These are reasons for restraint not censorship. But if the media do not exercise restraint, pressure may well build up for imposing censorship, as the hysteria about terrorism is increased or when a specific incident occurs in which media coverage has some demonstrable (or even plausible) link to a large number of deaths or injuries.

How should the media exercise restraint? The Report of the Task Force on Disorders and Terrorism[12] in the United States recommended that the appropriate approach is summarised by the principles of *Minimum intrusiveness* and *complete, noninflammatory coverage*. Some of the suggestions for coverage of terrorist incidents which encompass these principles include:

1. The use of a 'pool' of reporters to cover the situation on behalf of all news organisations.
2. Self-imposed restrictions on lighting, use of cameras and other special newsgathering technologies.
3. Limitations on direct interviews with hostage-takers during an incident.
4. Avoidance of enquiries to reveal tactical information that would be detrimental to police operations if disclosed.
5. Delaying the reporting of details which may inflame the situation.
6. Avoidance, where possible, of reporting that emphasises the sensational aspects of the incident.
7. Reliance upon official police spokespersons.
8. Balancing of coverage of self-serving terrorist propaganda with contrasting information from official sources. (Note that it should also be possible to reduce political violence by balance in the opposite direction in other instances. That is, on many controversial matters it is apparent that the 'establishment' or official view gets the majority of media coverage. There should be increased provision for public access to the media so that alternative views can be put, thus minimising the chances of people using violence to get their point across because they are denied the opportunity to put it through the normal channels.)

These suggestions, although they would not all be acceptable to the media at least provide a reasonable basis for discussion between the media and the police. (There are some important problems with some of the suggestions. For example, how are 'pool' reporters to be chosen and by whom? Also it is unnecessarily restrictive to limit news sources only to official spokespersons.) In the United States a number of major media organisations have promulgated their own guidelines which accord in some degree with the Task Force's suggestions.[13] The major points in many of the guidelines issued by major media organisations are:

1. That reporters should resist becoming participants in terrorist events. (Note, however, that the guidelines are silent as to how and specifically do not place a ban on interviewing terrorists during an incident. Because of the dangers of such communications, this is a major omission.)
2. That the guidelines attempt to provide senior executives with greater control over the organisations coverage.
3. That adherence to traditional journalistic values is stressed – stories should be accurate, reported fully, avoid sensationalism, and maintain a sense of balance.

Within the media community there has been significant dissension even over the issue as to whether broad, self-imposed guidelines are an evil which is set in the balance against the 'right to know'. A significant portion of media opinion holds that terrorist spectaculars should be covered live if need be, and at great length if warranted, with no specific or general restrictions. It is argued that even general guidance such as given in the existing guidelines subvert the principle of informing the public and would erode public confidence in the openness of the media – 'what else are they keeping from us?' It is also argued that potential terrorists may well escalate their acts to such an extent that massive media coverage is unavoidable. Each of these criticisms is, however, only true to a point. It is unlikely that public confidence in the media would be diminished significantly by adherence to guidelines such as those issued by many major news organisations (especially given public knowledge of the realities of news production anyway). Escalation is not likely, either, because the guidelines do not advocate even a necessary reduction in the time allotted to terrorist news but rather foster changes in timing and emphasis. Escalation is only likely if direct media manipulation by regulation is imposed. The trouble with such guidelines as exist is that they essentially avoid the moral questions surrounding the journalists' role. By adopting a pragmatic, commonsense approach they give no advice about moral standards to be applied. As one commentator has noted:

While these guidelines seem to represent sincere attempts on the part of the news organisations to do something rarely attempted in the news industry – to make reporting conventions explicit and concrete – these standards offer little moral assistance to journalists reporting an issue that is replete with moral dilemmas. The pragmatic approach bears a fatalistic element as well, based upon the assumption that journalistic practice cannot be changed without damaging the virtue of journalism itself.[14]

It seems apparent that the media still have some way to go in developing their own guidelines. It should be acknowledged that it is extraordinarily difficult to resolve the conflict of having rules which are inflexible enough to provide true guidance, yet flexible enough not to provide a rigid strait-jacket that does indeed share some of the dangers of censorship. Maybe the conflict cannot be resolved. But one cannot but help feeling that there has yet to be sufficient dialogue both within journalism and between the media and the authorities to really answer the question. To quote Jaehnig again:

The conclusion is paradoxical. News media coverage of terrorism suggests a moral, not a legal question. But the greater the collaboration between journalists and terrorists, the greater will grow community fears and calls for legal restraints that will intrude upon what journalists regard as their libertarian position. Only by forsaking this tradition, in developing a new ethical posture that will voluntarily control and intellectually regulate the instrumentality, can journalism preserve itself.[15]

In addition to (and overlapping with) voluntary guidelines there are four other policy decisions that may help both preserve the media's independence and overcome some objections to their treatment of terrorism. These are:

1. To consider matters relating to the timing of news. Temporary withholding of news may be legitimate in some instances such as kidnapping.
2. Making deliberate attempts to balance coverage (an extremely difficult goal to attain) may help counteract some of the negative effects of terrorism.
3. To acknowledge that news tailoring is a fact of everyday news production and focus on reporting that might be expected to lessen tensions and aid the negotiating process.
4. To accept that the media have an important role to play in public education and at times other than during terrorist incidents to feature items regarding the ethics of using violence for political ends, the legitimate needs of law enforcement in a democratic society, the non-romantic side of terrorism and the existence of avenues of dissent. Part of this role must also encompass a vigorous determination to investigate and report on the injustices and inequalities in society which, if left to fester, may be the cause of acts of terrorism.

Summary

It has been argued that terrorism is a reality which is here to stay. Sometimes it is a real threat, but mostly it is not. Some of the practices of the media tend to make it a greater threat than it is and invite their own regulation by so doing. Often it is our reactions to terrorism which may constitute the primary danger, not terrorism itself. Some of the behaviour of the media constitute more of a nuisance and an offence against good taste and sensitivity than offences which place the community in jeopardy. There is no present case for government regulation of the reporting of terrorism. However, the warning signs are there for the media to see. To continue to report on terrorism as they have in the past is to invite regulation. The media must adopt a more specifically ethical stance and must attempt to evolve sensible and workable self-control mechanisms. Lest it be thought that these comments are unduly critical of the media, let it be said that there are others that are at fault. In many cases police and other official agencies have been overly secretive and unhelpful. Many police forces have attempted to repair this deficiency by establishing media liaison units, inviting the media to training courses for hostage negotiators, and so on. Further, it must be said that most media coverage is not irresponsible (although one would not be so kind on the issue of sensitivity) and that the media have often cooperated with the authorities so as not to exacerbate an already difficult situation. However, it is not true to say that only a few fringe media outlets have indulged in the practices criticised above. Partly because of industry pressures and partly through ignorance most of the media can be faulted to some degree. What we must ensure is that criticism of their actions is kept in proportion. J. Bowyer Bell summed it up well when he wrote:

if open, democratic societies in the West cannot protect the liberty of us all from a handful of gunmen, accommodate legitimate dissent, and repress the politics of atrocity under the law – if we cannot tolerate the exaggerated horror flashed on the evening news, or the random bomb, without recourse to the tyrant's manual – then we do not deserve to be free.[16]

10

The role of the army in counter-terrorist operations

In recent years, debate has been stirred by the deployment of the armed forces on internal security duties in a number of British Commonwealth countries. In the most noteworthy cases, these deployments have been occasioned by terrorist activities. Since 1969, large numbers of British troops have served in Northern Ireland attempting to contain the activities of the IRA and various Protestant terror groups. In 1970, Canadian Prime Minister Pierre Trudeau invoked the War Measures Act enabling the Federal Government to saturate the Montreal region with troops in an attempt to locate terrorists from the Front Liberation du Quebec (FLQ) who had kidnapped the British Trade Commissioner, James Cross. This Act remained in force for six months and gave sweeping powers of detention for questioning to the security forces. In February 1978 a bomb exploded at the Commonwealth Heads of Government meeting in Sydney, Australia, killing three people. Fearing for the safety of the conference participants, the Federal Government authorised the use of a large number of troops to guard transport routes and to provide security for the meetings. In May 1980, a team from the British Special Air Service (SAS) Regiment assaulted the Iranian Embassy in London, effecting the rescue of hostages being held there by terrorists. All of these incidents have caused considerable discussion about the role of the armed forces in aid of the civil power in response to a terrorist act. This chapter will outline some of the main features of this debate, particularly as they pertain to countries with a basically British police and military heritage.

The events outlined above illustrate the necessity to decide quite clearly what are the specific roles of the police and the armed forces[1] in internal security matters in a democratic society. Having delineated these roles it will be possible to specify the circumstances (if any) under which joint police and army operations are desirable or necessary. Until recently many people have considered such matters to be only of academic interest in countries with an essentially British military and police heritage. With the formation of Peel's 'New Police' in London in 1829 the British army progressively reduced its internal security activities, and in the twentieth century has only infrequently been used in a confrontational situation with the public. The British public is therefore unaccustomed to thinking of the army as an internal security force. The absence of armed troops in civilian security roles and the tradition of non-interference of the armed forces in politics in Great Britain have made discussion of civil-military relations somewhat less than an urgent topic of debate.

Circumstances have changed, however, in the past decade. British troops have been deployed on internal security duties in Northern Ireland and have participated in a number of highly publicised anti-terrorist exercises at London's Heathrow airport. The increase in the vulnerability of industrialised society to attacks on a few critical points and processes, and the increasing levels of political violence have forced many commentators to consider what possible part the army plays in future periods of violent political strife. In Britain the debate has been stirred particularly by the publication in recent years of a number of books by senior serving officers which detail and justify internal security roles for the army.[2] In Australia similar considerations and the aftermath of the Hilton incident have prompted similar debate. To a large extent, however, the debate has consisted of shrill calls for the formation of specialised army or para-military units to deal with terrorist situations and equally loud condemnation of such suggestions as being inevitably a grave threat to civil liberties and our democratic processes. Proponents of either view seem not to have carefully analysed the type of problems which face or are likely to face us in the internal security field. Neither have they reasoned through the type of force which will be best suited to cope with these problems.

Police and army roles in a democratic society

As well as designing responses to specific contingencies, it is also necessary to delineate some basic political philosophies about the roles of police and army in liberal democracies. Edmonds argues that there are two roles which may be differentiated when the armed forces are used in internal security situations.[3] These are the maintenance of law and order and the compulsion of citizens to conform to political or governmental directives. As Parsons argues, the use of the armed forces in the maintenance of law and order may, but does not necessarily, involve the use of coercion or compulsion.[4] This is not the case when the armed forces assume a political role for it is precisely their monopoly of physical force to coerce or compel people for sectional, as opposed to national, interests that is at issue. To put the distinction another way, it is a question of intervention versus imposition. Edmonds claims that the distinction is an important one because it helps prevent us leaping automatically to the conclusion that the use of the armed forces on internal security duties is a bad thing *per se*.

If legitimate, there is no reason why a society should not be policed by the military completely; indeed in some under-developed countries for purely practical, as opposed to political, reasons, this is the case. In others, tradition plays a major part as does the prevailing political philosophy.[5]

It follows that there are no definitive answers to questions about the internal security roles of the armed forces and, therefore, each society should be analysed on an individual case-study basis. It should also be apparent that the answers for any particular society may change as conditions and socio-political philosophies change.

In the British context it may be argued that there is a considerable separation between the police and the army and that legislative checks and balances, tradition, and the good sense of the armed services hierarchies provide such good protection against the illegitimate use of the armed forces in an internal security role that there is really no problem to discuss. Those who see an armed services role based on hypothetical projections of situations likely to arise in the future also see no particular problem because they are confident that the armed forces will do their duty and act as necessary (that is, become involved in internal security operations). Many 'liberal' critics are worried not about an armed forces role *per se*, but more about its extent and its consequences for civil liberties. Those who are opposed to the capitalist system see the use of the armed forces in a law enforcement role as merely reflecting the determination of the ruling classes to maintain the system through coercion. For many such critics, even law enforcement by the police is seen as coercion of this type and therefore they would acknowledge no distinction between a law enforcement and a political role for the armed forces or the police. For them, both forces fulfil coercive political roles. It is obviously very difficult for many to analyse the situation without their views being determined entirely by their ideology. Of course, a debate over such issues can never be divorced from a political viewpoint and the present discussion will reflect the belief that appropriate roles for the police and the army should be sought broadly within a liberal democratic framework.

The nub of the view to be advanced in this chapter is that in the present political situation in Britain (except in Northern Ireland) and Australia the armed forces are in general an inappropriate agency to use in an internal security role. As far as possible internal security should be a police function and the respective roles of police and army should be delineated as clearly as possible. Too much emphasis should not be laid upon the presumed historical reasons for this position. While many commentators claim that the police should be the only significant internal security force because they have traditionally been so, this ignores the fact that police in the British tradition are a relatively recent innovation. It also ignores the use of the army to quell civil disturbances until even more recently. Furthermore, it seems foolish to insist that police–military relations should remain static and firmly bound by tradition. Whilst tradition is important, a blind adherence to it could severely limit a society's ability to adapt to changing circumstances. In the extreme, such inflexibility could well contribute significantly to the collapse of such a society.

It is argued here that in the present political and social circumstances in Britain and Australia the police and the army have significantly different roles, functions, and philosophies which enable them to perform in quite different spheres. It is argued that this division is functional and that dysfunctions would arise if uncontrolled overlap developed between the two organisations. A number of arguments may be advanced in support of this position. Probably of foremost importance is the doctrine of 'minimum force *versus* maximum violence'. The principal of the use of minimum force is central to all British-tradition police forces. 'In essence it has meant the use of the minimum force necessary to deter, restrain, or, if necessary, contain violence, and to preserve public order.'[6] The aims of minimum force are to protect the public, avoid the escalation of violence or confrontation where such can be avoided, foster public support for the police by displays of restraint and impartiality, and bring about the termination of a threatening situation with the minimum amount of personal and physical damage possible. This ethos may be contrasted with that which pervades the actions of the army. As a rule the army is trained to apply the maximum force that is necessary to take an objective and eliminate an enemy. The army need not usually be worried about causing damage or loss of life, gaining or maintaining public support or avoiding confrontation. It seems obvious that, in a society which is not accustomed to the sight of heavily armed detachments, on public-order duties supported by armoured vehicles and with little usual contact with the public, the army is unsuited, both by training and doctrine, to an internal security role. In countries such as Britain and Australia where the accepted emphasis in dealing with public order disturbances is on restraint the appearance of armed troops would indicate a new order of problem. If troops are ever so committed the authorities will need to be very sure that such change has indeed taken place. While there are some disturbing trends which indicate that a sensible precaution would be to prepare contingency plans for such events, we must be very careful that we do not allow unnecessary incremental steps to be taken which will eventually lead to military involvement without a deliberate policy decision to invoke a radical change in internal security operations.

Militarisation of the police

One of the most problematic areas which could contribute substantially to the move to military involvement in the absence of a deliberate policy change is that of the militarisation of the police. Again, the argument is not that some degree of militarisation is bad *per se* but that an imperceptible move in this direction *is* if it occurs without adequate justification and conceptual analysis. In Britain the formation of the police Special Patrol Groups has caused considerable controversy because of their alleged para-military nature and in Australia recent years have seen the emergence of quasi-military units within police forces, with the formation of such units as the Victoria Police's Special Operations Group, the South Australia Police's Special Tasks and Rescue Force, and the Counter-Terrorist Unit within the Australian Federal Police. In their submission to the recent Protective Security Review, the Australian Federal Police proposed that they should expand their unit into a highly specialised counter-terrorist reaction force. This suggestion was rejected by Mr Justice Hope.[7] The suggestion is also being voiced that we should consider the establishment of a so-called 'third force' – a para-military organisation which occupies the middle ground between police and army. Other suggestions are that a counter-terrorist reaction force be established in the army (based on the existing SAS capability) and, further, that the army in general be trained in internal security duties. Each of these options needs to be examined carefully and rationally in order to evaluate the extent to which any of them should be implemented. The remainder of this chapter will attempt such an examination.

It may properly be argued that many of the questions surrounding the best organisation of resources for internal security duties awaits the development of a comprehensive classification of such overlapping areas as law enforcement, policing, internal security, public safety, and so forth. Until such a classification (by function or by skills and knowledges) is evolved which could inform decision-makers of appropriate groupings there will always be confusion of role, creation of organisations or units because of bureaucratic or personal empire-building, and inappropriate allocation of resources. There are a number of areas in the public safety/public security field which currently present problems of this nature and for which an adequately developed classification would be an invaluable problem-solving tool. Unfortunately, the development of such a classification awaits further research. In the meantime, while some general statements of principle can be made as a basis for discussion, it must be remembered that they are subject to amendments in the light of the classification when it is produced.

In liberal democratic states there are a number of commonly accepted reasons for the police being assigned the primary role in internal security. Some of these reasons are bound in tradition or political philosophy, others are merely practical. However, the increase of terrorism, the changing nature of political violence, and the impact of the writings of contemporary European revolutionary[8] and counter-revolutionary theorists[9] have contributed to the belief that internal violence is an increasingly probable and more threatening phenomenon and that the armed forces are certain to be called upon at some time to deal with it. While the specific concern in this work is the army's role in counter-terrorist operations, this problem can only be viewed in the wider context of the army's role in countering social violence generally. Within this context, the argument will be presented that the use of the armed forces to maintain peace and order within democratic societies in the British tradition should be very strictly limited and that the emergence of any para-military organisations to fulfil this role should be particularly carefully monitored.

The role of the police

The major position to be advanced is that the police are the most appropriate body to maintain internal law and order and that the use of the armed forces in this role is generally inappropriate. The first reason advanced in support of this proposition is that the police have a special mandate both in constitutional theory and in organisation and training to control civil disorder. The office of constable, in particular, confers special powers on the police (particularly powers of arrest) which are much wider than those given to any other citizens. Of great importance, too, is the fact that a police officer is duty bound to support the law if the law conflicts with orders from superior officers. In constitutional theory, members of the military forces have the same status as any other citizen who intervenes to suppress civil disorder (indeed at common law soldiers, as citizens, have a duty to intervene). However, the soldier is in an anomalous position in that he is also subject to military law. He is not an individual citizen, but part of an armed group under orders. Lord Diplock has noted that the view of soldier as citizen may give rise to an imperfect understanding of the soldier's rights and duties. In a judgement concerning a British soldier in Northern Ireland who had shot and killed a fleeing person Lord Diplock said:

In theory it may be the duty of every citizen when an arrestable offence is about to be committed in his presence to take whatever reasonable measures are available to him to prevent the commission of the crime; but the duty is one of imperfect obligation and does not place him under any obligation to do anything by which he would expose himself to risk of personal injury, nor is he under any duty to search for criminals or seek out crime. In contrast to this a soldier who is employed in aid to the civil power in Northern Ireland is under a duty enforceable under military law, to search for criminals if so ordered by his superior officer and to risk his own life should this be necessary in preventing terrorist acts.[10]

It could have been argued until recently that, in liberal democracies in the British tradition, circumstances were unlikely to emerge in which large numbers of armed soldiers would be deployed in a civilian security operation. Most argument has centered, therefore, on the position of a small, relatively discrete unit (such as the SAS) being involved in a contained operation involving the use of force to dislodge terrorists from some stronghold. However, the deployment in specific emergencies of a large number of ordinary troops with no special training in internal security duties and in contact with the general public has become a reality in Northern Ireland, Canada and Australia. These operations raised many of the questions of the rights and duties of soldiers being considered here. Questions concerning the rights of soldiers to erect roadblocks, direct citizens, search persons and property, arrest people, and use force to carry out these functions suddenly become less than academic.[11] In particular the incidents revealed that the powers of soldiers in a civilian security context are ambiguous and ill-defined and could well place individual soldiers in positions of personal liability which are quite unreasonable. As part of the solution to this problem in Australia, Mr Justice Hope has recommended[12] that when members of the armed forces are acting in aid to the civil power in an internal security operation they should be deemed to have the powers of Commonwealth Police Officers but that they shall 'act only as part of the Defence Force and shall be individually liable to obey the orders of their superior officers as if they were being used for the naval, military or air defence of the Commonwealth or of the several States'.[13] This provision would place the soldier in a less invidious position than that currently obtaining but considerable effort would need to be put into educating and training soldiers in the powers and duties of constables. In fact, it is not entirely clear exactly what limits may be placed on police officers' powers to stop and search persons, man roadblocks, etc., and these are matters that also need clarification.

Apart from the constitutional preference for police as guardians of internal order, what other reasons may be advanced for limiting the internal security role of the armed services? (After all, if deemed appropriate, legislation can easily be enacted to give the military wider powers, and even primacy, in internal security operations.) One of the more important reasons is the necessity for the police to maintain as close a relation as possible to the public. This has a number of implications. Because the police normally operate in the community they are likely to have the necessary intelligence information to enable them to cope with threats to social order. Because they are seen as a positive force by many sectors of the community, information is likely to be forthcoming which an organisation such as the army, with no normal experience in the community, would find difficult to elicit. Further, if the armed services were to become involved in internal peace-keeping generally (as opposed to providing a strike force to counter a particular terrorist act) they would have to develop their own intelligence network in the community, such as the British Army has done in Northern Ireland. This would constitute a major and, to many a threatening change in civil-military relations which would need considerable justification. In general, it would only be thinkable when the civil police force had lost all hope of maintaining internal order. However, a serious question arises here. If the internal security situation appears to be deteriorating and if the military appear likely to be assigned an increasing role, at what point should they start an intelligence-gathering exercise? The example of the United States Army in the late 1960s gathering information on several hundred thousand American citizens is apposite. It illustrates the necessity to make quite explicit the conditions under which military aid to the civil power will be invoked. In this way, there will be less chance of ambiguous situations leading military officers to consider it their duty to start pre-emptive public order intelligence-gathering activities of their own.

Problems caused by the use of the army

The criticisms directed at the use of the army in a counter-terrorist role illustrate some further problems with employing armed troops on public order duties. First, the wide deployment of armed and uniformed troops implies an extremely serious terrorist threat which could easily be used by the terrorists to their own propaganda advantage. This is even more true if armoured vehicles are involved in the operation. There are situations in which armoured vehicles are necessary, but the commitment of such vehicles could add significantly to tension and would appear far too lethal. When the use of armour is justified, it will sometimes be best to commit wheeled, as opposed to tracked, armoured vehicles. Apart from their operational advantages in urban environments,[14] wheeled armoured vehicles do not have the same psychologically negative impact that tracked vehicles (such as tanks) do. As one military writer has noted: 'tracked armoured vehicles are commonly identified with tanks by the mass media and are branded by them, as well as political agitators, as massive instruments of oppression, which inhibits their use for internal security'.[15] The use of armed troops, then, particularly with armoured support and operating in situations which may bring them into contact or conflict with sections of the public may, unless carefully controlled and fully justified, incite further violence rather than quell it. To commit troops is to admit that more narrowly targeted and less violent methods have failed (or would fail if used).

For those concerned with power within the state the use of armed troops also poses worries. In countries in the British tradition the police and the armed forces bear significantly different relations to the central government. In essence, the police are under local control, whilst the armed forces exist to defend the interests of, and are controlled by, the central government. Taken together with the constitutional and command structure differences between the two organisations, the difference in control suggests to some that the armed services are more likely to be used for political purposes unacceptable in a democracy than for the legitimate maintenance of law and order. In discussing the situation in Britain, Edmonds argues that more local control of police is

a positive asset to any society for it emphasises the maintenance of law and order being a community responsibility, emanating from within; it is to be preferred to law and order imposed from without, under central Government direction. It is important to leave the Armed Forces out of this sphere of public life, since they can in no functional way be an integral part of it.[16]

While it is true that in a federal state such as Australia or Canada there are differences between the States (or Provinces) which suggest that some police forces are theoretically more liable to political direction than others,[17] it would seem obvious that they are less liable to such direction than would be the armed forces. For many critics, this is an important reason to limit the role of the armed forces in anti-terrorist operations to specific strike actions, rather than expanding their duties to include the keeping of public order.

With these objections in mind, it should also be recognised that other analysts see a legitimate role for the armed services in terrorist and other internal security situations. Such analysts contend that there are significant trends towards the increased and widespread use of political violence which will either seriously strain police resources or for which traditional police methods will prove ineffective. These predictions tend towards seeing a Northern Ireland-type situation duplicated in other places. What this means is that a situation could develop in which 'the rule of law is significantly at variance with the values and aspirations of the people, or when society at large fails to accommodate or adjust sufficiently to economic or social change'.[18] In other words, when consensus breaks down and when social discipline and cohesion are diminished we may expect an upsurge of terrorism and political violence. If such a situation emerged, the government would have to seriously analyse its own policies to ensure that they were not the fundamental cause. In order to keep up with changing social conditions our legal, economic, and political systems have to change to reflect the changed circumstances and aspirations of the citizens. New mechanisms of dialogue between citizen and state will need to be designed and must be used before any attempts to have recourse to coercive measures. Coercive action in the absence of consensus – particularly those actions likely to be carried out by the armed forces in a prolonged emergency situation – could well pose greater long-term dangers to the fabric of a democratic society than the evils they are supposedly designed to negate. The problem is one of balance. On the one hand, a too eager invocation of military aid to the civil power could easily slip into repression (or at least serious, and non-essential, abuse of civil liberties). On the other hand, too great a concern for democratic sensibilities could well produce a weak and vacillating response which eventually could lead to the destruction of democracy. It behoves governments and citizens to carefully consider their obligations and actions. There seem to be three main aspects of such an analysis. The first is to create specific policies which clearly outline the roles expected of the police and the armed forces and, where necessary to enact legislation to give effect to these policies. The second is for the government and various pressure groups honestly to analyse their policies in order to evaluate the extent to which they fail to accommodate peoples' expectations or rights. Governments in particular need to be more cognisant of the consequences of policies which affect employment opportunities, education, the environment, social roles, and other obvious causes of major disaffection. Effective communication is one of the major avenues to genuine political goodwill. Finally, in the event of political violence we need to develop a calmer approach as a society to looking for immediate solutions. In particular, we need to avoid the over-reaction which has characterised the response in many parts of the world. As is discussed in two other chapters, intelligence agencies and the media have important places in this process. The media need to develop a restrained and honest approach to the reporting of terrorist acts. The sensationalism and emotionalism which is the hallmark of much reporting in this area both distorts reality and places inappropriate pressures on government decision-makers in crisis situations. The intelligence agencies make a vital contribution to assessing the seriousness of any particular threat and it will be necessary to evolve systems which ensure democratic control of such agencies without restricting their activities to such an extent that they are ineffective. There is a danger that the recent revelations of the illegal and, sometimes, undemocratic and dangerous activities of intelligence agencies could produce a backlash which will destroy the legitimate activities of these organisations. This must be avoided at all costs because without detailed intelligence it is not possible either to take effective counter-measures against terrorism or to evaluate adequately the threat posed by any particular act or series of acts. Without the latter capability it is all too likely that governments will err on the side of over-reaction. This increases substantially the probability of the armed forces becoming involved in counter-terrorist operations on a wide scale.

A 'third force'

One suggestion which has been widely discussed as a potential solution to the problem of involving the military in civilian security operations is the creation of a so-called 'third force' or para-military force.[19] This means a force which is either a significant unit of a police force charged with para-military duties or a separate para-military organisation. 'Para-military' refers to

activity akin to that of the military's, but at the same time not performed by a military agency; although this activity is similar in certain respects, it is nonetheless of a scale much smaller (for example, usually light firepower capability) and less all-encompassing than what is denoted 'military'. Normally, paramilitary forces deal with challenges or threats to internal defence and public order, albeit this does not preclude an external defence role. A paramilitary force is usually designed as a mobile, and in some respects self-contained, organisation with a command structure not unlike that of the military's. It may also perform an intelligence role and riot control duties, although these are not, strictly speaking, paramilitary functions.[20]

There are a number of existing models for such a force. The best known are the third forces of Europe. The French have an anti-riot organisation named the Compagnies Republicaines de Securite (CRS) which is a highly mobile police security force under the control of the Ministry of the Interior. It is a section of the uniformed branch of the Police Nationale, which is the police force responsible for policing cities with populations of 10,000 or more. The CRS is complemented by another mobile security force called the Garde Mobile which is part of the Gendarmerie Nationale, a military force with mainly police duties. The Gendarmerie polices the rural areas of France and towns of less than 10,000 population. Although recruited and funded by the Ministry of the Armed Forces, the Gendarmerie functions under the Ministry of the Interior when operating in aid to the civil power.

In West Germany, each of the ten *Länder* (States) have police forces, one of which is a public order unit known as the Bereitschaftpolizei (emergency police). In addition, following a constitutional amendment in 1972, a para-military police force called the Bundesgrenzshutz (Federal Border Guard) which operates under the federal Ministry of the Interior, may be used to cope with acute internal crisis situations. It was a unit of the

Federal Border Guard (GSG-9) which effected the rescue of passengers from a hijacked airliner at Mogadishu, Somalia in October 1977. Most other European countries have a third force or public order police force, the best known of the remainder being the Carabinieri in Italy, and the Marechaussee in the Netherlands. In Asia the Thai Border Patrol Police and the Malaysian Police Field Force are regional examples of paramilitary police.

A number of advantages can be cited for the third force concept. The most obvious advantage is that such an organisation is especially trained to deal with such difficult situations as riots, terrorist incidents, or insurrections. It does not suffer from the problem of conflicting missions, which is the case with both the army (whose primary mission is external defence) and the police (whose primary mission is law enforcement/crime prevention). Such a unit would be highly trained in special skills, not involved in routine police work and, therefore, ready to respond in force at very short notice. This combination of attributes should make them much more effective than either the police or the armed forces as an internal security force. Being able to call out a third force reduces the possibility of having to call on the army, who with their training for war might be expected to use excessive force in some circumstances. It also removes the police from the most serious confrontations with the public, thereby preserving their basically peace-keeping reputations.

While these arguments seem sound, in both the historical and the current political context in Britain and Australia, there are stronger arguments against the proposal. In the first place, the establishment of a third force (be it an independent organisation or a larger, more specialised, and more heavily armed version of current police anti-terrorist units) could only be justified by a significant increase in political violence. There is no strong case to be made for such an increase at present. Under current police organisation, large numbers of police can be rapidly assembled for public order duties if the need arises. While it could be argued that the police themselves should receive more specialised training in crowd-control and riot-control techniques, there are dangers in becoming exclusively specialised in this area. If personnel are assigned solely to public order duties, they lack contact (except in the negative sense) with the public whom they become in danger of seeing – and being seen by – as an enemy. Further, specialised anti-terrorist/anti-riot training, in the absence of the experience of general police work, may tend to lead personnel to use more force than is necessary. There has been much criticism of third forces in this regard, notably of the CRS.

For example, the CRS in Paris in 1968 earned for themselves graffiti all over the walls – 'CRS-SS' – implying that the helmeted, visored and padded clothing worn, combined with a rifle-butt-swinging image, was more akin to the German SS than a police force.[21]

A further danger is that the existence of a third force may in itself exacerbate political conflict. For example, its existence may well tempt a government to use it to break up industrial protests or interfere in industrial disputes in situations or in ways in which either the police or, more particularly, the armed forces would not have been used in the past.

There are still other general problems with the concept of a third force. One is that such organisations 'blur the distinction that should be maintained between the soldier and the policeman'.[22] Another is that to be effectively on call and to be continuously in training, many European countries have found that it is necessary to have third force personnel established in barracks, which further sets them apart from the public and, if part of a police force, severely limits their deployment on other police duties. As it is possible to provide localised saturation coverage by ordinary policemen in a terrorist emergency, a specialised organisation seems unnecessary. As Bowden notes

Such a mode of response [the deployment of a routine police anti-terrorist squad] has the very considerable additional benefit of preventing the whole of a force from becoming obsessed, as has happened in much of Latin America, with terrorism and counterinsurgency operations to the detriment of their routine tasks.[23]

A further drawback to basing third force concepts on models in other countries is that the police traditions and problems of those countries are not comparable to countries having a British police model. For example, in Europe, the existence of para-military units is a natural development of the system of policing which has evolved there. In contrast to the British tradition of the police as 'citizens in uniform', the police in Europe have always been set apart from citizens and have had overtly political functions.[24] The police tradition in France and Germany, for example, is much more tied to public order duties than is the case with the British tradition. The development of specialist public order units was, therefore, a natural consequence of European systems and not the departure it would be if a para-military force were established in England or Australia. It is interesting to note that the only British attempt to establish para-military police (in non-colonial situations), the Royal Irish Constabulary (RIC) and the Royal Ulster Constabulary (RUC), resulted in the collapse of the forces through their becoming too communalised.[25] In the case of the RIC, the effect was to destroy the force altogether. The RUC, on the other hand, was so incapacitated that it had to hand over domestic order-keeping to the British Army in 1969, and is only now beginning to be able to exercise its proper functions again.

In fact, if one analyses the police forces created by the British, it is obvious that they seldom followed the traditional model of the English 'bobby'. The forces established in Malaysia, Palestine, Rhodesia, and elsewhere, were all para-military organisations. But if the functions that such forces fulfil are analysed, it is immediately apparent that many of them are inappropriate to either the British or the Australian situation (e.g. border surveillance, counter-insurgency operations, policing remote areas, intelligence-gathering, or even acting as a counter-balance to the army to reduce the likelihood of *coups d'état*[26]).

A balanced response

On balance, then, it appears that there is at present insufficient justification for the establishment of a third force in Britain or Australia. The response to terrorism should be primarily a police responsibility. Ideally, specialised police units, well-equipped and trained, should be maintained, but should be spread either throughout the ordinary police divisions (on the model of the New Zealand Armed Offender Squads) or the personnel rotated back to general duties after a tour in a specialised unit (on the model of the Metropolitan Police Special Patrol Groups in London).

With that accepted, however, clearly there are still situations which a police anti-terrorist squad will be unable to handle on its own because of lack of firepower, particular military skills, equipment, or tactical mobility. In the absence of a para-military unit, joint police–army contingency plans are obviously appropriate for such situations as heavily armed terrorists threatening to blow up a hijacked airliner or major installation, or kill hostages. In his *Protective Security Review*, Mr Justice Hope outlined the types of situations in which he considered the use of armed Defence Force personnel would be appropriate. These situations were:

(a) the assault of buildings, aircraft, or other forms of public transport seized and held by terrorists, with or without hostages;
(b) cordoning off or otherwise protecting large areas where terrorists may seek to enter by means of violence, as, for example, an airport; and
(c) situations involving large or remote areas or areas outside police control, such as the sea, or very large numbers of personnel, or requiring special skills or equipment, where the police are unable, adequately or at all, or within imperative time limits, to do what is required.[27]

If the army is to be able to operate effectively in such situations it must prepare for them thoroughly. It has been argued that the army lacks doctrine in the field of low-intensity operations (which includes anti-terrorist operations) and that there is a corresponding training deficiency.[28] If general units of the army are to be used for some of the non-specialist operations outlined above, these short-comings will need to be remedied. Obviously, for the specialised operations, intensive training will be required. In Australia, as in Britain, the SAS has been assigned the specialist anti-terrorist role. As the SAS rescue of the hostages from the Iranian Embassy in London in May 1980 illustrated, a highly trained military unit is an extremely effective final back-up when normal police methods are insufficient. By way of contrast, the failure of the United States rescue mission to Iran in April 1980 illustrates the thin line between success and failure and underscores the absolute necessity for exemplary planning, training and execution. In both the Australian and the British context, the army is the most appropriate agency to be tasked with this burden.

If this reasoning is accepted, there are still a number of matters which the government will have to resolve before a satisfactory basis is laid for military aid to the civil power in response to terrorist attack. In general, these revolve around the questions of command and control of military forces and the rights and duties of individual soldiers. A number of the recommendations in the *Protective Security Review* go some way towards resolving these issues. However, the *Review* does not get to grips with the mechanics of outlining what powers soldiers should exercise or what legal position the soldier is placed in for obeying an order of a superior officer, not manifestly illegal, which subsequently leads to a criminal charge or a suit for damages. The necessity to resolve these and related questions has been cogently discussed by Robin Evelegh in his book on the problems of the British Army in Northern Ireland.[29]

As a basis for detailed policy planning, then, the following principles can be enunciated. The containment of terrorism should as far as possible be a police matter dealt with by existing police forces. Each police force should have a unit which is able to deal with public order situations involving firearms, explosives, and/or hostage-taking. In the absence of widespread social disorder there seems no justification for the establishment of a para-military third force to act as a riot control or light infantry anti-terrorist organisation. In extreme situations with which the police are unable to cope it should be acceptable to call upon the armed forces. If large numbers of armed personnel are called out they should have received adequate training in both civilian security operations and their powers and duties. Legislation should be introduced which requires the recall of Parliament to oversee the use of troops exceeding prescribed limits of numbers or duration of service in aid to the civil power. The army should be tasked with the counter-terrorist reaction force role and should be the only agency to possess such a capability.

Two final points may profitably be added to this discussion. The first is that the above analysis is based on an assessment of the current and immediately foreseeable political and social situation in Britain and Australia. In particular, the objection to the introduction of a para-military third force is based on the assumption that there are presently no situations which the police are unable to handle (with or without selective military aid). If the situation should change, as some predict, and a significant lessening of social cohesion and consensus led to widespread threats to social order, the arguments would need to be re-assessed. As long as we can avoid a third force, we should do so. However, the proposal will need to be reviewed periodically and not merely rejected on the basis of prejudice. There is nothing *inherently* wrong with the suggestion. It is only suggested that it is an unnecessary and inappropriate step in the present circumstances.

The second point has to do with public awareness of counter-terrorist policy. There are sound reasons for keeping secret all the details of operational contingencies and capabilities and many issues of policy. However, because of the particular public misgivings which may be aroused by some instances of military aid to the civil power there is a strong case to be made for public education in this field. As Sir Robert Mark emphasised in his 1978 report on policing to the Australian Government,[30] the general guidelines governing the invocation of military aid to the civil power should be widely publicised so that there is no misunderstanding of the Government's intentions or of the roles, rights, and duties of the police and the army.

11

The legal regulation of terrorism: international and national measures

It has been argued in earlier chapters that contemporary terrorism is, increasingly, an international as well as a domestic phenomenon. Because of the delicate nature of international relations, attempts to control terrorism at a global level will always tend to focus on legal and treaty obligations rather than action-oriented measures. The diplomatic and political implications of, for example, an international anti-terrorist strike force are such that suggestions of this kind are never likely to be translated into reality. Rather, the only suggestion that has any hope of gaining acceptance is one which places treaty obligations on nations to act in a prescribed way in a certain situation (for example, agree to bring to trial any captured terrorists, or agree to extradite them to the country of origin). And as will be shown, even this avenue is fraught with such dangers as to seriously jeopardise its eventual success.

As discussed earlier one of the central problems bedevilling international cooperation is the definition of terrorism. Because treaties are couched in legal terms they rely heavily on definitions acceptable to all parties. Since the issue of what constitutes terrorism is one of the most important unsolved problems in debates about terrorism, the attempts to arrive at a definition for international treaty purposes epitomise the confusion and dissent which surrounds the whole subject.

Until the twentieth century there have been no efforts at international cooperation to control terrorism, even though many governments in the nineteenth century were seriously challenged by terrorist campaigns. It was the advent of international terrorism which prompted efforts to gain international agreement on a concerted approach to the suppression of terrorism. The hijacking of aircraft, the kidnapping and murder of diplomats, military personnel, and business executives, the conduct of highly publicised terrorist acts by individuals of one country in the territory of another, and the spectre of nuclear blackmail have all pressured authorities to seek for common agreement in trying to contain these incidents and their consequences. In the past, particularly because of the absence of an effective, coordinated, and rapid-reaction news network, terrorist acts were localised and specific. Today, many are spectaculars mounted to draw world-wide attention to the terrorist cause. Because less emphasis was placed on publicity, past terrorist activities generally took place within the borders of the country against whose government the activities were directed. If conducted in a foreign country, the acts of violence were generally limited to attacks on individuals or installations of the home country. As such they represented little threat to the internal security of the country in which the attack occurred because they did not seek to change the policies of the host country nor force it to make concessions (for example, release prisoners, provide money, or guarantee safe passage).

However, the advent of a closely interconnected international community, modern and efficient transportation systems and instantaneous transmission of news around the globe has altered the situation dramatically. Terrorist theory now emphasises the ease with which many goals can be achieved by exerting pressure on the target government through third parties. So an airliner carrying passengers of many nationalities may be hijacked in order that the governments representing these individuals will put pressure on some target government to accede to the demands of the hijackers. Similarly, hostages may be taken in one country to provide spectacular publicity for problems in another. Thus, the Black September terrorists perpetrated the incident at the Munich Olympics in September 1972 in order to publicise the plight of the Palestinian peoples. At the same time the terrorists attempted to use an incident in Germany to force the Israeli government to release 200 imprisoned Palestinians. The Israelis refused, but the West German government promised the terrorists safe passage to Egypt with their hostages. In fact, of course, German sharpshooters tried to eliminate the terrorists at Furstenfeldbruck airport and in the ensuing massacre all the hostages (nine), five terrorists, and one policeman were killed. In this case, although the situation was used to make demands, it appears that the primary purpose was to bring world-wide attention to the Palestinian cause. In this aim the terrorists were entirely successful.

Acts such as the Munich massacre, the embassy sieges in such places as the Hague (where members of the Japanese Red Army took over the French Embassy in September, 1974), Stockholm (where six members of the Baader-Meinhof group occupied, and eventually blew up, the West German Embassy in April 1975) and London (where the Iranian Embassy was taken over by Arab terrorists proclaiming freedom for Khuzestan in May 1980), the hijacking of international airliners, the blowing up of oil refineries are acts of modern times. Although they have historical parallels it has been shown in earlier chapters that they are significantly different acts in the present context. The motivations and consequences of contemporary acts of terrorism make them a greater threat to both national sovereignty and international order than they ever were (or, indeed, could have been) in the past. Many acts are possible only because of modern technology and increasingly the motive behind terrorist acts is a millenarian one. This latter development is accompanied by a widening acceptance of the view that there are no innocents and that the fight must be taken all over the world. It seems to be the case, too, that persons espousing such views utilise terrorism as the tactic of nihilism and desperation, with all that this implies for lack of restraint.

Because of these striking changes many people turn to international law as a force which could play a significant role in the suppression of terrorism. The first attempts to stimulate international cooperation took place within the League of Nations. Following the assassinations of King Alexander I of Yugoslavia and French Foreign Minister Louis Barthou in Marseilles on 9 October 1934, the League considered two measures dealing with terrorism. The first was the 1937 Convention for the Prevention and Punishment of Terrorism which criminalised international incidents involving heads of state and other internationally protected persons. It also proscribed destruction of the public property of and injuries to the citizens of one country by citizens of another. A second convention, that for the Creation of an International Criminal Court, gave signatories the option of committing persons accused of terrorist offences for trial in an international court established for the purpose. However, the Conventions never became operative because an insufficient number of nations ratified them.[1]

Part of the reason for the non-ratification of the Conventions was the impending Second World War which soon engulfed many of the members of the League of Nations and temporarily made terrorism a minor issue. But at least as important a reason was the perennial problem which has undermined subsequent attempts to frame international treaties on terrorism, namely, the definition of terrorism. Many nations had misgivings about the breadth of the definition proposed in the Conventions. The United Kingdom, for example, declined to ratify them 'due to an anticipation of the difficulty of framing the relevant domestic legislation'.[2]

The United Nations and the regulation of terrorism

The subsequent efforts to gain an international accord on terrorism through the United Nations have faced the same difficulties of definition upon which the League of Nations' attempts foundered. The increasing seriousness of international terrorism prompted UN Secretary-General Kurt Waldheim to request on 8 September 1972 that the UN General Assembly should consider 'measures to prevent terrorist and other forms of violence which endanger or take innocent human lives or jeopardise fundamental freedoms.'[3]

The difficulties that consideration of this proposal were going to encounter were already evident when the General Assembly decided on 23 September 1972 to include an amended version on its agenda. The amended agenda item requested the study of:

Measures to prevent international terrorism which endangers or takes innocent human lives or jeopardises fundamental freedoms, and study of the underlying causes of those forms of terrorism and acts of violence which lie in misery, frustration, grievance and despair and which cause some people to sacrifice human lives, including their own, in an attempt to effect radical changes.[4]

The major problem with this amendment was that the insistence of concentration on causes of terrorism made it almost inevitable that no immediate action would be taken against nor condemnation made of terrorism. The difficulty was pointed out in a UN Secretariat document which noted that:

The effort to eliminate those causes should be intense and continuous, as mankind, despite its intellectual powers, has not yet succeeded in creating a social order free from misery, frustration, grievance and despair – in short, an order which will not cause or provoke violence. Yet terrorism threatens, endangers or destroys the lives and fundamental freedoms of the innocent, and it would not be just to leave them to wait for protection until the causes have been remedied and the purposes and principles of the Charter have been given full effect. There is a present need for measures of international cooperation to protect their rights as far as possible. At all times in history, mankind has recognised the unavoidable necessity of repressing some forms of violence which otherwise would threaten the very existence of society as well as that of man himself. There are some means of using force, as in every form of human conflict, which must not be used, even when the use of force is legally and morally justified, and regardless of the status of the perpetrator.[5]

The fact that international measures had been agreed upon in order to control other forms of violence, without first having agreed upon their 'causes' was pointed out by Erik Suy, who was the chairman of the Sixth (legal) Committee of the 27th Session of the UN General Assembly. He asserted that:

in reality, a simultaneous study of 'causes' and 'measures' is a condition impossible to sustain. One of the most frequent manifestations of acts of violence is air piracy: yet, measures have been found without studying the causes. Further, the Commission on International Law has prepared a draft convention on the protection of diplomats without first having elucidated the reasons for the acts of violence directed against them. The demand to consider the question en bloc was in reality nothing more than a manoeuvre designed to reduce terrorism to a simply political question and to prevent concrete measures from being adopted.[6]

The problems of insisting on finding causes first became apparent following the establishment by the General Assembly of an Ad Hoc Committee on Terrorism to deliberate on the motion.[7] Because of the method of operation resolved upon by the Committee (that is, they decided to operate by consensus rather than by vote) together with the fundamental political differences existing between blocs of nations represented on the Committee, no success was forthcoming at getting to grips with the fundamental issues. Neither in the areas of definition nor remedies were any workable solutions arrived at.

The problems inherent in international debate on this topic are further illustrated well by the fate of the United States draft resolution and convention on terrorism submitted to the General Assembly on 25 September 1972. The essence of these proposals lay in an attempt to extend the range of crimes to include acts not covered under existing international accords (such as the Hague Convention for the Suppression of Unlawful Seizure of Aircraft) but without becoming enmeshed in the thorny issues of aggressive acts carried out in the context of a people's right to exercise self-determination (for example, in civil wars or colonial insurgencies). The United States draft Convention for the Prevention and Punishment of Certain Acts of International Terrorism was hailed as having achieved success in:

localising internal conflict situations by providing international measures for the punishment of those zealous revolutionaries who seek to dramatise their cause by acts of terrorism in foreign countries.[8]

Article 1 of the United States draft was:

1. Any person who unlawfully kills, causes serious bodily harm or kidnaps another person, attempts to commit any such act or participates as an accomplice of a person who commits or attempts to commit any such act, commits an act of international significance if the act
(a) Is committed or takes effect outside the Territory of a State of which the alleged offender is a national; and
(b) Is committed or takes effect
    (i)   Outside the territory of the State against which the act is directed, or
    (ii) Within the territory of the State against which the act is directed and the alleged offender knows or has reason to know that a person against whom the act is directed is not a national of that State; and
(c) Is committed neither by nor against a member of the armed forces of a State in the course of military hostilities; and
(d) Is intended to damage the interests of or obtain concessions from a State or an international organisation.

By thus trying to avoid placing constraints on wars of national liberation, the United States hoped to avoid interminable wrangling over the definition of terrorism. However, the Afro-Asia block in the General Assembly, together with the Arab states, carried out an intensive lobbying campaign to oppose the United States draft. When it became obvious that its proposals would not gain the necessary support, the United States switched its backing to a compromise proposal sponsored by Australia, Austria, Belgium, Canada, Costa Rica, Great Britain, Guatemala, Honduras, Iran, Japan, Luxembourg, New Zealand, and Nicaragua. This compromise replaced the call for a conference of plenipotentiaries in 1973 to draft a convention, with a three-stage process involving (1) asking the General Assembly to request the International Law Commission to draft a convention, (2) having the General Assembly debate this draft in the autumn of 1973, and (3) convening a special conference 'as soon as practicable' to adopt a convention. At the same time, there was a provision for the president of the General Assembly to appoint an ad hoc committee to study the underlying causes of terrorism.

However, before this draft resolution was voted upon, yet another resolution, sponsored by 16 African and Third World nations,[9] was introduced. Whilst making passing critical reference to violence, the resolution was more concerned with affirming 'the inalienable right to self-determination', supporting the 'legitimacy' of the national liberation 'struggle', and condemning 'repressive and terrorist acts by colonial, racist, and alien regimes'. There were no definite proposals on measures to control international terrorism, merely a suggestion that a committee be established to study both the underlying causes of terrorism and 'proposals for finding an effective solution to the problem'.

When the resolutions came up for discussion in the Sixth Committee, it was decided to vote on the 16-power draft ahead of the (primarily Western) 14-power draft. The Afro-Asian draft was adopted by a vote of 76 to 34 with 16 abstentions, thus consigning the 14-power draft to oblivion. One expert on United Nations' matters, Professor Seymour M. Finger, has claimed that:

Had the 14-power resolution been voted upon first, it might very well have received the support of the Soviet Union, since its representative endorsed the idea of the ILC's [International Law Commission] drafting an international treaty combatting terrorism. It is even conceivable that the 14-power draft might have won a majority, but the bloc pattern of voting prevented a test by ballot.[10]

When the General Assembly considered the draft resolution in December 1972, it approved it and decided to appoint a 35 state Ad Hoc Committee on International Terrorism.

An important document considered by the ad hoc committee was an analytical study of states' observations on terrorism,[11] which was submitted by the Secretary-General for their analysis at the direction of the General Assembly. Most states which had submitted written responses claimed to be opposed to acts of international terrorism. Even the Soviet Union adopted this stance, subject to the qualification that: 'It is unacceptable to give a broad interpretation to the term international terrorism and to extend it to cover national liberation movements, acts committed in resisting an aggressor in territories occupied by the latter and action by workers to secure their rights against the yoke of exploiters.'[12] It is pertinent to note that this proviso is not inconsistent with the United States draft resolution, indicating that the Soviet Union might eventually have agreed to some form of it had the Afro-Asian bloc vote not blocked consideration of the 14-power draft resolution. Of the 34 states who submitted written comments, only Syria and Yemen took positions which indicated that a workable convention on terrorism could not be arrived at.

However, the deliberations of the ad hoc committee, which met from 23 July to 11 August 1973, were characterised by fundamental differences between the members. Syria (ironically) considered that the focus should be on state terrorism. Other states insisted, as they had at previous debates, that the international community should be concerned with uncovering the causes of terrorism, rather than trying to devise punitive measures to eliminate it. Yet other states, while acknowledging that analysis of causes and devising of control measures were both necessary, argued that the latter did not need to await the outcome of the former. It was noted that in their domestic legislation, states did not wait for the underlying causes of crime to be identified before enacting penal laws.[13]

Similarly irreconcilable views were advanced as to what measures were appropriate to control terrorism. Some states favoured initial action at the national level, some stressed the desirability of bilateral agreements, and others favoured multilateral treaty arrangements. In an attempt to tease out these differences, the ad hoc committee established three sub-committees to examine, respectively, the definition, the underlying causes, and measures for the prevention of international terrorism. The results were predictable and are described by Finger in the following terms:

In the first subcommittee, it soon became evident that there was substantial disagreement as to whether or not a definition was either necessary or desirable. In the second, there was a rerun of the debate as to whether measures could be undertaken to restrain terrorism parallel with efforts to deal with underlying causes or whether elimination of the causes must precede such measures. Again, no consensus or compromise was reached.

This same conflict was repeated in the third committee. In addition, there were differences as to whether to aim for a general convention or a series of conventions, each related to a specific kind of act, for example, the taking of hostages for political extortion, the kidnapping of diplomats, or the sending of letter bombs. There was also a dispute on whether such conventions should cover state terrorism.[14]

As a result of their inability to agree on basic issues, the report of the sub-committee to the General Assembly amounted to little more than a summary of divergent views. As a consequence no convention on terrorism emerged and all the citizens of the world were left with to comfort them were a lot of empty and high-flown phrases. States were invited 'to become parties to the existing international conventions which relate to various aspects of international terrorism . . . [and] to take all appropriate measures at the national level with a view to the speedy and final elimination of the problem'. All very well as far as it goes. But there followed the obligatory warning that States should 'bear in mind' the provisions relating to 'the inalienable right to self-determination and independence . . . in particular the struggle of national liberation movements'.

Thus, as Green comments:

By wording its resolution in this fashion, the General Assembly has clearly elevated the right to self-determination above human life. Moreover, while apparently condemning acts of terrorism, it has bluntly asserted that if undesirable acts – which some might describe as terrorism – are undertaken in the name of self-determination or national liberation, then such acts are beyond the scope of condemnation and are legal.[15]

After a lapse of some time, the ad hoc committee was reactivated and met again between 14 and 25 March 1977. But again, its report[16] reflected the same differences as the initial meetings revealed, and no further progress appeared to have been made. Since then, the Western countries have become so discouraged with this avenue of securing international agreement on the control of terrorism that in December 1978 they all either voted against or abstained on General Assembly Resolution (32/147) continuing its existence.

While the United Nations has failed to reach agreement on the general control of terrorism, it has managed to finalise two conventions dealing with specific issues in this field. On 14 December 1973 the General Assembly approved the United Nations Convention on the Prevention and Punishment of Crimes Against Internationally Protected Persons, including Diplomatic Agents. This Convention mandates that signatories make the international commission of acts listed in the Convention offences under domestic legislation. The acts referred to are the murder, kidnapping, or other attack upon the person or liberty of internationally protected persons (or attempts or threats to do so, or being an accomplice to such acts), or the violent attack upon the official premises, private accommodation, or means of transport of internationally protected persons.

However, once again the United Nations hedged its bets. The resolution to which the Convention is annexed expressly provides at paragraph 4 that the Assembly 'recognises that the provisions of the annexed Convention could not in any way prejudice the exercise of the legitimate right to self-determination and independence . . . by peoples struggling against colonialism, alien domination, foreign occupation, racial discrimination and apartheid.'[17]

Given the latitude which may be taken in interpreting this provision the Convention is seen to be very weak. One might ask in what way the Convention differs from existing agreements on diplomats and government officials, such as the widely known 1961 and 1963 Vienna agreements on diplomatic and consular relations. The difference lies in the obligation to punish or extradite offenders. However, the 'self-determination' exception makes this innovation carry much less weight in practice than appears on paper. A further weakness is the problem facing all such Conventions, namely that of persuading all nations to ratify them. In the case of this Convention, only 40 nations had ratified it by mid–1979. Thus, even in its watered-down version, the Convention does not apply in many parts of the world.

The second matter on which the United Nations has reached a measure of agreement is that of hostage-taking. This area was raised for discussion by West Germany with its introduction of a draft convention on hostages. Germany sought to depoliticise the act of taking hostages in order to avoid the difficulties which had arisen in the earlier discussions on the United States draft resolution discussed above. This approach had recently been successful to a large degree in negotiating the Council of Europe Convention on the Suppression of Terrorism, but that was a case of a regional agreement with the negotiating parties sharing broad values and concerns, a factor which is conspicuously absent from the larger international scene. As a consequence, debate in the Sixth Committee (to which the draft convention was referred for discussion) began to take on the usual bloc attitudes apparent in earlier United Nations discussions of terrorism. On 15 December 1976, the General Assembly established an Ad Hoc Committee on the Drafting of an International Convention Against the Taking of Hostages, and this committee, consisting of 35 member states, began meeting on 1 August 1977 in an attempt to seek a consensus on the West German proposals.

The early meetings of the ad hoc committee followed the course which one now expects of such debates. The Western-aligned bloc argued that a convention, such as proposed by Germany, must be based on the principle of *aut dedere aut punire* (extradite or punish) with no allowance being made for the political motivation of hostage-taking. To do so, they argued, 'would amount to legitimising a crime which was repugnant to the conscience of mankind or would maintain a climate of tension between the States concerned . . . which an organisation whose main purpose was the maintenance of peace between peoples should avoid at any cost'.[18] The Italian representative argued that a convention such as proposed by West Germany was the best way of combating hostage-taking because 'the only effective means of reducing, if not eliminating, that kind of criminal activity was to ensure that the perpetrators fully understood from the outset that they could not escape without severe punishment'.[19]

The African and Soviet blocs, on the other hand, felt that the West German proposal represented 'only one aspect of violence and might well delay consideration of an overall solution to a problem which affected the sacred rights of human beings, their lives and freedom'.[20] The Tanzanian representative raised the now common issue of the legitimacy of violent struggle with the demand that the convention:

should recognise the legitimacy of the struggle of national liberation movements and the inalienable right of freedom fighters to take up arms to fight their oppressors. The oppressed peoples and colonial peoples who were held in perpetual bondage could not be stopped from taking oppressors hostage, if that became inevitable.[21]

In the ensuing meetings of the ad hoc committee, much of the discussion revolved around opposing views on national liberation movements and were characterised by a number of inter- and intra-group disputes. At its final meeting of 1977 the committee adopted a report which was so equivocal that the Mexican representative felt constrained to point out that Mexico had no objections to it 'because it could hardly object to something that did not say anything'.[22] The committee also adopted a draft resolution recommending that the General Assembly invite it to continue its work, a recommendation which was accepted in Assembly resolution 32/148 on 16 December 1977. At further meetings in 1978, the ad hoc committee again became embroiled in the same contentious issues, but eventually a number of compromises were reached and a report agreed upon, as was another recommendation to the General Assembly that its work continue in 1979.

Following the adoption of resolution 33/19 extending its mandate, the ad hoc committee began meeting again and finally agreed upon a draft convention with a recommendation that the General Assembly consider and adopt it. On 17 December 1979, the General Assembly adopted the general report and the draft convention without amendment, so that the Convention is now open for signature and will come into force thirty days after the deposit of the twenty-second instrument of ratification. However, according to some experts, it is unlikely to be generally ratified and, even if it were to be, would be largely ineffectual. For example, Aston argues that the Convention fails to close the gap in existing legislation against hostage-taking.[23] Only those acts which are of an international nature are covered, so that each state is left to its own initiative or desire to enact legislation against purely internal acts. Even if the act satisfies the international criterion, it must also involve demands on a third party – a conjunction which experience has shown is not always the case. For example, of 33 incidents of hostage-taking in Western Europe between 1968 and 1978 which involved an international element,[24] 11 involved no demands at all.

A further problem is that because of the insistence of the Soviet and Third World blocs that a dichotomy must be recognised between terrorist and national liberation groups, the enforcement provisions contained in the West German proposal were not accepted and were so watered down that Article 14 of the Convention now specifically states that there shall be no impairment of the right of asylum.

Finally, there appears to be a direct conflict between the Convention and the Additional Protocol I of June 1977 to the Geneva Conventions of 1949. Article 12(1) of the Hostages Convention recognises hostage-taking by national liberation movements as a legitimate part of their struggle as defined in Article 1(4) of the 1977 Geneva Protocol. However, Article 75, s.2(c) of the Protocol expressly prohibits the taking of hostages by national liberation movements at any time and in any place whatsoever. It would appear, therefore, that ratification of the Protocol precludes ratification of the Convention.

The situation is, thus, conceivably little more resolved than it was without the Convention. As Aston comments:

While it was perhaps too much to have expected the United Nations to have been capable of taking effective action against a phenomenon on which opinions and views are so strongly held and so utterly divergent, the Convention remains an unfortunately accurate reflection of the realities of the present world. Nor is the legislation against terrorism a panacea. Concerted action aimed at eliminating or at least identifying the underlying sources of structural violence, goal frustration, and socioeconomic inequalities that are often blamed as the precipitants of terrorist behaviour will undoubtedly help. Nonetheless, the fact remains that acts of hostage-taking will continue, and probably increase, because it is a proven, effective means of focusing the attention of a largely uncaring world on causes and issues generally overlooked. More despairingly, it has become glamorous.[25]

If the United Nations is unable to arrive at a workable accord does this mean that international efforts in this area are doomed to failure? It may be that the answer lies in regional agreements or agreements limited to specific problems. A number of attempts along these restricted lines have resulted in agreements in recent years. Although they may have some advantages over the United Nations attempts, it is fairly obvious, though, that they suffer from many of the same problems and deficiencies, as will be shown. To date, there have been two successful regional attempts to formulate Conventions against terrorism. In 1971, the Organisation of American States (OAS) agreed upon the Convention to Prevent and Punish the Acts of Terrorism Taking the Form of Crimes Against Persons and Related Extortion That Are of International Significance. The Convention focussed on murder of public figures and kidnapping for ransom. These acts are to be regarded as being of international significance regardless of their motivation. The country having jurisdiction has the responsibility to decide whether or not the Convention applies in any particular case. If it is decided that it does apply, the offender may be extradited. If extradition is not possible, then the onus is on the country of detention to try the offender. As with the United Nations 'self-determination' exception, the OAS Convention seems to be mitigated by a provision which re-affirms an inalienable right to asylum. Although some scholars [26] are of the opinion that granting of asylum was not envisaged in respect of terrorist acts – particularly kidnapping and murder – the provision is at least open to considerable interpretation. Again, the final problem is that of getting all OAS members to ratify the Convention.

The European Convention on the Suppression of Terrorism

The second existing major anti-terrorist Convention is the Council of Europe's 1977 European Convention on the Suppression of Terrorism. This may on paper be seen as an advance on previous Conventions in that it strips many offences of the protection afforded by the classic 'political exception clause' (that is a clause which exempts from the criminal category those acts which are politically motivated). Article 1 of the Convention[27] declares the following offences to be outside the purview of a political exception clause:

1. Offences within the scope of the 1970 Hague Convention for the Unlawful Seizure of Aircraft.
2. Offences within the scope of the 1971 Montreal Convention for the Suppression of Unlawful Acts Against the Safety of Civil Aviation.
3. Serious offences involving an attack against the life, physical integrity, or liberty of internationally protected persons, including diplomatic agents.
4. Offences involving kidnapping, hostage-taking or serious unlawful detention.
5. Offences involving the use of bombs, grenades, rockets, automatic weapons, or letter or parcel bombs where peoples' lives are endangered.
6. Attempts to commit any of the above offences, or being an accomplice to such offences or attempts to commit them.

Article 2 stipulates that other particularly serious acts involving innocent persons may also be regarded as non-political. Much of the Convention deals with provisions for extradition and Article 7 states that refusal to extradite under the terms of the Convention requires the detaining State to initiate prosecution of the offender. On the face of it, the European Convention seems a worthwhile contribution to international attempts (or, in this case, regional) to combat terrorism. However, as with other cases, it is flawed by the fact that not all members of the Council of Europe have ratified it and that it contains no enforcement provisions for breaches by signatories. Thus, there is no guarantee that it will be adhered to in the cruel test of a crisis. And one member of the Council, France, has already demonstrated that it would sooner refuse extradition of a terrorist than stand up to its international obligations. (In 1977 France permitted Abu Daoud to leave the country knowing that he was wanted by both Germany and Israel for his part in the Munich massacre.) In general, it can be expected that many, if not all, nations will put national self-interest before international treaty obligations in a crisis. This is the fatal flaw in international regulatory attempts.

In spite of these reservations, it may be, as Paul Wilkinson has pointed out that:

the European Convention represents the *optimal mechanism* for European cooperation in the fight against terrorism, given the present condition of international relations. Rather than expending more time and effort in discussing fresh institutions or mechanisms we should pursue the more modest aim of making the existing machinery work effectively. Moreover, there is no doubt that recent efforts by the Council of Europe and the European Community toward a greater degree of convergence in the jurisdiction, legal codes, and judicial procedures of the European states could immeasurably assist in smoothing the path for closer judicial cooperation and an effective implementation of the Convention on the Suppression of Terrorism.[28]

Other international treaties

For completeness, a number of other international treaties also need to be discussed. There are three major Conventions on hijacking in effect. The 1963 Tokyo Convention on Offences and Certain Other Acts Committed on Board Aircraft dealt with the question of jurisdiction over hijacking whilst an aircraft was in flight. During the flight, the Convention states that the country of registry of the aircraft has jurisdiction, regardless of where the aircraft is. During the flight, authority over the would-be hijackers is exercised by the aircraft commander who is authorised to hand the hijacker over to the local authorities upon landing, if they will accept responsibility. The Convention then allows the receiving State the option of returning the hijacker to his state of origin or to the state of registration of the aircraft. The Convention did not address itself to the political aspects of hijacking and the subsequent issue of right of asylum.

The next Convention to be signed dealt with the apprehension and punishment of international hijackers. The 1970 Hague Convention for the Suppression of Unlawful Seizure of Aircraft expressly made hijackers subject to extradition to either the country of registry of the aircraft, the country where the aircraft, with hijacker on board, landed, or the country whose citizens charter a plane without chartering the crew. If the hijacker is not extradited, he is to be tried in the detaining country.

The third aircraft agreement, the 1971 Montreal Convention for the Suppression of Unlawful Acts Against the Safety of Civil Aviation, was mainly concerned with various acts of sabotage. It requires signatories to extradite or prosecute persons who commit acts of sabotage or in other ways damage or destroy aircraft or who endanger the safe operation of an aircraft by damaging or destroying installations or air navigation services. The Convention also covers acts of violence on board an aircraft, and giving false information that endangers the flight of an aircraft (this provision being principally directed at bomb hoaxes).

Even though these measures are a move in the right direction it is hard to see what real effect they would have on many political hijackings. The most obvious drawback is that most of the states which are the well-known sanctuaries of political hijackers are not signatories to the Conventions. Even if all nations were signatories, however, such measures suffer from the fundamental weakness of a lack of an enforcement clause. There is simply no mechanism by which States who do not fulfil their obligations under the Conventions can be sanctioned. Of course, given the political realities, if an enforcement clause were added many, if not all, of the present signatories would withdraw their support. Thus, many feel that it is better to have an accord which at least sets out some requirements, albeit unenforceable, than no such agreement at all. But the fact remains that such Conventions are effectively no more than collections of high statements of principle devoid of any real impact. It is quite obvious that political terrorists have not been deterred by the existence of the Conventions. They have not been deterred because they reasonably believe that their actions will not be subject to the written restrictions.

The only agreement on hijacking that appears to have had any measurable impact has been the 15 February 1973 Memorandum of Understanding between Cuba and the United States which dealt with the return of boats and aircraft and the prompt extradition of certain categories of terrorists (including hijackers). This was in response to the widespread commandeering of air and water craft by anti-Castro Cubans escaping to the United States and the regular hijacking of American aircraft to Cuba. However, it might be argued that this agreement (which is no longer formally in force) was possible only because Cuba recognised that the majority of the hijackers were criminals or mentally deranged individuals and not politically motivated revolutionaries. It is also frequently overlooked that the Memorandum contained a clause allowing both governments to exercise discretionary rights to grant political asylum. Nevertheless the agreement serves to illustrate how effective a measure can be if the signatories enforce its provisions. During the formal existence of the agreement it was 100 per cent successful.

In the final analysis it appears that even in the limited area of aircraft hijacking, international agreements are unlikely to be very powerful for the foreseeable future. Attempts to give teeth to such agreements are almost bound to follow the path of the proposed convention submitted by a number of Western nations at the 1973 conference of the International Civil Aviation Organisation (ICAO). This accord would have authorised sanctions against States not honouring their treaty obligations. The proposed sanctions include suspension of aviation rights under the 1944 Chicago Convention on International Civil Aviation, the International Air Services Transit Agreement, and other relevant agreements. It was also proposed to allow suspension of all international air navigation to and from an offending State. Predictably, however, the measure was not agreed to.

If nations do not take it upon themselves to exercise responsible sanctions such as those suggested at the ICAO Conference, the future is likely to see pressure being exerted at critical points by non-State organisations. In a book on the illegal diversion of aircraft, McWhinney[29] suggests that the potentially most effective way to punish countries aiding or harbouring terrorists is for private organisations such as professional associations and unions within the aviation world to impose their own sanctions. He notes how quickly an El Al airliner hijacked to Algiers was allowed to leave the country in 1968 when the International Federation of Airline Pilots threatened to boycott all flights into or out of Algeria. In 1972 the Federation announced a worldwide stoppage of its members if the United Nations failed to add to existing conventions enforcement clauses against nations offering sanctuary or failing to prosecute hijackers.[30] Although the deadline passed and a stoppage by pilots of eighteen airlines ensued, the Federation failed to gain any action. Nevertheless, the potential for a concerted action against a specific target country has been demonstrated and will no doubt one day be exploited when the inability or unwillingness of governments to act becomes too gross to ignore.

Perhaps one bright cloud on an otherwise dark horizon was the statement on aircraft hijacking issued at the conclusion of the Bonn Economic Summit on 17 July 1978.[31] The Declaration read:

The heads of state and government, concerned about terrorism and the taking of hostages, declare that their governments will intensify their joint efforts to combat international terrorism.

To this end, in cases where a country refuses extradition or prosecution of those who have hijacked an aircraft and/or do not return such aircraft, the heads of state and government are jointly resolved that their governments should take immediate action to cease all flights to that country.

At the same time, their governments will initiate action to halt all incoming flights from that country or from any country by the airlines of the country concerned. The heads of state and government urge other governments to join them in this commitment.

Although this Declaration does not constitute a formal treaty and the determination of the signatories has yet to be tested in a crisis, the tone of the document is encouragingly firm. The intent, if acted upon, would be of significance because the signatories represent approximately 70 per cent of the non-communist world's air traffic. Although Wilkinson has commented that 'a cynic might note that aircraft hijacking was no longer the major terrorist threat by July 1978; action had really been needed in 1969–73 when the menace was at its peak',[32] it seems likely that, for reasons advanced elsewhere in this book, aircraft hijacking will enjoy a renewed vogue in the coming years, and the determination of the Bonn declarants will indeed be put to the acid test.

The failure of international measures

An examination of attempts to regulate terrorist behaviour through international treaties and conventions reveals, then, that there is little hope of nations effectively coming to grips with the problem as a collectivity. There are two obvious reasons why this should be so. The first is the ambiguous nature of struggles of 'self-determination'. As Green comments:

There seems little chance of terrorism being controlled on anything like a universal basis so long as international organisations or individual states are prepared to apply a double standard whereby they confer legality and respectability upon acts of violence that are committed by those with whom they sympathise, especially when they can be presented in the language of the new international order that places self-determination and independence above any other principle or obligation.[33]

And there seems little chance of the world's nations agreeing on what does and does not constitute a legitimate struggle for self-determination. The major source of confusion seems to stem from the equation of self-determination and terrorism. There is no necessary equation here and, as Paust has argued, before any international convention has a chance of success it will be necessary to make clear that provisions such as those contained in the US draft Convention on the Prevention and Punishment of Certain Acts of International Terrorism 'do not proscribe activities compatible with the UN Charter, such as permissible revolution, self-determination, anti-colonial struggles, and quests for independence or other macro-political purposes'.[34] Nevertheless, there is a long road to travel before this principle will be accepted. At the moment it is difficult even to see the end of the road, let alone make the journey.

The second major obstacle to be overcome is the reluctance of nations (including those who would otherwise wish to support an anti-terrorism convention) to give up their right to grant asylum to those who commit politically motivated offences. Although some legal scholars see this as a separate issue, it is inextricably bound to the definitional problems discussed earlier. If nations can agree on what acts fall into the category of terrorism there are few circumstances under which one can imagine a State wishing to grant asylum to someone it agrees should be labelled 'terrorist'. Dugard notes that: 'When a person commits an act which threatens the stability of other states or undermines the international order, he ceases to be a political offender and becomes a criminal under international law, like the pirate or hijacker.'[35]

This philosophy is exemplified in a nineteenth-century English decision, *In re Muernier,*[36] which held that an anarchist could be extradited because he was an opponent of all governments, not of just one government. Again it becomes obvious that the central issue in the control of terrorism is the definition of the phenomenon itself. If nations could agree on at least a limited definition of terrorism which included only specific acts in specific circumstances the groundwork would be laid for a successful international convention. It would still be necessary to ponder such issues as enforcability, but until the definition is settled such issues are almost irrelevant. Franck and Lockwood suggest at least two possibilities which could lead to agreement in limited areas.[37] The first is to work towards a convention which prevents the export of violence to countries not party to the conflict. This seems to be a reasonable goal which might profitably be pursued. But it must be expected that some countries will claim that states which are not a direct party to the conflict are involved in an indirect or underhand manner. Such claims will always be a danger to the success of any such convention. Sometimes these claims will be true, such as when a foreign intelligence agency is secretly involved in the internal affairs of the primary target nation. Sometimes they will be true merely because of ideological perspective, for example, an industrial nation may be seen as involved because of the activities of its transnational corporations.

The second suggestion is to press for a convention for the control of particularly offensive, but narrowly defined acts. A primary example would be the use of the international mails to despatch letter bombs and other explosive devices. The taking of innocent, civilian hostages could be another example. (Although here there could be severe problems in that some nations who support terrorist organisations would undoubtedly argue that nobody who had anything to do with the target country can be regarded as an innocent. In fact, some would go further and claim that there are no innocents.) Thus, again, while this suggestion has merit and should be pursued, it is unlikely because of its limited nature to be a significant deterrent to international terrorism. At best, if agreement could be reached between all nations, it could limit some specific forms of terrorism.

The conclusion that must be reached from a survey of international attempts to counter the terrorist threat is inevitably a depressing one. Given the realities of ideology, political and economic self-interest, and individual personality there appears no hope of the international community agreeing upon a definition of terrorism which will be at all meaningful. The best that can be hoped for is a series of definitions of limited acts which may reduce the scope of terrorist activity. But it is unlikely that such definitions will encompass the more frightening or threatening forms of terrorism. At a regional level, there seems more hope of obtaining a measure of agreement among nations with a common interest or facing a common threat. The recent European Convention on the Suppression of Terrorism is such an example. But even here it is likely that signatories to such agreements will not have the political will or ability to act as they have agreed to do. Since no sanctions may be applied for such breaches any such convention will be merely a paper tiger. The most hope of success seems to lie in bilateral agreements between nations who feel compelled to act to safeguard their own interests. Although these too are fraught with the perils of exception clauses and unenforcability they are likely to withstand more pressures than other agreements. The future is likely to see a proliferation of these arrangements as nations feel more threatened about specific dangers.

Whatever agreements transpire in the foreseeable future, however, it is clear that international law is not going to play a significant role in the suppression of terrorism. The failure of international law could itself have serious consequences. It is likely that the more obvious becomes the impotence of nations to cope in a concerted manner with terrorism the greater will be the probability of non-governmental bodies taking unilateral action. The most obvious example would be the International Federation of Airline Pilots successfully carrying out its threat to suspend airline operations to and from nations supporting or harbouring terrorists. Other powerful organisations such as trade unions could also exert considerable pressure. Although such actions may be desirable in the short-term (to the extent that they were, in fact, successful in achieving their aims) the consequences for international order are unpredictable. It is potentially dangerous, given our current ordering of affairs, for 'non-state actors' to be able to exercise significant, direct power over international affairs. (Of course, significant 'non-state actors' such as transnational corporations already exercise more power in international affairs than do many nations. This, in itself, is highly undesirable and, where possible, limits should be put on such power. But it would be even more undesirable to increase the number of organisations wielding significant power – usually for very short-term purposes – merely because the inability or unwillingness of governments to act galvanises them into utilising their, so far, unrealised manipulative potential.) After all, this is one of the primary objections to the use of international terrorism. Surely our aim should be to make our governments responsive to the needs of their people so that they may be accepted as the conduit of the people's will. If this perhaps unattainable goal is not reached the people will turn to various representative groups, whether they be terrorists, corporations, trade unions, or powerful professional associations in order to make their demands known and in order to achieve the ends they desire. If nations cannot agree upon ways to control terrorism (and many other matters of international concern), as seems to be the case, we can expect to see an even more confused and dangerous international environment with a myriad of pressure groups vying with governments and with each other to achieve their own limited and short-term goals. It is not an encouraging view of the future but current international efforts to control terrorism would suggest little else.

The use of domestic anti-terrorist legislation – the West German case

Although questions of definition are also a problem in the case of domestic anti-terrorist legislation they do not pose the same blocks to action as they do in the international forum. They may be the cause for vigorous debate in the legislature or may provoke dissent and discussion within various community interest groups (such as civil liberties organisations), but in the final analysis the government has the power to decide upon a definition, unilaterally if necessary, and take legislative and administrative action. As long as a government has sufficient consensual support or rules by sufficient coercion it may introduce anti-terrorism legislation which can effectively be used. In this section two recent instances of domestic anti-terrorist laws will be discussed in order to show how different nations have sought to provide their security agencies with powers to prevent or suppress terrorist activities. Although many countries either have specific sections of general laws covering terrorism or have enacted specific anti-terrorist legislation[38], the cases of the Federal Republic of Germany and the United Kingdom reveal something of the range of measures adopted by liberal democracies and will be discussed here.

In the Federal Republic of Germany (West Germany) the activities of extremist, terrorist groups such as the Baader-Meinhof group prompted the federal government to enact a number of specific anti-terrorist measures which together probably amount to the most repressive anti-terrorist legislation in existence in a liberal democracy. The process began in 1968 with some changes to the Basic Law (which confers legislative power upon the Federal Parliament, decrees judicial organisation, etc.). The changes related to court organisation, the assignment of judicial competences, the exercise of powers by the Executive in the absence of parliamentary approval, the power to commit the Federal Border Guard throughout the federal territory, the power of the Federation to issue instructions to *Land* (State) governments, legislative authority to place restrictions on freedom of movement, and other measures. These changes set the background for some more specific provisions.

The provision that has provoked the most outspoken international discussion is the so-called *Berufsverbot* (job-ban) or *Radikalen-Erlasse* (terminations of radicals) policy. Basically, this is a process for judging the suitability of individuals to be hired for or to maintain a tenured (*Beamte*) status in the German civil service. 'Berufsverbot refers to the non-hiring, termination, refusal to admitted to tenured (Beamte) status, and other disciplinary actions against civil servants at all levels whose loyalty is in doubt. Such doubt is usually based on alleged behaviour which is legal, yet questionable.'[39] The criticism of these regulations internationally merely on the basis of their existence ignores the fact that similar provisions exist in many (if not most countries). For example, the United States Code contains the following provision which is very similar to the German one:

An individual may not accept or hold a position in the Government of the United States or in the government of the District of Columbia if he –
(1) advocates the overthrow of our constitutional form of government;
(2) is a member of an organisation that he knows advocates the overthrow of our constitutional form of government.[40]

The difference in the German case no doubt lies in the enthusiasm with which the Government applied the restrictions and the criteria they used to make decisions resulting in refusal to hire or termination of civil service appointments. Oppenheimer, reporting the results of a survey of victims of the regulations conducted by the *Aktionskomitee gegen Berufsverbote*, has shown that the most tenuous connections with terrorist or extremist groups have been used to justify refusal to hire or dismissal.[41] For example, a woman faced disciplinary action because her *husband* was a lawyer for an accused terrorist; a number of persons suffered because they signed petitions; a doctor was barred from his hospital for protesting the dismissal of another doctor, and so forth. It is suggested that the regulations encourage malicious or mistaken complaints (for example, a social worker was accused by a colleague of distributing communist leaflets; it was found upon investigation that it was a case of mistaken identity and in any case the leaflet did not exist) and are used to suppress opinions which the government finds undesirable (particularly criticism of the government itself). The basic assumptions of the restrictions seem to be twofold. First that subversive elements can be easily identified and rooted out of positions within the civil service. And second, that if people are prevented from committing minor acts of protest, like writing critical letters to the newspapers, belonging to organisations critical of government policy, and signing petitions they will probably not make the jump to more serious acts of political dissent, such as violent protest or acts of terrorism. Both assumptions are highly suspect. The second, in particular is not only suspect but, if wrong, highly dangerous. As Oppenheimer asserts:

The delegitimation of conventional forms of criticism and dissent can thereby foster the paradoxical condition of a society in which the large majority of the population not only lives relatively well, but supports the repression of the minority of dissatisfied, thus virtually forcing that minority to undertake a politics of either total apathy, or total opposition in the form of terrorism.[42]

Ironically, it could be the case that provisions such as these contribute to a social climate in which terrorism flourishes. The question of what constituents make up the German social climate which has been the background to a unique brand of domestic terrorism (at times overflowing into international terrorism) is a complex one to which no satisfactory answers exist. Although a number of commentators[43] have attempted such an explanation, or parts of one, it is outside the scope of the present work to examine their arguments. Whatever the causes, however, the West Germans have responded to the wave of terrorism with a panoply of measures far greater than that in evidence in other liberal democracies. Apart from the Berufsverbot regulations West Germany has also introduced a number of specific anti-terrorist provisions.

Between 1974 and 1978 a number of significant amendments were made to the Criminal Code which aimed to give the security authorities greater powers to combat terrorism.[44] The most important provisions are contained in Sections 129 and 129a of the Criminal Code. Section 129(1) provides for up to five years incarceration for anyone who forms an association whose aims or activities are directed towards the commission of an offence, or who participates in, recruits for, or aids such a criminal association. These provisions are qualified in Section 129(a), entitled 'Forming A Terrorist Association'. Section 129(1)(1) provides penalties of imprisonment from six months to five years for anyone forming an association whose aims or activities are directed towards the commission of specific crimes, or who is a member of, recruits for, or aids such an association. The crimes listed are: (1) murder, homicide, genocide; (2) offences against personal freedom listed in Sections 239a or 239b of the Criminal Code; or offences constituting a public danger under other various sections of the Criminal Code. In addition to imprisonment, the Court may forbid a person found guilty under this Section from holding any public office or acquiring any rights from a public election for a period ranging from two to five years. Ringleaders of such associations may be imprisoned for up to ten years.

Another provision of the recent amendments is Section 88a of the Criminal Code which punishes support of offences against the Constitution. Imprisonment for up to three years awaits 'anyone who disseminates, publicly issues, placards, produces or otherwise renders accessible a text that supports an unlawful act named in section 126, or who obtains, provides, keeps, offers, announces, praises, or attempts to import or export it within the spatial jurisdiction of the German Criminal Code'.[45] To qualify as a text coming within the purview of this provision, the text must be judged capable of encouraging the willingness of other persons to commit offences against the existence or safety of the Federal Republic of Germany. Similar provisions exist for publically or in an assembly advocating unlawful acts named in Section 126. Other punishable offences are the 'glorification of violence' (Section 131) and public 'approval of criminal acts' (Section 140).

In addition to changes to the Criminal Code, the West German Government has also introduced some controversial changes to those parts of the Criminal Procedure Code that apply to the detention and trial of suspected terrorists. Sections 231a, 231b, and 255 of the Criminal Procedure Code allow the court to hold hearings in the absence of the accused if he 'intentionally and wilfully causes his own unfitness to stand trial'.[46] This provision was introduced to cope with organised hunger strikes staged by terrorist prisoners which sought to delay or stop the legal proceedings. The extreme behaviour of some terrorists in court was also a contributing factor.

The provisions which drew most critical comment when they were introduced, however, were those relating to the exclusion and surveillance of defence lawyers. Under the amendments, a defence counsel may be excluded from the trial of a suspected terrorist if he is suspected of: (1) having participated in any offence; (2) misusing his right of contact with the incarcerated client in order to commit an offence or to endanger the security of a penitentiary; (3) aiding and abetting an offence; or (4) endangering the security of the State.[47]

The exclusion order is made by the Higher Regional Court or by the Federal Court of Justice, and so the court before which the case is pending cannot itself rule on an order. Both the accused terrorist and the excluded lawyer may appeal against the order.

Because the German authorities had evidence of the traditional free correspondence between a lawyer and his client being used to convey illegal material to and from incarcerated terrorist suspects they introduced the

Contact Ban Law (Kontaktsperregesetz) in September 1977. This provides that where there is immediate danger to life, limb, or liberty of an individual where terrorist involvement is suspected, a *Land* government or the Federal Minister of Justice can forbid any contact, written or oral, between imprisoned terrorists and their lawyers if it is considered that this action would avert the danger.[48] The ban is valid for 30 days, but must be upheld by a state court after 15 days or it automatically expires. A new contact ban can be put into effect after the expiration of 30 days.

In situations where it is not considered necessary to exclude contact between lawyer and client, Section 148 of the Criminal Procedure Code provides for control of written communications between the two. Oral communication between accused terrorists and their lawyers remains confidential. Finally, Sections 137 and 146 of the Criminal Procedure Code decree that the number of defence lawyers cannot exceed three per accused person.

A final set of provisions enacted in West Germany relates to police powers to deal with terrorist threats. Under Section 103 I of the Code of Criminal Procedure, the police may search an entire building if they have reason to believe that a person is inside who they suspect has committed an offence under Section 129 of the Criminal Code (described earlier).

An amendment to Section III of the Criminal Procedure Code allows police, under certain conditions, to establish roadblocks in order to carry out identity checks. The conditions are (1) that the police must possess sufficient evidence that offences under Sections 129a and 250 of the Criminal Code have been committed; and (2) the roadblocks must be necessary either to apprehend the alleged offender or to obtain evidence relating to the offence. Finally, Sections 163b and 163c of the Criminal Procedure Code prescribe the conditions under which identity checks can be made.

This survey indicates the very extensive laws which have been brought into effect in the Federal Republic of Germany which are aimed specifically at terrorist organisations. An analysis of the laws of a number of other European nations reveals that similar provisions exist in many of them.[49] The major difference appears to be that they are not exclusively aimed at terrorist groups and that, in some cases, the legal or procedural impediments to their use are greater than they are in Germany. The German amendments are essentially ad hoc responses to emerging situations rather than a coordinated and long-term plan for dealing with instances of violent social unrest. As such they are over-reactions. Opinions are sharply divided on whether or not this is the case. For example, Bakker-Schut[50] sees the new laws as the phantom of a new fascism, the International Commission of Jurists has criticised the Federal Republic for endangering the rule of law,[51] and Amnesty International's German Section wrote to the Federal President in October 1975 informing him that the laws were making it increasingly difficult to persuade Germans to sign even the most unobjectionable petitions, such as one aimed generally at 'the abolition of torture in the world'.[52] On the other hand, Moons believes that 'the laws in question are designed to preserve the established democratic government and that they do not seriously restrict the constitutional rights and liberties of the individual'.[53]

Whether or not the particular circumstances in Germany in the 1970s justified the introduction of these measures there is a clear danger of their use being extended to cover acts of political opposition short of terrorism. The security authorities will always see the necessity for such powers (and sometimes they will indeed be necessary) but the duty of the government is to balance the extent of the response with the seriousness of the problem and the rights of its citizens. To the extent that governments introduce legislation similar to the German examples above, it is vital that there exist legal checks to balance the powers given and preferable that the provisions should be repealed when the emergency has passed. The real danger in such legislation is not so much that a government of good intention will allow its security forces to abuse their powers but that they will convince themselves that legal solutions to the terrorist problem are possible. At best, they are only stop-gap measures. The pity is that in many instances governments seem almost to have stopped thinking about the 'why' of terrorism once they have introduced police and judicial measures to try to contain it. They fail to see that containment is not equivalent to understanding and solution.

The British legislative response to terrorism

While the West German provisions are extensive many people will be of the opinion that such a response is not unexpected in the German social and cultural context. It is interesting, therefore, to compare the German case with that of the anti-terrorist legislation of the United Kingdom, which is seen as being traditionally more tolerant of political dissent and subject to less threat from domestic and international terrorists. Apart from provisions in many laws which may be applied to terrorist acts, the United Kingdom has enacted a major piece of anti-terrorist legislation, the Prevention of Terrorism (Temporary Provisions) Acts of 1974 and 1976.

Following two bomb explosions in Birmingham pubs on 21 November 1974 in which 20 people died, and 180 were injured the Home Secretary, Mr Roy Jenkins MP, introduced the Prevention of Terrorism (Temporary Provisions) Bill. This followed a week of public outcry at the bombings characterised by calls for a ban on the Irish Republican Army (IRA – the perpetrators of the act) and for increased police activity against the IRA, demands for the death penalty for convicted terrorists, and even attacks against Irish residents and property in England. The Bill was subject to only 12 hours' debate in a single night in the House of Commons (and by the House of Lords the following morning), was approved without a division, and became law on 29 November 1974. The Act, which contains a number of provisions which differ considerably from most British law, was severely criticised on a number of counts. Foremost amongst these were that the legislation was hastily drawn up in response to crisis, had no precedent in British law, and was passed in an emotional atmosphere which allowed it to evade the scrutiny which it deserved. Of these criticisms, only the last may be valid. While the Bill was introduced immediately following a terrorist outrage it had, in fact, been in preparation for some time. The basis for the Bill was to be found in contingency plans drawn up by the Home Office following a bombing at the Old Bailey in March 1973 and which had been refined over the intervening period. In addition, it could not be said to be unprecedented because its provisions were similar in most respects to the Prevention of Violence (Temporary Provisions) Act 1939 which had been introduced in response to an earlier IRA bombing campaign. The fact that so little critical scrutiny was afforded the Bill, however, worried (and still worries) many people, including some who support the idea of the legislation. The most outspoken criticisms, however, have been reserved for the actual provisions themselves.

The major features of the Act were that it:

1. Proscribed the IRA and made display of support for it illegal. Gave the Secretary of State the power to exclude from Great Britain, Northern Ireland, or the United Kingdom persons suspected of connection with terrorism.
2. Gave the police powers to arrest suspected terrorists and detain them for 48 hours in the first instance, with the possibility of an extension for a further five days authorised by the Secretary of State. At a port or airport, the police were empowered to detain suspected terrorists for up to seven days in the first instance, with the possibility of a further extension authorised by the Secretary of State.
3. Gave the police powers to carry out security checks on travellers entering or leaving Great Britain.

The Act was the subject of a good deal of criticism, particularly from civil liberties groups. The National Council for Civil Liberties (NCCL) objected to the provisions for the following reasons (among others):[54]

1. That emergency provisions such as these abandon the usual due process protections by giving the Home Secretary powers which cannot be

challenged in the courts. This increases the probability that an innocent person will be deprived of liberty on the basis of evidence which would not satisfy a court of law.

2. That the Act reverses the tenet that a person is innocent until proven guilty. Under this Act the accused must establish his innocence.
3. That the experience of such emergency powers in Northern Ireland has shown them to be counter-productive.
4. That the danger of abolishing traditional safeguards as an emergency measure is that the new procedures will come to be accepted as the norm.

On 25 March 1976 the 1974 Act was replaced by Prevention of Terrorism (Temporary Provisions) Act 1976 which was only slightly different from its predecessor. An additional offence was created of contributing or soliciting contributions towards acts of terrorism as was withholding information relating to acts of terrorism or persons committing them. The Prevention of Terrorism (Supplemental Temporary Provisions) (Amendment) Order 1979 decreed that from 18 April 1979, the time police may detain a person at a port or an airport on their own authority was reduced to 48 hours in line with other locations (with the Secretary of State able to authorise an extension of detention of up to five more days). The Prevention of Terrorism (Temporary Provisions) Act 1976 (Amendment) Order 1979 added the Irish National Liberation Army to the list of proscribed organisations.

Because of public criticism of the Acts the Government appointed Lord Shackleton to review their operation. His report, published in August 1978, recommended that the Act should continue in much its present form.[55] The most controversial aspect of the report was the bland acceptance of the use of the powers of detention.[56] The question of reversing the onus of proof involved in holding suspected terrorists is a vexing one. On the one hand, the security officials feel they cannot tell the detainee the precise nature of the information against him because that could prejudice security or an informant's life. On the other hand, the detainee, not knowing what the evidence is against him, is in an extremely difficult situation when trying to prove his innocence. There is no easy solution to this problem. It is certainly the case that to reveal sources and specific information could be dangerous if the detainee is in fact involved in a terrorist organisation. However, if he is not, it is all too easy for prejudice on the part of the investigators to result in severe distress to the innocent party (to the extent of having him excluded from Great Britain where his family, friends, and employment may be). This is particularly a danger where there is no way of verifying the evidence against the detainee. The Act tries to cope with this in the case of Exclusion Orders by appointing an Advisor to the Secretary of State who reviews the case following the making of an order and makes recommendations to the Secretary. But the excludee has no right to counsel, no right to have access to the prosecution's evidence, and is not informed of the charges, information, or evidence against him. As Lowry sums up the situation:

The exclusion order must merely show that the excludee has a right to make representations, but not the grounds on which the order was made, thus leaving the excludee in total ignorance of his 'wrongdoing' and making it difficult, if not impossible, to set out his objections to the order. No standard of evidence is required by the Act. In addition, the Home Secretary may disregard the advice of his advisor if he chooses.[57]

In view of the traditions of British law which this violates and the fact that effective police action has curtailed the violence it does not seem justified to continue to operate these powers in this way. The concept of an independent tribunal established to hear allegations of misuse of the Act should be seriously considered. Some of the cases collected by NCCL at least suggest that the Act has been used to exclude people on flimsy evidence with no clear danger apparent. Some avenue should exist for seeking redress if wrong has been done in these cases.

Another serious criticism of the operation of the Act is that because it is not subject to critical scrutiny it is being used for purposes outside of its intended ambit, notably to collect low-grade intelligence and to intimidate those whose political views, although not illegal, are not approved of by the authorities. An example given by Lowry illustrates the latter point:

although the selling of Republican newspapers is not an offence, the vendors could be arrested and held under Part I. Clearly, from the police standpoint, disseminating information of a Republican nature, albeit not in support of terrorism, is itself grounds for reasonable suspicion of support, assisting, or contributing to a proscribed organisation.[58]

The suggestion that the police use the Act to justify 'fishing expeditions' for intelligence gathering is supported by published statistics on the operation of the Act. For example, in the first quarter of 1979, 207 of the 279 persons detained under the Act (i.e. 74 per cent) were not subsequently charged or excluded. Further, although the Act is meant to be a temporary one (as indicated by its title) it is routinely continued each year. Thus, the Prevention of Terrorism (Temporary Provisions) Act 1976 (Continuance) Order 1980 continues the Act in force for a period of 12 months from 25 March 1980. Since no evidence has been produced that the Act is, in fact, effective in preventing terrorism it seems justified to call for such evidence or for a discontinuation of the Act or a revision allowing inspection by the Courts or some tribunal. As Lowry concludes:

England may conceivably be correct in the use of draconian pretrial measures against suspected terrorists and others but until the pretrial detention process in

England under the [Prevention of Terrorism] Act is opened to judicial and other impartial scrutiny, these powers remain an unjustified departure from common law principles.[59]

Many analysts of terrorism, including the present writer, would argue that there are circumstances in which legislation giving the security forces more extensive powers to stop, question and, if required, detain people is necessary. If such circumstances exist, legislation modelled after the British Act seems reasonable and likely to be effective. However, is it a fact that current circumstances are so desperate that they warrant the overturning of normal judicial review of the police? It is submitted that the answer is no. At the very least if it can be demonstrated convincingly that the Act is necessary some effort should be made to compromise strict security considerations in order to provide a form of review or oversight of the administration of the law. The necessity or desirability of such a review may change as times change. But at present it is appropriate to temper security with an explicit adherence to the normal standards of British justice.

12

Counter-measures against terrorism: the intelligence function

The clandestine nature, organisational principles, and tactics of terrorist groups pose particularly difficult problems for security authorities. In order to take preventive measures, pre-empt planned attacks, deal successfully with terrorist incidents in progress and, when possible, prosecute terrorists they need information. The information they need is not readily available. The only way to obtain it is by intelligence-gathering techniques. This chapter will seek to outline the features of terrorism that make intelligence-gathering vital to counter-terrorist operations and to briefly indicate the types of intelligence techniques which are used in the struggle against terrorism.

The importance of surprise

A well-organised and coherent terrorist group strives for secrecy in order to maximise the advantages afforded by surprise. It should be noted that in order to be effective, surprise need not be total, although effectiveness may be directly related to degree of surprise. The US Army definition of surprise recognises this. Surprise is defined as: 'Striking an enemy at a time and place and in a manner for which he is unprepared. It is not essential that the enemy be taken unaware, but only that he becomes aware too late to react effectively.'[1]

Terrorist tactics focus on utilising surprise to achieve the following aims:

(1) To create a situation for which police and security authorities are unprepared. If authorities have not anticipated general situations they will not have developed coherent response policies, obtained necessary counter-technologies, practised appropriate responses, selected and trained appropriate personnel, and so forth. All of these factors could contribute to official indecision, vacillation in policy, poorly coordinated and inappropriate responses and similar deficiencies which make the resolution of any particular incident problematic.

(2) To force security authorities into hurried or ill-considered actions. This aim is intimately related to lack of preparation for dealing with terrorist

incidents. If the authorities have no coherent and established policies and response hierarchies, it is probable that forces committed to the action will either be ill-trained and ill-equipped for the task or lack sufficient direction. Particularly important is the evolution and clear articulation of basic governmental policies to be effected in terrorist situations. In their absence there is a great danger of vacillation which could engender confusion and lack of confidence within the security forces, a situation which can easily be exploited by terrorists and which severely affects efficiency of counter-terrorist operations. Further, a prime aim of many terrorists is to force the government to adopt harsh and repressive measures, in short to over-react. Such a situation is very likely to eventuate in the absence of clearly thought through policies and graded response hierarchies.

(3) To dislocate or disperse security forces. By maintaining secrecy, terrorists seek to ensure that security forces are spread widely over all possible targets so as not to allow a concentration of forces at a particular target to be attacked. An alternative strategy is to spread disinformation so that security forces are concentrated at a location which is not the intended target.

(4) To allow deployment of terrorist elements in unexpected strength. Particularly at critical points in a terrorist campaign it is advantageous to be able to increase the size of a terrorist force unexpectedly, thus catching the security forces off balance either by overwhelming them at one location or being able to deploy in a number of locations simultaneously. Since an increase in manpower requires time, particularly if training and indoctrination are necessary, it is obviously necessary to maintain secrecy over the period of the build-up in order to be able to exploit its maximum potential.

(5) To allow assault from an unexpected direction. In particular, to the extent that secrecy is preserved, a terrorist group is able to exploit the advantage to be gained by a change in tactics or type of target. Surveying terrorist events over time, it is difficult to resist the impression that terrorists follow fashions or fads in their choice of tactics. Thus, at one point in time assassinations will figure predominantly, at another time hostage-taking will predominate, at another hijacking of aircraft, and so forth. Of course there are practical reasons for such fluctuations. Foremost amongst them is that as a technique is shown to work, more extremist groups will utilise it. But as they do so, police forces will develop procedures, personnel, and technologies to counter that particular threat. As the cost effectiveness of the technique rises, the pressure is on the terrorists to explore the use of less risky techniques or attack against less protected alternatives. Thus while hijacking of aircraft was a popular technique in the late 1960s the frequency of such acts declined significantly with the introduction in the early 1970s of security checks on baggage, passenger screening, and other techniques.

This led to an emphasis on alternative methods of exerting pressure such as bombings, siege situations, and kidnappings. These tactics have also shown changes in frequency as security has been increased at critical locations, hostage-negotiation techniques have been developed, and aggressive counter-measures have emerged. However, it is likely that each technique will regain its popularity as time passes. The trend is already evident in the case of aircraft hijacking. In the late 1970s very few politically motivated hijackings were successful. Gone were the spectaculars such as that mounted in the Jordanian desert in 1970. (In that event, two aircraft were hijacked over Europe on 6 September 1970 and taken to a disused desert airfield called Dawson's Field. A third aircraft was forced to Cairo, where it was destroyed, and a fourth, an El Al Boeing 707, escaped when security agents on board thwarted the takeover attempt. On 9 September a BOAC VC-10 was hijacked and taken to Dawson's Field to join the first two captive planes. The aircraft were all blown up by the terrorists following the eventual release of the passengers in exchange for the release of Palestinian terrorists imprisoned in Switzerland, the United Kingdom, and West Germany.) However, security measures tend to become slack if there is no continuing and obvious threat and if they are not tested frequently. So it is inevitable that a degree of slackness and lack of vigilance has slipped into aircraft and airport security operations. In 1980 there has again been a spate of politically motivated aircraft hijackings with a number of successful hijackings of aircraft from the United States to Cuba occurring within a time span of a few weeks. It is reasonably certain that these defences will again be tested in the future by political terrorists.

(6) To facilitate exploitation of unexpected timings. Again the combination of secrecy and spread of inaccurate information can lead the security forces either to attempt to maintain a constantly high level of vigilance (which is impossible to achieve for significant periods of time and can cause over-reaction or inefficiency) or to be put on alert when no attack is in fact imminent. To the extent that the latter tactic is successful the terrorists attempt to blunt the reactions of the security forces in the hope that when a genuine alert occurs they are less likely to respond quickly and efficiently.

(7) To capitalise on the use of unexpected tactics. This point relates to the earlier aim of assault from an unexpected direction. However, in this case the aim is to cause maximum disruption by a leap in tactics rather than by a mere change of direction. In intelligence analysis much emphasis is placed on tracking escalations in the activities of particular groups in an effort both to predict the future actions of those groups and to be able to accurately ascribe to a group an act which has already occurred. As a rule such prediction and ascription is possible because escalation of activities follows a reasonably discernible pattern. However, if a terrorist group is able to

decide upon changes of tactics outside of the normal limits (an extreme example would be to move from random bombing to nuclear blackmail) and is further able to equip and organise itself to employ those tactics without alerting the authorities to the changes, the problems for security officials could be extremely severe.

Terrorist organisational features

In order to achieve these aims, terrorist groups enforce strict security and frequently organise themselves in such a manner as to limit information flow even within their own organisation. The more successful terrorist organisations are either numerically small and/or are structured into small cells, typically with only three to ten individuals to each cell. Cells may then be grouped into columns which are assigned a specific support, political, or military function. This columnar form of organisation has been exploited successfully by the Tupamaros in Uruguay,[2] the FLN in Algeria,[3] and Castro's guerrillas in Cuba.[4] Within such a structure particular emphasis is placed on security of communication. Secrecy, mobility, and flexibility are maximised, but overall direction is still possible (and sometimes tightly exercised) by the terrorist hierarchy, although each cell typically has a reasonable degree of operational independence. Some organisations permit smaller groups to exercise individual initiative in selection of particular targets or timing of operations, although usually within the framework of an overall scheme or set of objectives. Further, such latitude is only possible in a relatively large-scale terrorist campaign. If such independent decision-making is allowed it complicates considerably the intelligence problems facing the security authorities by necessitating penetration of more units than would be required if precise directions for targeting and timing were issued by the central leadership.

Other relevant organisational features of terrorist groups include para-military structures and the rigid enforcement of discipline (to the extent of having enforcement or internal security units which will execute members for offences against the organisation's code). Security is enhanced by ensuring that few (often only one) members of each cell are fully aware of the extent of links to other cells or the identity of other members. This compartmentalisation of cells may be achieved by using a system of *dead drops* to communicate between cells (that is, a location such as an airport locker, telephone booth, or post office box where a communication can be exchanged without either the sender or receiver meeting). Security may be enhanced further by deploying *cut-outs* to deliver and collect the messages (a cut-out is a member of the organisation whose sole function may be to pass messages, usually not knowing either the source of the message, its content, or its recipient). The advantages of such an organisational structure have been summarised by Wolf in the following way:

> The cellular-columnar type of clandestine organisation is particularly suited for use by a broadly based terrorist movement that, because of its size, has to be particularly cautious of infiltration by the police and the possibility that its captured colleagues might provide law enforcement agencies with information that would lead to the arrest of other members of their organisation. In addition, the cut-out system insures that terrorists do not know each other's true identity, that communication from different cells is minimised to include only task assignments and operational orders, and that movement is relatively secure.[5]

In addition to these organising principles, many terrorist groups are not unaware of the more complex techniques employed by intelligence and security agencies and some are adept at developing covers, forging papers, and devising anti-infiltration procedures. Further, it has been known for terrorist groups to adopt the 'sleeper' technique in which individuals or units are strategically placed and then activated some time in the future when circumstances make them of operational value.[6]

However, these techniques all form part of the compartmentalised structure which while enhancing security under most circumstances is not without its difficulties:

> Once an armed cell involved in an operation with other cells is temporarily disrupted by a sudden weather change, a police action, or a missed rendezvous, it is most difficult to re-establish control, since terrorists from different cells do not know each other. Also terrorists must have egos that permit them to render great obedience to an unknown leader and plan for operations that they are not permitted to undertake without permission from a higher authority. Consequently, a terrorist organisation cannot move without the absolute and unswerving cooperation of all its members. Thus, compartmentalisation, which facilitates the survival of a terrorist organisation on the one hand, is its major operational liability on the other.[7]

The features of terrorist organisations described in the foregoing pages reveal the necessity for high-quality intelligence as a basis for prevention, containment, and counter-measures in a terrorist environment. It is only by analysing comprehensive and accurate data that the security authorities will have any hope of identifying and locating terrorist groups before they are able to mount operations or effectively coping with terrorist incidents in progress. In particular, data need to be collected on existing and emerging extremist groups and individuals, the aims, political alignments and motivations of terrorist organisations, their logistic and financial structures and resources, and their organisational features.

As has been noted, surprise is the cornerstone of successful terrorist operations. Since the security forces are almost always stronger than those of insurgents, the latter seek to minimise their disadvantage by choosing the time, location, strength, and method of attack. Since in a complex industrial society the number of potential targets is far greater than can economically (or even physically) be protected against terrorist attack, if secrecy can be maintained the considerable initial advantage to the security forces is significantly eroded. As Kerstetter notes:

Interception of the terrorist prior to his attack thus becomes a key element in a rational response to the threat of terrorism. Interception requires timely and accurate information about the activities of those directly involved in terrorist activities and, equally important, about their network of supporters who provide shelter, equipment, and other assistance.[8]

The place of intelligence

The criticism of intelligence agencies notwithstanding,[9] intelligence *is* the first line of defence against political terrorism. Although, as recent debates about domestic intelligence gathering in the United States of America,[10] Australia,[11] and Canada[12] have shown, there is considerable public concern about the recording of sensitive information by security agencies, it is clearly the duty of a properly elected government to collect and analyse as much information as possible about extremist political groups. Since many such groups openly espouse the overthrow of democratically elected governments such targets therefore have a legitimate right to defend themselves. The precautionary measure of intelligence gathering is therefore justified, as long as it is carried out within the limits of the law.

The public disquiet, however, arises not from such obvious cases, but from evidence that extensive files are maintained on organisations which do not espouse the terrorist cause or method and do not seem to be obviously linked to terrorist activities. However, as Kupperman observes, 'it is virtually impossible to tell when a formerly obscure or inactive group will suddenly spring into prominence. (The incident of March 1977 in which Hanafi Muslims terrorised Washington with three separate sieges illustrates this point.)'[13] There is thus an argument for keeping information on groups not believed to be directly implicated in terrorist activities. The dangers in keeping such data though are primarily of two types. The first danger is that this justification is used as a mandate for placing almost any person or group under surveillance, sometimes using intrusive methods and technologies. The second and more important danger, is that information collected under this justification may be used for purposes other than tracking terrorist activities and assisting in the detection and prosecution of terrorists.

Unfortunately debate over these extremely complex and problematic matters has tended to polarise into simplistic extremes. On the one hand, the supporters of intelligence agencies see all criticism of intelligence gathering as a left-wing inspired plot to undermine and destroy the Western security intelligence effort. This view, argued *in extremis*, as it frequently is, ignores the reality that intelligence agencies have been guilty of documented abuses of their powers (or, more frequently, have stepped outside the limits of their powers and have acted illegally). Further, any organisation, however well intentioned, can suffer from a siege mentality which alters its perceptions of events. It is quite reasonable, and indeed necessary, for informed and reasonable criticism to be levelled at both deficiencies. It must be conceded too that internal subversives and foreign, unfriendly governments do use such arguments to render our security intelligence less effective. But this is good reason to accept and act upon reasoned criticism in order to maintain public confidence. It is no excuse for the wholesale rejection of critical analyses and the cover-up of abuses and excesses.

On the other hand, there are very many critics of intelligence services who see only the most malevolent of motives in their activities. They point to the potential for repression which exists when files are held on many people. They demonstrate how information collected for one purpose has been improperly used for another purpose. They argue that the conservative nature of security intelligence agencies makes them inherently undemocratic. And they argue that many such agencies grow without justification, expand their activities and their influence until they become a law unto themselves, an independent state within a state. The only remedy, they say, is to abolish such agencies.

Again, it must be conceded that a good case exists for each of these arguments. However, abolition is not the only answer. An alternative is better control. Now this is very easy to propose, and much more complex to put into effect, especially given the entrenched opposition. Nevertheless, there are threats to modern democratic societies, both internal and external, and their reality cannot be denied. It is also true that intelligence is at the core of any defence against such threats. Therefore, it behoves all supporters of democratic states to search for ways to control intelligence-gathering without either exposing democracy to abuse from its presumed protectors or weakening the effectiveness of defences against its assailants. Some of the principles that might be applied have been set out in a number of inquiries into security services. Primarily they include a system of checks and balances (including operating standards and principles of accountability) which is designed to promote citizen confidence in intelligence agencies and to control the collection and dissemination of sensitive information.[14]

It is up to both authorities and citizens of democracies to make such a system work. It is true that many find the necessity to collect information on citizens repugnant. But as Mr Justice Hope pointed out: 'Whatever justification there may be for their fears, it is difficult to see what alternative any responsible government would have to seeking the best available intelligence about those who plan or desire to use terrorist violence as a political instrument.'[15]

The nature of counter-terrorist intelligence

What then is the nature of counter-terrorist intelligence? The Australian *Joint Services Staff Manual Glossary*[16] sets out the following steps by which information is assembled, converted into intelligence, and disseminated to users.

These steps are in four phases:
A. Direction
    Determination of intelligence requirements, preparation of a collection plan, insurance of orders and requests to information collection agencies, and a continuous check on the productivity of collection agencies.
B. Collection
    The systematic procurement and selection of information pertinent to a given intelligence problem.
C. Processing
    The step whereby information becomes intelligence through evaluation, analysis, integration and interpretation.
D. Dissemination
    The conveyance of intelligence in suitable form (oral, graphic, or written) to agencies needing it.

Each of these steps raises complex issues which can only briefly be mentioned here. Obviously the foundation of counter-terrorist intelligence is laid by a carefully thought through collection plan which sets out the requirements and collection procedures. The collection process itself raises many civil liberties issues which have been touched on earlier. However, from an intelligence point of view, the vital issues revolve around designing procedures which will in fact yield data of operational value. Once the data have been collected they are evaluated for reliability, sensitivity, timelines, and appropriateness, and data not meeting criteria set out in operating standards should be screened out. Once the raw data have been screened, the retained data may be collated with existing information.

It is the analytic and processing step which follows that is said to be the 'heart' of intelligence. It is at this point that the information collected can be turned into a product of operational value. Probably the most common form of analysis is target analysis. This involves identifying potential targets and the conditions that are likely to lead to an attack upon them. The analysis may also include an evaluation of the manner in which potential targets will respond to attack, in particular how easily intimidated they may be. It may also extend to estimating the effects on others in the event of an attack on a target. The latter types of target analysis are examples of the rapidly growing area of psychological assessments. Thus there now exist a number of persons expert at designing profiles of the 'typical' executive, victim, hijacker, etc., or of specific individuals. Profiles are a potentially useful weapon as a screening device or as an intelligence base during the course of a terrorist incident. But they are only at an early stage of development and many attempts at profiles may be severely criticised on the grounds of superficiality. Further, a number of examples may be found of profiles continuing in use over long time spans. To be useful they should be subject to continuous revision to take account of changing circumstances and individual behaviours. If properly developed, the hope is that psychological assessment will be able to discover the social conditions that a particular individual or group seeks to manipulate. Thus Wolf notes:

Meaningful psychological assessment means the analyst should detect – and recommend ways to influence – trends among the general public and within "special target" populations. For instance, when an analyst can determine that kidnapping is falling into disrepute among the people the terrorists hope most to influence, the analyst is earning his keep. He must then suggest how to take advantage of that feeling – or suggest that as bad as kidnapping is, it would be worse if the terrorists switched from abduction to assassination.[17]

Related to both target analysis and psychological evaluation is another technique, propaganda analysis. Many analysts claim that examination of a terrorist group's propaganda gives many of the most significant facts about those groups. Using methods such as the SCAME formula[18] (an acronym for source, content, audience, media, effect) to analyse propaganda can produce data to feed into target analysis and psychological evaluation. An analytical framework can then be used to integrate data from all three analyses and direct an analyst's attention to data gaps that might be filled. A typical framework is given below:[19]

(a) type and nature of operation
(b) relationship to revolutionary process
(c) organisation
(d) ideology
(e) propaganda classifications
(f) tactics
(g) weapons
(h) targets
(i) audience
(j) media coverage

The increasing use of computers to construct associational matrices among a number of data items promises to allow fuller utilisation of intelligence data to see links between events and people and to make predictions about future acts. A number of specialist counter-terrorist computer applications have been developed[20] and are currently being refined.

Having collected and analysed counter-terrorist intelligence it then remains for it to be disseminated. It is often claimed that security procedures and the bureaucratic process prevent the flow of information to those who could most successfully use it (or if channelled in the right direction, that the information arrives too late). Sharing of intelligence is a sensitive political issue, particularly when it involves sharing with overseas agencies. But if intelligence is to be of operational value much thought must be given as to who is to receive it and how the information is to be passed on in a timely manner. Some intelligence commentators claim that in many democratic societies intelligence sharing and dissemination is not conducted in an efficient manner and is a matter requiring urgent attention.[21]

With these general comments on the role of intelligence in mind it is possible to examine some of the areas in which a specialist counter-terrorist intelligence function is necessary. The primary objective of internal security intelligence is to prevent terrorism developing beyond the incipient stage. Current intelligence methods generally in use are necessary but not sufficient. Especially in dealing with potential high-technology terrorism (for example, involving the use of stolen nuclear or biochemical material), the need exists for intelligence systems designed specifically to deal with terrorist activities. Mengel in his analysis of high-technology terrorism argues that we should rely on general intelligence for purposes such as identification of groups and individuals and their *modus operandi*.[22] However, he sees as essential the existence of a specialised intelligence function related to high-technology threats. The early detection of high-technology terrorism should be a high priority in view of the potential consequences of such incidents. Mengel suggests that a specialised unit should collect, analyse and evaluate the following indicators:

1. Theft of radioactivity monitoring equipment.
2. Theft or loss in shipment of a biological culture.
3. Theft of chemicals clearly associated with the manufacture of dangerous agents.
4. Theft of explosives and/or bomb components.
5. Purchase or theft of unique filters.
6. Purchase or theft of special handling equipment (e.g. protective clothing, isolation chambers, glove boxes).
7. Abduction of persons with high-technology backgrounds.
8. Rental of isolated facilities.
9. Purchase of laboratory equipment suitable for chemical, biological or nuclear experimentation.
10. Suspicious purchases of chemicals.
11. Indiscriminate targeting by terrorists.

12. Increased acquisition of funds by terrorist groups.
13. Increased terrorist liaison and coordination.
14. Increased expenditures by terrorist-connected groups.
15. Unexplained sickness or unusual diseases reported for treatment.

If any of these indicators (or more particularly, groups of indicators) appear, decision-makers will be in a position to set in motion pre-planned activities, decide upon appropriate responses and attempt to match the pattern of activities with general intelligence indicators to establish the group involved and the nature of the threat posed.

At this point it might be useful to very briefly describe some of the intelligence techniques which might be utilised in such cases. In police planning it has been common to examine terrorist target patterns to analyse potential future targets. Although this technique has not been very effective in apprehending terrorists it has been a valuable way of detecting security weaknesses in potential targets. Also it seems likely that the increased security measures that have frequently followed such evaluations have deterred some terrorist activities by increasing the risk attaching to particular targets.

There exists, however, a technique called *escalation trend analysis* which goes further than target pattern evaluation and builds upon sequences of acts by a single group in the hope that, when taken as a whole, the characteristics of events may provide predictive indicators of future events. This sort of analysis is based on an understanding of the political nature of terrorist organisations and their goals. Terrorist actions are always related to the ultimate goal of producing political change. The means by which this goal can be reached can be depicted in four sets that run along a progressive continuum as illustrated in Fig. 1.

If demands are highly specific they entail a government either performing,

Fig. 1. Four sets of means by which terrorists attempt to reach their goals. (From *Disorders and Terrorism*, Report of the Task Force on Disorders and Terrorism, US National Advisory Committee on Criminal Justice Standards and Goals.)

Target selection \ Specificity of demands	High	Low
Discriminate	Bargaining	Political statement
Random	Social paralysis	Mass casualties

or failing to perform, some act. A hijacker who demands the release of political prisoners in return for the safety of hostages is an example of this means.

Political statements, that is slogans such as 'freedom for everyone' exemplify the demands that are very unspecific.

If we look at the target selection factors, we can see that highly discriminate targeting is usually associated with bargaining and political statements and often will involve little or no violence. Targets are chosen because of their importance and the corresponding willingness of the coerced parties to negotiate for them, or because they are readily identifiable as opponents of the terrorists or their goals. Random target selection, on the other hand, is typical of those groups who want to create social paralysis or mass casualties. Historically, and for strong tactical reasons, terrorists have seldom resorted to random target selection early in their campaigns. Indiscriminate attacks are usually tried only when bargaining and political statements have failed. Random targeting is usually accompanied by significant increases in the level of violence.

Social paralysis is typically associated with high levels of specific demands. As Mengel has pointed out:

The random targeting that accompanies social paralysis is indicative of a group that has failed to achieve its ends through bargaining and political statements using less destructive violence. Terrorists who are motivated to employ social paralysis as a means usually do not care about publicity as a means of gaining popular support for their position. They appear to believe that the higher level of violence associated with social paralysis, through random targeting, enables them to achieve more specific demands. These activities bring the activities directly to the anonymous citizen. The IRA attacks in London subways in mid-March 1976, is illustrative of the type of attack that terrorists so motivated undertake.[23]

The final category covers means involving mass casualties, which are usually employed when support declines, a campaign has failed, or in times of intense frustration. Generally, acts involving mass casualties are indicative of a terrorist group's realisation that:

1. They do not have a position of strength from which bargaining can be successful.
2. The public will no longer respond to statement-(propaganda-)related attacks.
3. Popular support has been lost because of the social paralysis caused by previous attacks.

To the extent that the security authorities understand the dynamics of the situations that have just been described they then employ escalation trend analysis as an intelligence tool. Typically, terrorist activity has escalated as shown in Fig. 2 (which is Fig. 1 with a directional arrow added). In other words, in many terrorist campaigns terrorist activity escalates through a series of steps, each of which involves progressively more violence – the steps being from bargaining to political statements to social paralysis to mass casualties. To the extent that this generalised pattern is followed, tracking the activities of terrorist groups may provide excellent predictors of their future targets and means of attack. Such an analysis could indicate when a group has or will escalate its activities. It is just as important to monitor when a group does not escalate to more destructive or violent terrorism, because this may indicate either a deficiency in resources or that the group does not consider that its objectives will be met by indiscriminate targeting – information which is vital to tailoring specific measures and strategies to counter the activities of specific groups.

A related form of trend evaluation – objective trend analysis – provides information about the potential a particular group has for escalation to the employment of high-technology terrorism to gain their objectives, but without the escalation of means shown in Fig. 2. This situation is described as follows in the *Task Force Report on Disorders and Terrorism*:

> For example, a group may continue to be motivated to bargain for certain objectives, but be frustrated in attaining them using conventional terrorist tactics. Recognising that more extreme means are inappropriate to their objectives, the only options open to the group are to abandon the quest or to seek greater leverage – an option satisfied by the use of high technology. Election of this latter option does not necessarily indicate the direct employment of high technology, but the likelihood of a coercive threat is significantly increased as the group's inability to achieve its ends and an unwillingness to escalate direct violence results in frustration.[24]

A well-organised intelligence unit should be able to track the attributes of individual groups. The actions of such groups should be analysed for trends which will give some idea of their potential for high-technology terrorism.

As well as tracking and analysis of current terrorist movements there is

Fig. 2. Escalation of means by which terrorists attempt to reach their goals. (From *Disorders and Terrorism*.)

Specificity of demands / Target selection	High	Low
Discriminate	Bargaining	Political statement
Random	Social paralysis	Mass casualties

also a need for an historically based analytic system from which predictions about future terrorist operations may be made. There are a number of such systems in operation which analyse data that have been previously collected, collated and evaluated. The major coded categories of one such system[25] are as follows:

Code category 01: information relative to an international national or internal (domestic) symbolic act executed in a particular locale on a specific date, hour and time of day.

Code category 02: information which provides an associable basis between the terrorist act and a stage of a revolutionary process: planning, action, consolidation.

Code category 03: information relative to the perpetrating organisation and its membership, its foreign or domestic criminal associations and particularly its clandestine apparatus which is constructed to help members prepare and execute direct action and propaganda operations and cover them when tasks are completed.

Code category 04: information relative to the ideology of zealous and resolute individuals who are intractably committed to a cause which they believe just.

Code category 05: information relative to techniques utilised by a terrorist group to influence political behavior and thereby to permit them to manipulate the population and to fight effectively with few resources.

Code category 06: information relative to the extra-normal tactics used by terrorists (kidnapping, bombings, assassination, etc.) and their weapons.

Code category 07: information relative to the targets attacked by terrorists; specifically aspects of target vulnerability, the adverse impact that target destruction or restriction will have on a specific group, or the positive impact that the destruction of a specific target will have upon the image of the group responsible for assaulting it.

Code category 08: information pertaining to the propaganda goal of a terrorist group; specifically how it is manipulated to enhance the public visibility of a terrorist group or used to create an atmosphere of a perpetual, widespread and ever-increasing fear among a particular segment of a population or a population at large.

The information, when coded in this manner, can then be computer-analysed to discover patterns from which projections of terrorist behaviour can be made and to reveal strategies which have been most successful in dealing with specific combinations of factors in terrorist incidents. Projections such as the following are possible from such an analysis:

(a) purpose, reason or cause of the event;
(b) nature of the situation;
(c) groups and/or individuals involved;
(d) number of persons expected;
(e) locations affected;
(f) time and/or duration of the event or situation;
(g) potential for disorder;
(h) effect upon the law enforcement agency, the jurisdiction it services, visiting dignitaries, other individuals, etc.;

(i) significance of the event or situation;

(j) evolving patterns and trends; and

(k) recommendations for consideration of the law enforcement agency's top management concerning possible actions to be taken.

While much of the emphasis in the present discussion on intelligence has focussed on its pre-emptive role the same information is vital to the successful conduct of a terrorist incident in progress. Intelligence is the key to judging the credibility of an actual threat and to deciding on the appropriate tactics to employ. Apart from hard data such as number of individuals involved, location and layout of incident situation, weapons possessed, etc. intelligence agencies are rapidly developing expertise in the area of behavioural science intelligence skills. These skills are particularly useful in assessing threat credibility. Russell, Banker, and Miller point out some of the questions which behavioural science may be called upon to answer:

How do we assess whether a group that presumably has a high-order operational capability or mass disruptive potential will, in fact, resort to its use? What characteristics of individual terrorists and groups exist or can be determined to aid us in assessing probability of execution, hoax potential, level of resolve, willingness to negotiate, motivation, and so on? In general, how do we know when to call the terrorists' bluff and when to negotiate or consider entering some other relationship with them rather than suffering the *possible* consequences of a mass disruption or destructive act?[26]

Apart from psychologists, psychiatrists, and other experts who are researching behavioural patterns, responses in stressful situations, etc., other professionals such as psycholinguists are now being employed by intelligence agencies as part of the counter-terrorist effort. Such people are developing techniques to analyse threat communications in order to provide an amazing amount of data about the terrorists, their intentions, and their potential behaviours.[27] It is to be expected that such innovative uses of behavioural science will characterise more and more of counter-terrorist intelligence in the future.

Summary

In summary, this very brief analysis of the role of intelligence in counter-terrorist operations has shown that current, accurate intelligence is vital both in planning to prevent or pre-empt terrorist actions, and in the conduct of operations against terrorists in a threat situation. It is likely that the future will see a greater emphasis on developing sophisticated modelling procedures which can be used as predictors of terrorist targets and methods and a much heavier involvement of behavioural scientists in intelligence work in the course of terrorist incidents. A further likelihood is the development of wider sharing of intelligence between intelligence agencies and security authorities both within each country and between countries or groups of countries. However, such arrangements will be proceeded with only cautiously in view of the political implications of some possible intelligence-sharing arrangements.

13

Handling hostage situations

In recent years hostage-taking has become a favourite tactic of political terrorists. Largely because of the intense publicity surrounding terrorist hostage/siege situations hostage taking has also bourgeoned as a tactic of mentally unstable and criminal individuals. Because of its high profile, the publicity surrounding it and the extreme actions which governments have been prompted to take as a consequence of hostage situations they exemplify many of the policy issues surrounding anti-terrorist operations. In this chapter, therefore, some of the basic factors considered by those responding to hostage situations will be outlined to illustrate some of the issues raised in preceding chapters as they apply to one particular terrorist activity. It is stressed that this analysis is not a practical guide to hostage response measures. Rather its purpose is to alert the reader to the types of policy issues which arise from a practical terrorist problem.

There are a number of possible ways of classifying hostage-takers,[1] each of which may be used for different analytical or decision-making purposes. At the most general level, Dr John Stratton,[2] Director of Psychological Services for the Los Angeles County Sheriff's Department, has identified three broad groups of hostage-takers and characterised them as follows:

1. *The mentally ill hostage-taker.* Primarily because of the high media exposure given to hostage/siege situations it has become increasingly apparent to mentally unstable individuals that taking someone hostage guarantees individual recognition by the news media, the opportunity to exercise power and, to many the most important feature, the power to put the police into a defensive posture. For those with suicidal tendencies a hostage or barricade situation is often seen as a spectacularly successful method of bringing about one's demise. Stratton points out that psychiatrists and psychologists tend to categorise such individuals by using such labels as paranoid, psychotic, schizophrenic, and delusional. He argues that these terms promote in the layperson a view that the mentally ill hostage-taker cannot be reasoned with. This is unfortunate, because in a hostage situation, the hostage-taker must be communicated with and interventions must be attempted. The hostage-taker may be mentally ill and prone to violence, but

may also be very intelligent. He may have developed his own specialised view of the world and how it operates within the context of a complex delusional system. It is, therefore, very important for the negotiators who communicate with the hostage-taker to try to understand that individual's world. This may be extremely difficult but if the negotiator can begin to make some identification with the hostage-taker it may make it possible to begin to understand why the following sorts of reasons, enumerated by Stratton, spark off hostage events:

1. An individual whose mother died of cancer would take a tobacco executive hostage to make the world aware of the evils of smoking.
2. An individual having multiple problems who receives a foreclosure notice on his house would enter the loan company to hold those responsible for removing him from his house.
3. A man who considers himself useless, the world meaningless, and who wants to die, would make a big scene with the police in an attempt to have them kill him in a grandiose spectacle rather than commit uneventful suicide.

This list of (actual) examples could go on forever, because in many cases the individuals involved are people with limited personal power who feel their problems occur because they are being persecuted by the world or significant segments of it. Their feelings of frustration, helplessness, and lack of worth may overwhelm them so that they feel they must strike back by taking power and control over someone or some organisation that symbolises their problems. We can also, for practical purposes, include in the mentally ill group those who take hostages under the influence of drugs or alcohol.

The parameters are endless in considering the mentally ill hostage-taker and such an individual is probably the most difficult to deal with because of the element of irrationality or loss of control (due to drugs, for example) present. For this reason, the use of psychological or psychiatric expertise is encouraged in such cases.

2. The criminal hostage-taker. Criminals who take hostages (with the obvious exception of kidnappers) usually do so as a last resort. Sometimes the police response to a crime in progress may be sufficiently rapid that the offender is trapped with what appears to him to be no alternative but to take a hostage in an attempt to bargain his way out of custody. Incidents such as the one upon which the book and movie *Dog Day Afternoon* was based illustrate well the effect on criminals when police arrive unexpectedly at the scene of a crime in progress.

While criminals are generally rational when committing a crime they obviously do not want to be arrested and may display somewhat less than their usual reason when the police corner them. However, in many cases it is possible to discuss with them that fact that the crime committed is not as serious as kidnapping or murder. With current judicial sentencing practices and the operation of the parole system, the ordinary criminal given a little time and reason, will frequently come to the conclusion that surrender will save his own life and perhaps lead to only a minimal time in prison. Some criminals caught in such a situation, however, may try to convince the police that they are political terrorists rather than robbers, for example, and this may complicate the situation exceedingly. This was the case with the famous Spaghetti House siege in London in 1975. On September 28 three men armed with a sawn-off shotgun and two pistols burst into the Spaghetti House in Knightsbridge with the intention to commit robbery. In fact, two of the men were black militants who were fringe members of a black extremist group and the leader was a convicted armed robber who also supported black militancy. However, in spite of their connections with an extremist organisation it was apparent that the three were there as armed robbers not terrorists.

The plan was to raid this particular Spaghetti House early on a Sunday morning when Davies, the leader, knew that the managers of a number of Spaghetti Houses in London gathered to cash their takings. However, when the robbers entered the premises one of the managers was able to escape and literally walked straight into a police officer with a two-way radio. Within a minute-and-a-half the police were knocking on the back door. Once the robbers realised the police were there they forced their captives downstairs into a small storeroom and shut themselves in with them. They then began planning how to get out. It took them nearly a week to decide that the only way out was to surrender.

These three weren't entirely stupid, however, because at first they claimed they were members of the Black Liberation Army and hoped to bluff their way out by forcing concessions to terrorists. So the situation when senior police officers arrived was that three BLA terrorists (not three armed robbers) had eight hostages.

Davies revealed who he was, which turned out to be important information, stated they were with the BLA and demanded that the Home Secretary should listen to their demands. What they got was the local Police Superintendent who extracted a promise not to shoot anyone and negotiations began. Davies demanded the release of a number of black militants in custody at Brixton Prison and issued a number of claims on behalf of the BLA. The police had never heard of this organisation and it turned out, in fact, to be merely a figment of Davies' imagination. Negotiations reached the stage where Davies demanded that a plane be made available at London airport. It was because he failed to be precise about what sort of plane and what sort of range he wanted it to fly that made the police believe this was not a well-planned terrorist operation, but a crime gone wrong. So they prolonged the negotiations and conducted some excellent detective work relying to a large extent on information they got from cleverly worded conversations with Davies. The police found the car which the robbers had used and, on it, the fingerprints of Davies' unknown accomplices, which allowed their identification. This information in addition to following up what Davies let slip during the negotiations meant that the three could be positively identified as criminals not terrorists.

The police also managed to use their technical services to see and hear what was happening in the storeroom. It enabled them to know what sort of guns the criminals had, what condition they were in and, near the end of the siege, to know that despite their banging on the door and shouting that they were dying of hunger and thirst, they were in fact opening and consuming cans of food and drink stored in the room.

As the siege progressed, and the police had identified the men, a newspaper published a photograph of one of them. A copy was slid under the door of the room with some pertinent comments on it. However, the man it was about was asleep at the time and his comrades realised what was going on, tore the paper to shreds, and flushed it down the toilet. When the man woke up, the police asked him if he had seen the paper and having provoked dissension within the robbers' ranks, slid another copy under the door. They were able to observe that the man was visibly shocked to see the newspaper story. The final straw was when they heard on a radio given to them by the police that their two outside accomplices had been arrested. On day six the hostages were released and the gunmen surrendered (although Davies shot himself, but only managed to sustain serious wounds). Scotland Yard considered that the two most important factors leading to a successful conclusion were that they kept pressure on the gunmen all the time, continually emphasising that the responsibility for what happened was theirs, and that they made clear and stuck to a 'no deals' policy. Sir Robert Mark, who was then Commissioner of the Metropolitan Police, made it absolutely clear to them when he told them, 'There is nowhere for you to go except the nearest police station'.

The Spaghetti House siege was important for two reasons. First, it was one of two incidents (the other being the siege of IRA members at Balcombe Street, London in December 1975) in which the British perfected their approach to hostage negotiations, an approach which has been used successfully on many subsequent occasions. Second, it shows the overlap between political and criminal hostage-takers and shows why security authorities need to have a detailed knowledge of all types of hostage-takers if they are to properly assess the threat posed by any particular incident.

   3. *The social, political, ethnic, or religious crusader hostage-taker.*

Such a hostage-taker is generally a member of a group falling within the definition of terrorist and will have a strong sense of commitment to or belief in a particular idea or cause. Terrorist groups are usually numerically small, but extremely dedicated, even to death, to the furtherance of their beliefs and ideas. Whatever their particular movement's goal, professional terrorists have usually studied revolutionary tactics and effective methods of promoting and broadcasting the basis for their ideology or cause. They are often students of the specific use of terror as a tactic, studying in addition to their own ideology and revolutionary methods, such topics as police and security force procedures, societal reaction, other terrorists' approaches, and how to use their influential theatre to reach millions of people by gaining publicity through the media. Organisations which seek social change (e.g. the Tupamaros in Uruguay), political change (e.g. the Palestine Liberation Organisation), independence for ethnic minorities (e.g. the ETA Basque organisation in Spain), or religious reform (e.g. the Hanafi Muslims) are known to the world because of their outrageous violence and the publicity these acts have received through the news media. Such groups are the most difficult to deal with because of their total commitment. Although rational, they often enter a situation with set demands and identified limits as to what they are willing to do in the furtherance of their cause. Frequently members of these groups are committed to the extent that they will kill or die if necessary. Although situations involving terrorists are complicated by their determination, extensive planning, and ability to exert power effectively, experience has shown that alternatives to the original demands can often be worked out, frequently alternatives which concede little in political terms.

Within the three-way classification set out by Stratton it is possible to analyse each group in terms of specific factors which could determine the way in which security forces or police should react to terrorist sieges (or acts committed by unstable or criminal individuals who use or imitate terrorist tactics). A careful consideration of such an analysis clearly indicates different responses to different types of hostage-taking.[3] Since hostage/siege situations are a major form of terrorist activity (not necessarily in terms of frequency, but certainly in terms of impact) security forces around the world (be they police or military, depending on the country or the particular situation) over the past decade have been developing special negotiating procedures to cope with these situations in order to prevent the killing of innocent hostages or the granting of significant political concessions to the terrorists. The leaders in this field have been the British and the Dutch in dealing with political terrorists and the New York City Police Department in dealing with criminal hostage-takers. The development of hostage negotiation techniques is an evolving process with new approaches becoming necessary as new types of hostage situations emerge or as hostage-takers become aware of negotiating techniques and seek to minimise their effects. A number of specialised texts are available for police negotiators and yet other classified material contains detailed information on precise negotiation methods. Obviously it is inappropriate in a book such as this to detail negotiation techniques, not least because it has become obvious that terrorists change their tactics in response to information about what factors change the negotiating situation to favour the authorities. However, some general principles have now been well publicised in the popular and professional press and the reader may be interested to read some of the very broad guidelines which apply to hostage situations (particularly those with policy implications related to the topics discussed in the foregoing chapters).

Guidelines for hostage situations

1. Time

Time is the foremost factor in a hostage/siege situation. Developing rapport between the negotiator and the hostage-taker needs time. This is also true of the development of a relationship between the terrorists and the hostages. And it may be vital to the safety of the hostages that they do develop some sort of relationship with the terrorists. There is some evidence that if hostages are in fact shot, the first to go will be the person who has developed the least relationship with the taker. It should also be noted that terrorists are becoming aware of how development of rapport weakens their resolve to harm the hostages and some now force their captives to wear hoods and remain silent to prevent the relationship developing. (The problems of victims will be discussed in more detail later in this chapter.)

The first few minutes appear to be the most crucial because the emotional state of everyone, especially the terrorists and the hostages, is very unstable. Under these conditions reactions tend to be automatic, unpredictable, and excitable. But as time passes the nervous system cannot sustain the level of arousal and responses return towards normality. Initially emotion predominates and reason has little influence over behaviour. However, as time goes by, these two forces move toward an equilibrium point.

In order to ensure that equilibrium is reached it is necessary for law enforcement personnel to avoid performing acts which will elevate the terrorist's emotional state still further. The initial response should be to establish and secure the location and an outer perimeter and, unless particular circumstances dictate, to avoid shows of aggressive force that indicate an assault on the terrorists' position. Steps must then be taken to introduce a negotiator and to begin to slowly establish communication and rapport.

Another aspect concerning time is the nature of the procedures to be used after the emotionally high pitch has decreased and levelled off to a point where communication is possible. Stratton has identified two types of strategies, both of which have their supporters.[4] One view is that the negotiators should alternately raise and lower the hostage-taker's emotional levels so that he can experience numerous changes in emotional response in a short period of time and subsequently tire easily and quickly and be persuaded to surrender. The other opinion is that once an emotional equilibrium has been attained, it is best not to disturb the balance unduly, but rather to let the situation work itself out until surrender seems to the hostage-taker to be his only option.

Both of these approaches (and combinations of them) have worked in bringing about the surrender of terrorists without harm coming to the hostages. However, it seems likely that the second option, containment and waiting, will result in the saving of more lives in the long run. It is potentially dangerous to raise and lower a hostage-taker's anxiety, because it is extremely difficult to predict how any individual in a particular situation will respond to various kinds of pressure.

2. The negotiator

Selection and training of negotiators is of critical importance because they are the link between the law enforcement authorities and the terrorists. Many agencies have developed strict criteria for selection and put potential negotiators through comprehensive training and simulated hostage situations to prepare them for hostage incidents.

Primarily, the negotiator has to establish a favourable and supportive relationship with the terrorists. One of the goals of the negotiator is to develop his relationship as a neutral agent and not as a decision maker. He attempts to understand and reach some form of identification with the hostage-taker so that he can relay the perpetrator's case to the decision makers.[5] This procedure is time-consuming, but decreases the probability of irrational outbursts or uncontrollable emotional episodes and allows the relationship between taker and negotiator to develop more fully.

Generally it is recommended that one or two negotiators conduct all negotiations, otherwise it is difficult to establish any relationship. Negotiators should usually be middle-ranking officers who report to a decision-maker. This buys time because they always have to pass messages to their superiors. Other advantages are that unfavourable decisions may be accepted as not the negotiator's responsibility and therefore not ruin the rapport that has been established, and also the negotiator can concentrate on his immediate task and not be diverted by executive responsibilities.

3. Dishonesty as a tactic

The issue of whether or not to be honest during hostage negotiations is very difficult to resolve. Again there are two basic approaches. One view is that if you lie to save lives in one situation, particularly if the deception is reported by the media, the terrorists involved in the next incident will not trust any negotiators and peaceful solutions will be less likely. Proponents of this view believe that we must consider the long-term effects of such behaviour and not be persuaded by immediate gains.

The second approach places the value of human life in the present situation above possible (and unknown) loss of life in the future. Deception is seen as valuable if it works. It should be noted, however, that deception is more likely to be successful with mentally deranged or criminal hostage-takers than with dedicated and fanatical terrorists.

There is evidence to support both points of view and the dilemma is a difficult one. All that can really be said is that, while guidelines can be given, hostage negotiations must respond to individual situations and circumstances. Sometimes deception will work, will not be widely publicised, and should be used. However, as a general proposition it is probably best to try to avoid promising what cannot or will not be delivered. Particularly where a situation gains publicity and notoriety it is likely that the law enforcement response will be closely watched by future hostage-takers who will adapt their plans accordingly. Indiscriminate or stupid deceptions could well limit the options open to future negotiators.

4. Suggestions

Many authorities believe that negotiators should never make suggestions to terrorist hostage-takers because they may give them ideas they had not considered previously. For example, if in one of his demands a terrorist asked the police to provide him with a submachine gun, it would hardly be advisable to suggest that he take a .44 magnum instead. On the other hand, particularly as the siege wears on and the terrorist is anxious, tired, and suffering from clouded thinking, suggestions by the negotiator may ease some of the stress and be of benefit to the goals of the security personnel. Again, it is a matter for careful judgement at the scene.

5. Demands of hostage-takers

One of the most widely accepted principles in hostage negotiations is never to give something to the terrorist unless you get something in return. This principle has been successfully used to get hostages released for such otherwise trivial items as sandwiches and cigarettes. The only time when this restriction might be relaxed is very early in the negotiation when rapport is being established and a token meeting of a demand could be acceptable.

There are certain demands which are almost universally accepted as being non-negotiable. These include weapons, drugs, alcohol and, frequently, hostage-exchanges. Transportation is to be avoided if at all possible, but most agencies have contingency plans in case a particular situation arises when the moving of hostages becomes permissible.

These are just a few of the guidelines which would be discussed in training hostage negotiators and considered during a terrorist siege. It is important to remember, though, that every guideline may be altered to suit a particular situation.

The victims of hostage-taking incidents

No discussion of the psychology of hostage-taking would be complete without a brief look at the reactions of the immediate victims – the hostages.

Hostages are viewed by their captors not as individuals, but as negotiable commodities. They are a means to an end with no intrinsic worth other than their exchange value. The hostage-taker tries not to see the victims as individuals with personalities, wants, and needs, but only in terms of what they may be able to bring in return for their lives. Nevertheless, it is now apparent that the reactions of the hostages may have a very significant effect on the outcome of the situation. This has become particularly evident following the recognition of the relationship that develops between hostage-taker and hostages.

The subsistence and continued existence of hostages is dependent on the behaviour of the captors. As a result, whether hostages are to survive or not may depend on how they identify with and relate to the hostage-taker who has the ultimate control over their lives. There is great psychological pressure on hostages, therefore, to understand, cooperate or even love their captors in order to save themselves.

These changes in relationship between captor and hostage are often referred to as the 'Stockholm Syndrome' after an incident which occurred in a Stockholm bank in August 1973 in which four hostages (three women and a man) were held captive for six days. As a result of their captivity, the hostages soon began attempting to negotiate with the police on behalf of the bank robbers who held them and, ironically, for whose safety they began to fear. When the robbers decided to surrender, the hostages insisted on walking in front of them so that the police could not shoot them. In addition to the fact that they refused to testify against the robbers, one of the hostages divorced her husband and married one of the men who had held her hostage.

According to Mann there are three sequential stages in the reactions of victims to being taken hostage.[6] These are:

1. *Behavioural (coping) responses*. The first reactions are shock, panic,

weeping and hysteria. This gives way after a time to resignation, apathy, and passivity. Because both hostages and terrorists are very tense and jumpy for the first few hours this is the most dangerous time and negotiators or other officials should avoid any dramatic moves during this period.

2. *Emotional responses to captors*. Emotional changes may be immediate or long-term. The cycle is usually a change from fear or anger to ambivalence and then perhaps to understanding, friendship or attraction, and a hostage may eventually become emotionally dependent on the captor. This attachment may be reciprocated, particularly when women hostages are involved. This is of great significance to the hostage negotiator. The force that the terrorist exerts is due to the credibility of the threat to the hostage's life. If an emotional attachment is formed between hostage and terrorist that particular threat is greatly minimised because the terrorist is much less likely to kill a hostage who is no longer an impersonal pawn. Further, as time goes on, the terrorist may well become increasingly concerned about and feel responsible for the hostage's well-being which often allows the authorities to persuade him to make concessions. The implication for negotiators is that they should allow time for such relationships to develop. It may help to allow conditions to become uncomfortable so that the hostages and captors become more dependent on each other and perhaps view authority as a common threat.

Of course these principles are now beginning to become understood by some terrorists too and they take steps to prevent bonds forming between themselves and their victims. Some groups try to change guards frequently and enforce silence rules in an attempt to prevent communication. Others blindfold their hostages and/or wear hoods themselves. The psychological effects of these measures is to deindividuate the terrorist (hood) and dehumanise the hostage (blindfold). As events at the Munich Olympics and aboard the Dutch train hijacked by the South Moluccans in December 1975 showed, the survival prospects of hostages are very much lessened by the use of such tactics.

3. *Attitude change and brainwashing*. The third level of response is that involving changes in belief regarding the terrorist's ideology. In some cases such changes can occur within 30 hours. The changes go further than emotional responses to the terrorist as an individual, to encompass the cause for which he fights. There are two levels of change: small, subtle changes in attitude towards the terrorist's cause (for example, the attitudes expressed by the passengers and crew of a TWA plane held by Palestinian terrorists in Jordan for almost a month in 1970[7]) and, very rarely, massive changes in attitude ('brainwashing') which lead to wholesale embrace of the terrorist cause (for example, Patty Hearst). These changes are important because they make it even less likely that the hostages will be killed.

These effects are particularly important considerations in conducting hostage negotiations. As Mann concludes:

These responses tend to follow a distinct sequence and they are reasonably predictable for hostages in both kidnapping and hijackings, especially for female hostages who are being held as bargaining chips. These hostage responses produce effects on the terrorists. By keeping in mind the development of these responses, and by putting them to good use, the negotiator may be better able to save hostages and, in addition, win a more satisfactory settlement or outcome to the episode.[8]

That the dynamics of a hostage situation can change and demand new approaches was illustrated by the siege of the Iranian Embassy in London in May 1980. In that incident an assault team from the British Special Air Service (SAS) Regiment stormed the building following the execution of one of the hostages held by Arab terrorists demanding a free Khuzestan. In the ensuing action 19 hostages were released and five terrorists killed. The British operation followed the failure of days of the trusted methods of hostage negotiation involving the building up of a relationship between police and terrorists which, in the past few years, has resulted in the surrender of terrorists in seemingly similar circumstances. However in the siege of the Iranian Embassy the situation was somewhat unique in sieges to date.

The London siege revealed a disturbing exception to the traditional pattern which was one of the major factors which eventually led to strike action. The difference was that the Stockholm Syndrome did not become a pervasive influence. The principal reason for the failure to follow the usual pattern was that some of the hostages (in this case Iranian diplomats loyal to the Ayatollah Khomeini) were as fanatical as the terrorists. Some actively sought martyrdom. This combination, which we will almost certainly see more of in the future, completely changes the dynamics of a siege situation. Security authorities would do well to study the implications of such a change.

In the London siege most would agree that an armed assault was necessary and that the SAS were the appropriate unit to carry it out. (However, there is some evidence that negotiations might have had more chance of success had police intelligence about the frustration level of the terrorists been better or had political considerations dictated by the British Government not so limited the role of Arab ambassadors in an intermediary capacity). The success of the mission was a product of exemplary planning and thorough training, but the element of luck should not be overlooked. In each of the successful military rescues so far attempted, including those by the Israelis at Entebbe and the West Germans at Mogadishu, post-event analyses have revealed that things could very well have turned out differently had certain fortuitous events in each case not occurred. In the

London case the mission was jeopardised when a friction brake jammed on an SAS member's abseilling gear and left him dangling some way up the outside of the building under assault. The result was that explosive charges which were to be used could not be detonated without risk to his life and the entry to the building was delayed momentarily at a vital point in the operation. Fortunately, the operation succeeded and none can deny the skill of the SAS in mounting it. But such success should not encourage the expectation of high success rates with such operations which might lead to their increased use (as a progressively earlier option) in the future. The more special rescue operations there are, the more failures there are bound to be. This is not only because of the law of averages, but because easy recourse to special action forces will almost certainly lead to the commitment of less well trained forces with poorer planning and execution. The emphasis in the foreseeable future must still be on slow, patient methods with carefully planned and meticulously executed military responses as the last option.

The success of operations such as the London raid and its predecessors has naturally led to the establishment of similar units worldwide. At least one other incident involving a special action force has occurred since the London siege. In October 1980 Turkish commandos stormed a hijacked airliner rescuing 100 hostages and seizing the terrorists without loss of life or serious injury to the former. The organisation of counter-terrorist reaction forces was discussed in a previous chapter in which it was suggested that the best arrangement for the present is one which places the primary responsibility on the police but allows for the use of specialised defence force personnel in certain clearly defined situations. As far as possible terrorism should be dealt with as a law enforcement, not a military problem. The armed services should ensure that they retain an adequate capability to meet their responsibilities should they become necessary, but as a recent editorial in a leading defence journal warned they must beware of 'losing sight of the real roles of special force units and of the dangers inherent in such forces in a democracy in their rush to set up and display such units who are by way of becoming some form of international status symbol'.[9]

These considerations stress the importance of continuing to refine and update our hostage negotiation policies and techniques. Over the past decade or so there have been a number of 'vogue venues' for hostage/siege incidents, each necessitating special procedures. The considerations involved in negotiating over a radiotelephone with a hijacker in an airliner with a finite amount of fuel are obviously not the same as those involved when face-to-face negotiations with no time limit are the case. Apart from situational constraints we must also be aware of changes in technique necessitated by hostages and hostage-takers of different combinations, as illustrated by the siege at the Iranian Embassy in London. The events of 1980 indicate that in the immediate future there may be a preponderance of attacks on embassies but it might also be predicted that hijacking of airliners or trains will again become prominent in the next few years. The techniques developed to cope with these situations will need to continue to be refined and re-cast to fit emerging circumstances and it is expected that many of the projects described in the following chapter on behavioural science research will help fulfil this requirement. And, finally, governments should take steps to educate the public about hostage situations and the problems they pose both for victims and the authorities. In particular, it is desirable for governments to seek to act on the forces which in the course of hostage situations place such pressure on the authorities that their negotiating options are severely (and inappropriately) limited. Miller sums up the problem as follows:

The government may not have much control over the image of terrorism conveyed by the popular media. After all, terrorism is news and the media is there to convey the news generally in a form that sells copy. However, the government can make the public aware of the difficulties and problems faced in hostage situations. In this way, the public, while not exposed to the same information with which potential targets are provided, will have access to sufficiently high quality information that discussion can take place in an informed manner, leading to the type of environment that assists in maintaining intelligent and objective responses to a problem too easily caught up with emotional fervor. Such discussion, hopefully, will lead to a less vindictive response toward hostages who are compromised by the process of transference and to the establishment of public attitudes that will recognise that extinguishing liberty in the rush to combat terrorism only accomplishes for the terrorists what they are unable to accomplish for themselves.[10]

14

Counter-measures against terrorism: the role of behavioural science research

In Part One of this book it was shown that terrorism as a tactic is not a novel phenomenon. Yet presently we stand in danger of being engulfed by a flood of books, films, magazine and journal articles, conferences and symposia all devoted to defining, describing, understanding, or countering the 'threat of modern terrorism'. This flurry of activity suggests that we do not understand exactly what is the nature of the threat which is forcing many nations to devote to it more and more of their time and resources. In the first place, little consideration seems to have been given to the question of whether or not a 'real' threat exists or whether it may in some instances be essentially a product of fear and prejudice. Is it possible that many official reactions to terrorism reflect an unwillingness or inability to grapple with the inequalities in society or are a smokescreen designed to disguise repressive measures taken for unrelated political reasons?

It might be suggested that here is an important focus for behavioural science research. This is not the sort of research which will find favour with governments and security officials. For the former it may represent a dangerous challenge to their legitimacy and for the latter it offers nothing 'practical' in the way of the specific security measures they seek. However, the answers may well be in the long-term interests of the people and behavioural scientists should not let the representatives of the status quo define all the research questions. We need social analysts from a number of disciplines to answer basic questions of definition and motivation, on both sides of the terrorist equation. In particular, they should delve into the reasons behind a state, or a portion of its population, feeling vulnerable and threatened and for the motivations for various counter-measures to perceived or alleged threats. They need to examine the conditions in society which give rise to political violence and convey the implications of their findings to governments and the people.[1] Such issues should form an important priority for behavioural research.

Having acknowledged that particular area of research need, it is obvious, particularly in the short term, that behavioural science research has a significant contribution to make to the development of specific counter-terrorist technologies and responses. Without trying to trivialise or sidestep some of the definitional, political, and causal problems inherent in discussing terrorism, it is argued that there *are* valid reasons for supposing that current terrorist operations pose a greater potential threat than their historical forebears and that it is legitimate to seek ways to deal with the current situation (as long as we are not tempted to let short-term contingencies exclude consideration of the structural factors which may give rise to terrorism and which may require major social or economic changes to alter). The reasons for seeing contemporary terrorism as a new order of threat have been discussed earlier and it has been argued that most of the reasons are connected with the development of recent technological innovations and their impact on social organisation (and consequent potential for social disruption).

However, while many of the reasons for this change in terrorist potential are grounded in technological innovation and its consequences, the solutions, either long-term or crisis-oriented, are inescapably rooted in behavioural considerations. An excessive reliance on technological solutions, therefore, is unlikely to provide useful answers to many of the important questions surrounding terrorism. Since we are dealing with human behaviour it is vital that we assess the contribution which can be made by the behavioural sciences. It is the purpose of the remainder of this chapter to outline very briefly some of the important areas in which behavioural science has, or could have, a significant role to play in the investigation and control of terrorist activities. For ease of presentation the discussion will be rather arbitrarily divided into consideration of research and advice prior to, during, and after terrorist incidents, although it is obvious that many of the areas overlap and are inter-related.

Before outlining some of the specific research topics, however, it is useful to consider the research strategies which could be applied in counter-terrorist behavioural science research. Crelinsten has suggested a number of strategies among which are the following:[2]

1. *Data collection, surveys, descriptive classifications.* This involves the routine and continuous collection by a number of agencies of basic facts about terrorism. This information acts as a data base for specific studies. Ongoing collection systems would be established to track areas such as characteristics of terrorist attacks, details of terrorist perpetrators, basic frequency data on attacks, case histories of outcomes (successes and failures), incident logs, passage of domestic and international legislation dealing with terrorism, technical data on security arrangements and procedures, establishment and operations of anti-terrorist forces, and many others.

2. *Technological research and development.* The application and

development of technology to prevention and control programmes is a rapidly expanding industry. As will be discussed later there are a large number of behavioural considerations in the design, construction, and use of such technology. Crelinsten suggests that the prime areas for the development of new technologies or the application of existing ones are preventive screening methods, weapons detection and tracing, medical and emergency preparedness, intelligence operations, and surveillance.

3. *Cost-benefit analysis.* Crelinsten suggests that cost-benefit analyses are necessary in such areas as crisis management, use of specialised personnel, preventive target-hardening, effects of specific policies on incident management and public attitudes, use of military options or international treaties.

4. *Conceptual modelling.* This involves the development of specific models of terrorist and counter-terrorist behaviour in which clearly stated assumptions are made and the modellers assess the implications these hold for various aspects of prevention and control (for example, incident management, deterrence policy, negotiations, or use of special action units). The bargaining and indemnification frameworks devised by Bobrow are examples of such conceptual models.[3]

5. *Gaming, prediction, futuristics.* These are the logical development of the conceptual models and represent exercises in 'out-inventing' the terrorist. Examples are developing new modes of terrorism and their counters, and analysing the logical outcome of specific scenarios. Bobrow explains the differences between exercises, scenarios, and gaming as follows:

Unlike exercises, diagnostic games are not attempts to see whether the current operating system works according to rules or as efficiently as its advocates claim. Exercises may of course be useful to pursue the earliest suggestion for descriptive studies of the current situation. Unlike academic and scientific simulations, diagnostic games are not attempts to test hypotheses drawn from theories or to trace the workings of complex, explicit models. Diagnostic games are instead exercises in applied imagination. Most simply they involve the reactions of people who can 'represent' the types of participants in the real world when asked to deal with a novel situation within the constraints of a decision-making context. Imagination enters in conceiving of the situations, the types of participants who should be represented, and the decision-making context. While cumbersome, this definition indicates that we can use diagnostic games to explore differences that follow from alternative situations, sets of participants, and the environment for management. Unlike scenarios, the analyst does not try to conjure about these differences. Instead he observes behaviour in a management situation. And since there are participants, the opportunity exists for them to learn and acquire experience.[4]

6. *Correlational studies: relations between variables.* A number of possible correlational studies, essentially descriptive in nature, are possible aids to policy formation. It should always be borne in mind that positive

correlations between two variables do not necessarily imply causal relations and this should be noted when assessing the relevance of correlation studies. Some examples of such studies include correlations between frequency of incidents and public attitudes, granting of terrorist demands and incidence of future terrorist acts, policy changes and incident outcomes, decision-making organisational structures and incident outcomes, government responses to terrorism and other political consequences, and so forth.

7. *Case studies, specific topics.* A large number of topics for research fall into an interdisciplinary and multi-methodology category. The list is almost endless and includes analyses of proposals for international regulation, the structure of rapid reaction forces, the construction of selection tests for anti-terrorist personnel, analyses of the theoretical basis for various terrorist ideologies, and the dissection of specific incidents by way of case study. Many of these studies will utilise data flowing in from some of the specific research modes already discussed and will often be conducted on an ad hoc, short-term basis as input for policy making or strategy development. They underline the need for a broad approach to research and for the necessity for an organisation or structure which facilitates sharing of data and analyses.

8. *Public opinion surveys.* Most counter-terrorist experts emphasise the importance to policy makers of being able to assess public attitudes both towards terrorist groups and their activities and towards government counter-measures. Although the formal use of surveys and public opinion polls is currently fairly limited there is much useful information to be gleaned from them as long as the inherent weaknesses of such techniques are remembered. Crelinsten suggests that:

Attitudes toward government policy, terrorist threat credibility, incident management, etc. can be measured before, during, and after specific terrorist incidents which occur locally or are reported in the international news. A public opinion survey could provide some measure of the extent of perceived terror, the effect of terror on basic values, and the effect of incidents on public pressure for government action. Specific issues could also be studied through the use of opinion polls. These issues could include the definition of terrorism, the scope of intelligence operations in peacetime, or the relative merits of the military option vis-a-vis paramilitary law enforcement. In general, this technique is an important tool in assessing the degree of conformance between government policy and public opinion.[5]

9. *Evaluation research.* There are three types of evaluative research relevant to counter-terrorism. First is the evaluation of the performance of counter-terrorist procedures and personnel. Second is the evaluation of need. This includes such activities as threat and vulnerability analysis, and evaluation of the consequences of extreme counter-measures. Finally is the evaluation of capabilities (which often will amount to a cost/benefit analysis). It is possible to evaluate how well the government is conforming

to public expectations by matching an assessment of what can be done with an assessment of public attitudes. A mismatch indicates that the government should either take steps to live up to public expectations or to conduct a campaign to bring public expectations into line with actual capabilities.

It is obvious, then, that a wide range of research strategies are available and seem relevant to the specific area of behavioural science in its application to the development, operation, and refinement of counter-terrorist techniques. The remainder of this chapter will provide a brief insight into some of the research topics to which these strategies are being applied. It is not intended to give a comprehensive coverage of the field. Rather it is hoped that a selective review of some current and potential projects will demonstrate the relevance of behavioural science to the solution of practical problems. If this is achieved, perhaps more persons in responsible positions in the security forces and in relevant government agencies might be persuaded to commit much needed resources to this potentially valuable field.

The first line of defence against a potential terrorist attack is intelligence. Much of the emerging behavioural work in this field was touched upon in an earlier chapter and need not be reiterated here. The development of a number of predictors which may be combined with or direct intelligence operations is of interest though. The best known of these is the US Federal Aviation Administration's hijacker profile programme. Such profiles are still in a relative infancy in terms of being able to narrow down the potential target group but they are reported by their users to have demonstrated operational value.[6] Much important work is still to be done to refine these measures and make them more accurate predictors. (As an aside, it should be mentioned that profiles are only useful if those doing the screening use only the characteristics they are given. Otherwise screening can easily be subverted into bias against minority groups or persons exhibiting features that the individual screener finds distasteful. If this happens the instrument will obviously not perform its required function. The results will be that some individuals who should be screened out will be let through while, possibly, large numbers of innocent citizens will be unnecessarily inconvenienced – and in some cases have their individual rights seriously infringed. There is a lighter side to this problem too. One airline is reported to have engaged two psychiatrists as special security officers with orders to arrest anyone trying to board a plane who exhibited signs of mental instability. Unfortunately, within a few minutes of commencing duty one psychiatrist arrested the other.)[7]

Shaw, Hazlewood, Hayes, and Harris claim that behavioural science research tools can provide information on terrorist activities which would be directly useful for:[8]

1. Allocating resources – deciding when and where security forces are needed.
2. Identifying periods of greatest likelihood of attack on social order so that enhanced security measures can be implemented.
3. Estimating the extent of contagion from terrorist acts to determine the length of time during which extra security may be needed.
4. Identifying policies which are effective in deterring terrorism.
5. Identifying outcomes which are likely to cause or inhibit further terrorist attacks.

Data relevant to these problems can be produced because terrorist acts are amenable to statistical analysis. The events are highly publicised and are therefore identifiable. Major categories of events may be distinguished easily, for example, bombings, hijackings, hostage/siege situations, assassinations, etc. There are enough events to meet the assumptions of statistical techniques. Where this latter condition is not met, for example in researching attempts to penetrate or sabotage nuclear facilities, there are sufficient analogue events with major commonalities with the low-frequency occurrence event which can be subjected to analysis. For example, the Sandia Laboratories have developed an extensive methodology to determine a set of attributes of potential threats to nuclear programmes using analogue incidents as data sources.[9]

In the same way in which behavioural scientists have constructed perpetrator profiles, it is also possible to turn the same techniques to the construction of profiles identifying potential locations of terrorist actions. The analyst would start by constructing a list of likely profile attributes such as level of existing security, ease of access, value of target in propaganda terms, critical nature of target, numbers of people in target and surrounding areas, and others. A large number of different terrorist events which have already taken place would then be coded on the variables, and associational and clustering techniques applied to the resultant output. These techniques could then

produce information of the likely *combinations* of attributes present in targets. Separate analyses of different types of violence and trend analyses would also be useful. The result would be a straightforward profile describing likely targets. Taken together, the likelihood indices for actor, type of violence, and target will provide powerful decision aids to security officials around the world.[10]

The production of a target screening measure would allow day-to-day security measures to be varied with the most cost-effective allocation of resources. Contingency plans could be developed for periods when the profile indicated the requirement for enhanced security and such a profile might also be useful in crisis decision-making.

Shaw *et al*. have suggested a number of specific operational tools which are being or could be developed using analytical techniques largely developed within the behavioural sciences.[11] These tools include:

1. An index which forecasts the likelihood of terrorist acts by emotionally disturbed individuals based on indicators of general social stress. This index, if it could be developed, could be used as a general guide to security forces to enable them to take certain preventive actions (for example, increase security at government buildings, increase a visible police presence, etc.) at appropriate times of impending risk so as not to over-deploy scarce resources unnecessarily. Being realistic however, it is difficult to see the development of an index with sufficient accuracy in the foreseeable future which would fulfil the requirements set out by Shaw *et al*.

2. An index of social conflict which projects the likelihood of attacks on public order by terrorist groups motivated by ideological or ethnic considerations. The intention here is to produce a typology of groups likely to engage in terrorism. When the typology had been validated it could assist in the determination of whether and to what extent surveillance techniques or information collection would be warranted.

3. Projections of the scope and duration of contagious terrorism. In planning security resource allocation it is important to understand the dimensions of major acts of terrorism producing contagion effects. A specific study of some practical concern would be to examine this question. If relevant data could be produced they would materially assist by indicating when enhanced security precautions might be necessary and would also set likely boundaries on the contagion effect beyond which heightened security might be unnecessary.

4. Information on the impact of different outcomes of terrorist incidents. Shaw *et al* argue that:

The results of violent acts, perhaps even more than police policies during confrontations, can be expected to influence the likelihood of contagious violence. Systematic analysis of the effect of different outcomes on subsequent terrorist acts can be expected to produce important information of use to policy makers.[12]

A technique which has recently been suggested to have relevance to counter-terrorist planning is link analysis. 'Link analysis is a systematic behavioural approach to defining and describing relationships among entities (individuals, organisations, and locations).'[13] It is therefore a tool which may be employed to analyse organised threats to physical security and to evaluate physical safeguards employed against defined threats. Link analysis has recently been applied to the criminal intelligence process[14] and it is a logical step to extend its use into the counter-terrorism field. In fact a number of large United States organisations are currently developing link analysis techniques to assess the probability of penetration into facilities such as nuclear weapons storage sites.

Link analysis can be used to develop an understanding of potential terrorist threats by establishing the relationships that exist among the entities constituting a specific adversary and defining the relationships between different adversaries. Link analysis can tie into the intelligence system to provide the best possible description of an adversary which, taken in conjunction with other data, could be invaluable in assessing the nature and magnitude of a threat. It can also be used to evaluate physical safeguards. For example, a potential target facility can be analysed to identify the most vulnerable pathways into, within, and out of the facility and its associated safeguards. A computer-based analysis can define the facility's potential access entities (for example, doorways, hatches, fences, etc.) and links (the safeguards that would have to be successfully negotiated to pass through the access entities, for example, guards, sensors, monitors, alarms). By specifying the probability of successful passage through each link in the safeguard system, it is possible to produce a probabilistic' ordering of the most vulnerable pathways for both penetration and escape.

Obviously, one of the earliest links in the defence against terrorist attack is security – both physical and procedural. It is readily apparent that behavioural science may have a role to play in devising procedural security arrangements. But it is less obvious to many that behavioural science can also be highly relevant to physical security. Karber and Mengel argue that the behavioural sciences provide a methodology by which physical security can be examined across many areas that impact upon its success or failure.[15] They claim that:

Combining systems analysis and behavioural approaches, one is able to examine physical security from the requirements definition phase through test and evaluation and implementation of a security system. The behavioural approach provides a methodology which is flexible enough to explore not only system vulnerabilities but also adversary resources and adversary motivations in terms of their inner relationships in a particular environment.[16]

Contributions to physical security can take a number of forms. For example, there may be behavioural input into the design of security devices and systems. A recent study prepared for the Intelligence and Security Directorate of the US Defence Nuclear Agency (DNA) provides a good example.[17] The study attempted to identify techniques that might be useful in DNA's Forced-Entry Deterrent System (FEDS) Program for psychologically deterring nuclear weapon theft by terrorists. FEDS is defined as 'a system composed of one or more of several optional security elements, each of which is specifically designed to impact upon the human senses for the purpose of impeding, delaying, diverting or dissuading unauthorised entry, and if gained, seriously impeding an attempt to escape and remain undetected'.[18] The FEDS Program is investigating how psychological/ behavioural principles may be incorporated into hardware design and security system development with a view to increasing the probability of aborting an attempted terrorist attack primarily by manipulating human sensory, perceptual, and cognitive processes.

The security philosophy inherent in the FEDS Program provides a good example of the manner in which behavioural science inputs may add flexibility to a security system. Fig. 3 is a conceptual diagram of a nuclear storage facility. It conceptualises a series or progression of barriers from the periphery inward to the target (for example, a nuclear device). The figure represents a progression in both time and space because each boundary functions as a delaying mechanism designed to gain time for the mobilisation of defences. The functions of the barriers reflect an increasingly drastic and aggressive defence response as the target is approached. The extra-perimeter and perimeter barrier performs mainly non-injurious surveillance and delaying functions. At the centre, the FEDS will act in a disabling or destructive manner if necessary. Between these two extremes, the level of destructiveness provided by the barriers would be governed by considerations of effectiveness in deterrence tactics. It is here that behavioural science research is useful in devising techniques to disrupt communication or degrade decision making in the terrorist group. (In many circumstances, it could be more effective to disrupt the overall effectiveness of intrusion operations than to inflict severe bodily injury.) The use of behaviourally based measures also allows a greater range of options in dealing effectively, yet discriminately, with a range of threats on a continuum from low-level to worst-case threats. Information from psychological experiments on the

Fig. 3. Conceptual diagram of a nuclear weapons storage site: 1, extra-perimeter area (clear zone); 2, perimeter barrier; 3, inner barrier; 4, inner barrier; 5, nuclear weapons storage unit(s); 6, nuclear devices.

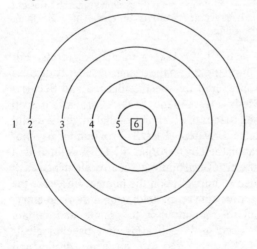

behavioural responses to noise, radiation, temperature, chemical agents, perceptual distortions, information overload and other factors provides a basis for the design and testing of a number of new and potentially useful security systems. As yet the effectiveness of behavioural factors in systems designed to deter a worst-case threat is not yet known. Research is, therefore, needed with the aim of: (1) developing mechanisms (devices) and techniques (procedures) subject to feasibility testing; (2) conducting controlled behavioural impact studies to determine the level of psychological deterrence achievable; and (3) conducting cost/effectiveness analyses.[19]

An example of a specific behavioural approach within this context is another DNA project which attempted to assess optimisation of Nuclear Weapons Storage Site (NWSS) security lighting through the application of established principles of psychological and behavioural functioning.[20] Specifically, the study examined factors involved in the design of security lighting systems which would achieve optimum conditions for intruder: (a) psychological deterrence, (b) visual detection and identification, and (c) visual incapacitation. The survey resulted in a number of highly specific recommendations concerning the design of security lighting systems as well as directions for further research and development.

A much overlooked contribution to the design of physical security systems comes from basic work in animal behaviour. Bailey and Bailey have described in some detail the dangers potentially posed by animals specially trained to circumvent security procedures and suggest that we need to engage in basic animal research in order both to produce and to counter novel ways of using animals to penetrate security systems.[21] Their report concludes that:

Animals are ubiquitous and generally not subject to close inspection. It doesn't take much imagination to see how an animal, particular a small bird such as a raven, or a small mammal such as a rat could be used to penetrate even a highly sophisticated security system . . . Programs studying animal sensory capabilities, locomotion and other attributes both physical and behavioural, should be supported whenever possible; especially applied research programs oriented toward practical applications. By knowing the capabilities of animals, understanding animal sensor mechanisms and how they may be compatible with man-made instrumentality, it will be possible to assess potential uses against our country and also to develop necessary counter-measures.[22]

In recent years there have in fact been some interesting instances of the application of basic animal research to practical security tasks. For example, drawing on experimental work with pigeons[23] Lubow has trained these birds to conduct surveillance tasks.[24] Other projects have trained animals to detect contaminants in water,[25] explosives,[26] and weapons.[27]

The development of physiological monitoring techniques for humans has also opened up some interesting security applications. Montor and Afdahl suggest that there is a direct relationship between human physiological factors and observed psychological performance.[28] They are developing techniques applying signal-processing techniques to neurological analysis which aim to determine physiological parameter differences between competent and incompetent security guards. If successfully developed, such techniques could be used to select and monitor the performance of guard personnel. Significant research is also being conducted in human factors laboratories which is designed to produce equipment and select personnel which improves the reliability and accuracy of security surveillance systems.[29] Other researchers are involved in analysing the psychological and physical deterrence effects of security arrangements.[30]

The area in which behavioural science has currently achieved a measure of acceptance is that of managing a crisis situation involving terrorists who have circumvented security measures and succeeded in attacking a target. Most crisis management teams already include such people as psychiatrists and psychologists. As was illustrated in the chapter on hostage negotiations, behavioural science advice has many practical uses in siege situations. However, behavioural science has a much wider potential contribution to make, particularly in the field of basic research into methods of threat evaluation and analysis of the effects of various responses on the actors in a terrorist situation. A number of systems are being developed as an aid to decision-making in a terrorist situation.[31] But there needs to be much more research conducted on the actual decision-making process. In particular we need more information on the effects of stress on crisis management teams and on the coping reactions which develop in response to stress. Some of this information is available from related fields[32] but behavioural scientists need to do much more to demonstrate its relevance to the decision-makers.

A number of random examples of relevant behavioural science research will serve to illustrate the wide range of potential applications in terrorist incident management.

1. Understanding the behaviour of terrorists and predicting their responses to situational changes is an important part of incident management. A programme in psycholinguistics developed by Dr Murray Miron of Syracuse University in collaboration with the Behavioural Sciences Unit of the FBI Academy is being applied to threat messages from hostage-takers to 'provide an understanding of those who use criminal coercion, as well as a rational management strategy for dealing with such a threat'.[33] By computer analyses of the written or spoken communications of terrorists the method shows great promise of revealing information about the origins, background, psychology, emotional state, and intentions of the terrorists.

2. In establishing rapport with a terrorist during hostage negotiations it is important to know how cultural differences affect relationships and

communication. Distance from the person, the use of intonation or gesture, and physical stance may all have different meanings for different cultures. Behavioural scientists are examining these differences and the information, when relayed to hostage negotiators will increase the probability of establishing a fruitful negotiating relationship with persons of different cultures.[34]

3. In large-scale terrorist emergencies where public panic is a danger, police may face a problem of how to communicate evacuation instructions in such a way as to minimise confusion and panic but maximise information value. Psychologists have recently been researching the science of preparing evacuation messages and many of the results are immediately applicable to terrorist situations.[35]

These three examples illustrate just some of the diverse areas that behavioural science may be applicable to. Since most problems of counter-terrorist operations are behavioural ones it is likely that the actual areas of applicability are limited only by the inability of many security officials to frame their problems in behavioural terms and of behavioural scientists to communicate the data they do possess in a form which is meaningful and practical to security officials.

The final broad area that behavioural science should impact upon is the aftermath of a terrorist incident. Particular emphasis should be placed on the victims, especially of hostage situations. First, it is necessary to provide the appropriate services to aid victims come to terms with their experience and help them return to normal life as soon as possible. Many victims are psychologically traumatised for long periods after the incident[36] and, in general, insufficient practical assistance or research is stimulated by their plight. Second, the debriefing of victims and the study of their coping reactions may add significantly to our ability to tailor rescue attempts to certain circumstances and to give advice and training to those who are at risk of becoming the victim of a terrorist-attack.

The foregoing survey of types of behavioural science research relevant to counter-terrorism reveals a vast reservoir of untapped knowledge. Much data already exists but needs to be translated into relevant language or applied from a different setting. Much data still needs to be collected, but the success of the exercise depends heavily upon asking the appropriate questions in behavioural terms. A note of warning is appropriate, however. The application of behavioural science is not a panacea. It will not provide all the answers. Further, if any of the research is to bear fruit there will have to exist a much closer appreciation and collaboration between the scientist and the practitioner than is often evident today. It will not be helpful to have academic solutions of no application to the real world, but neither in this complex area can society accept 'seat of the pants' decision making. What is necessary is a combination of common sense and experience integrated with applicable and realistic research data. The plea is twofold then. First, there needs to be a greater appreciation on the part of law enforcement and security experts and decision makers of the potential contributions of behavioural science. And, second, there must exist a greater appreciation on the part of behavioural scientists of the practical problems faced by security personnel.

15

The future of political terrorism

The analysis presented in this book has focussed upon identifying the nature of contemporary political terrorism and outlining some of the major policy choices involved in invoking a number of specific counter-terrorist measures. Many of these policy decisions will be made on an assessment of future directions in terrorism and the threats they will pose. Crystal-ball gazing in an attempt to forecast future actions is a pastime fraught with uncertainty and danger. A number of commentators have warned that *detailed* predictions are almost always inaccurate and it is also possible that those who predict events connected with violence may unconsciously underrate evidence which would lead to unexciting (that is, non-violent predictions). As Carlton has observed:

the least diverting prediction for the future of terrorism would be one that foresaw neither uncontrolled escalation nor deescalation after a dramatic reassertion of authority by sovereign states, but rather one that foresaw a continuing untidy pattern of incidents largely unrelated to one another and each of only transient significance to an increasingly unconcerned world.[1]

Bearing in mind these dangers we must ask ourselves how much value there is in trying to predict the future of terrorism. There are two reasons why such an enterprise should be attempted by as many analysts as possible. The security authorities will obviously be required to make such predictions and the danger is that they will be inaccurate in either of two extremes. On the one hand they may perceive no great change from the current situation when in fact significant, and threatening, changes are going to occur. In this case society may not be adequately prepared to meet the threat. On the other hand, and more likely given the inherently conservative nature of security decision-making, there may be a propensity to be overly pessimistic about the future. The great danger here is that based on pessimistic scenarios we will find ourselves sliding helplessly, and unnecessarily, into a repressive atmosphere which will engulf the entire functioning of society. To the extent that commentators outside the authority structure construct future scenarios for terrorism there will be more data available for the authorities to analyse which may help them reach realistic conclusions. Even if they choose to ignore such opinion it may inform the public so that they are able to evaluate the performance of governments and protest if policy seems to be heading towards either undesirable extreme.

In order to assess the future threat posed by terrorism we must return to the considerations addressed earlier in this book concerning the changes which have made terrorism a new force in analyses of world order. The main areas mentioned were transport and communications, weaponry, the effects on society of concentration of vital functions on a decreasing number of critical nodes, and changes in social structure and attitudes. It was concluded that developments in these areas have made terrorism a different and more sinister threat than it has been in the past. The question for the future is will these developments continue and will they magnify the threat which we already recognise is posed by terrorism?

In the area of transport and communications it is unlikely that we will see the sort of quantum leap in the foreseeable future which will increase the scope of terrorism in the way developments in the past two decades have done. Particularly in view of the energy crisis, airliners are unlikely to get much bigger (offering more sacrifices or hostages) or much faster (allowing better, more efficient operations). Although more locations may be accessible as communication routes expand the sorts of locations which are likely venues for terrorist spectaculars are already well served. However, better travel links will make it increasingly easy for terrorist groups to confer with their sponsors or with one another. As was discussed earlier, the democratisation of the means of travel together with the frequency of services and comprehensiveness of routes has given even relatively small and poor terrorist groups the opportunity to operate on a wider scale than in the past. However, it is conceivable that this trend will be slowed down now that travel costs have ceased their downward move and are rapidly escalating. This is particularly true of air travel, the mode of greatest relevance to terrorism. As air travel becomes more expensive we may again see decreasing access to it. This will not deter major terrorist groups, who have no financial problems, but it does reduce somewhat the probability of smaller, less obvious groups entering into the international picture.

The other important aspect of communications is the increasing scope and coverage of the news media. Particularly with the introduction of television in even the most remote and poor locations, more and more disadvantaged groups will come to be well acquainted with the tactics of terror and may well emulate them. Further, the greater access to remote locations possible for news crews makes it more likely that terrorist violence at hitherto unheard places will be widely publicised thus adding to the impression of widespread violence and danger. However, given the extent of news coverage which is already possible it seems unlikely that future developments will add significantly to the terrorist threat. Having escalated the threat by providing a medium (television) which gives instantaneous coverage to a terrorist spectacular we have reached a plateau which will not be exceeded by foreseeable changes.

It should be noted, too, that the revolution in communications has not been entirely in the terrorists' favour. Within any particular jurisdiction it is now possible to attain, store, and retrieve information about individuals on a scale only dreamt about in the past. And on a larger scale, the steadily expanding network of secure and rapid communications between countries allows information about terrorist movement and activity to be easily transferred between governments. On balance, then, it would appear that the threat caused by terrorism, having been made significantly greater by the transport and communications revolutions, is not likely to increase significantly in the immediate future because of future developments in these areas.

The same cannot be said, however, in the case of the development and availability of weapons. The rate of turnover of conventional weapons by the world's military forces has increased dramatically in the last two decades and many of these weapons are finding their way on to the open market. It is inevitable that in the future any group who is reasonably determined to do so will be able to purchase or steal powerful, conventional weapons. (Training to enable them to utilise them effectively is another matter. However, there already exist a number of elaborate training centres in such places as the Middle East and North Korea where terrorist groups from around the globe are taught to use modern weapons.) With the rate at which weapons now become obsolescent the arms which will find their way into the hands of a large number of terrorist groups will be very sophisticated by past standards (for example, precision guided munitions), capable of operation at a considerable distance from the target and with significantly increased destructive power.

To many people, the most frightening prospect for the future is that terrorist groups might gain access to and use weapons of mass destruction, specifically, nuclear, biological or biochemical weapons. Most attention to date has been directed to the possibility of some form of nuclear material falling into terrorist hands. There are a number of readily conceivable scenarios. One would involve the terrorist seizure of a nuclear facility with a subsequent demand that a government accede to certain claims under threat of having the facility sabotaged and releasing radioactive material over the surrounding countryside. The panic that followed the release of radioactive gases during the crisis at the Three Mile Island nuclear power plant in Pennsylvania in 1979 gives some indication of the potential impact of such a demand on a threatened population. The consequences for public order and for pressure on the government to take any steps (including complete acquiescence to the terrorists' demands) to avoid such an outcome are obvious. Given the level of security that has been shown to exist at some nuclear power plants in the past (although most countries have taken steps to improve security precautions in recent years) it is not inconceivable that a determined group of well-equipped and well-organised terrorists could assault and take over a nuclear facility.

Other scenarios involve the acquisition of a nuclear weapon by a terrorist group. A number of possibilities exist here. One is that a nuclear weapon state may supply a terrorist group with such a weapon. However, it is difficult to see a situation emerging in which the benefits accruing to a nuclear state would outweigh the potential costs or dangers of such a course of action. Theoretically more likely is the theft of a nuclear device from a military storage point. Although the security of nuclear weapons storage sites is generally excellent the danger exists that a determined commando-style raid on such a facility could succeed in capturing an intact nuclear device. The fact that a United States rocket could be smuggled out of West Germany, as occurred some years ago, indicates that subterfuge may also sometimes be successful. In addition, the proliferation of battlefield tactical nuclear weapons means that there are simply many more relatively portable nuclear devices to protect, with consequent difficulties for security.

Probably the most controversial possibility is that of terrorists being able to construct their own crude nuclear device. Experts differ as to the feasibility of such a project. Much of the data needed to design a nuclear bomb are freely available, as was documented by a highly publicised television science programme which in March 1975 featured a 20-year-old undergraduate from the Massachusetts Institute of Technology who designed a technically conceivable nuclear bomb.[2] But there is a vast difference between being able to design a bomb and being able to execute the design. The major difficulty would appear to be that of obtaining the necessary nuclear materials to make the device work. The theft of such material, either by hijacking or surreptitious removal over a long period of time is a possibility though. Given a combination of such material and knowledge of physics possessed by very many people, some experts consider that a credible nuclear device could be constructed. Willrich and Taylor argued that:

Under conceivable circumstances, a few persons, possibly even one person working alone, who possessed about ten kilograms of plutonium oxide and a substantial amount of chemical high explosive could, within several weeks, design and build a crude fission bomb. By a 'crude fission bomb' we mean one that would have an excellent chance of exploding, and would probably explode with the power of at least 100 tons of chemical high explosive. This could be done using materials and equipment that could be purchased at a hardware store and from commercial suppliers of scientific equipment for student laboratories.[3]

It would appear, then, that while some experts disagree about the ease with which a nuclear device can be constructed which could be successfully detonated, a sufficiently dedicated terrorist group could overcome the technical difficulties and construct a credible nuclear bomb. In all probability the capability already exists – and if not, it will soon do so. If this capability exists, then so too does the capability to fashion biological and biochemical weapons. In fact, most experts seem to agree that the latter pose less technical difficulties for a terrorist group. The question then arises, if the capability to use any of these weapons exists, why has no terrorist group tried to use them as a major bargaining tool?

There are a number of possible reasons. The first is that there are 'technical' problems in using, say, a nuclear device as a bargaining chip which are not only the technical problems of constructing the device. Jenkins has pointed out that there are problems over what demands could be made.[4] It would seem unlikely that any 'rational' terrorist group would 'waste' the potential leverage afforded by 'going nuclear' merely to effect the release of prisoners or demand a ransom. But if impossible demands are made it is unlikely that a government would accede (for example, dissolve itself) even under nuclear threat. The problem is one of the fulcrum of bargaining power. As Jenkins asks: 'How long can the threat be maintained? If the terrorists are unwilling to dismantle the threat by surrendering the device, governments are less likely to yield. If the terrorists surrender the device, how do they enforce their demands, particularly if these are for such things as changes in policy?'[5]

Probably a more important reason for the non-exploitation of weapons of mass destruction is that, to date, terrorist groups have operated under self-imposed political constraints. Although much popular writing on terrorism portrays terrorists as unscrupulous, insane, and having an insatiable lust for blood, this is far from the truth. Certainly, most recognised terrorist groups are neither nihilist nor composed entirely of psychotics whose only objective is killing people. On the whole, the major groups, particularly the nationalistic ones, have goals which can be articulated and may well be attainable in the long run. These groups are appealing to a constituency and are driven by goals which may be rationally explained even if the methods cause violent disagreement. The leaders of such groups are thus concerned with the relationship between ends and means. Jenkins reminds us that:

The capability of killing on a grand scale must be balanced against the fear of provoking widespread revulsion and alienating perceived constituents (a population which terrorists invariably overestimate), of provoking a massive, publicly approved government crackdown, of exposing the group itself to betrayal if terrorist group opinions on the political wisdom of mass murder are sharply divided. The groups most likely to have the resources, access to the requisite technical expertise, and the command and control structure necessary to undertake what for the terrorist groups is a large-scale operation are also those most likely to make such political calculations.[6]

To date, major terrorist groups have demonstrated what to some people would appear to be a paradoxical conservativeness in the methods of violence employed. During the past decade, terrorist acts have been repetitive and unimaginative, on the whole. As Carlton notes, 'they have shown but little ingenuity or enterprise in trying wholly novel methods of terroristic bargaining. On the contrary, one group has tried to imitate another in its techniques even to the smallest detail. In short, they have tended to behave as terrorists and guerrillas are supposed to behave in an urban or rural context.'[7] However, bearing in mind that killing is not usually the end in itself in terroristic violence and given the technical problems, both in constructing a weapon of mass destruction and in using it in such a manner that it is a successful bargaining tool, it should not surprise us that such weapons have not been employed to date. In essence, it seems that most terrorist groups do not see the killing of a few people (whether nominated 'enemies' or unlucky bystanders) as counterproductive, but have to date assessed the massacre of many people as being either out of proportion to their ends (for example, it is hard to see that the deaths of 5,000 people as opposed to five in a spectacular incident would generate more publicity given the total coverage which is now given to major terrorist incidents) or counter-productive to their cause (for example, provoking a publicly approved authoritarian crackdown and destroying what public support the terrorists may, in fact, have). If there is such a thing as an 'orthodox' terrorist, he or she is unlikely to be obsessed by killing large numbers of people. It could, therefore, be argued that there is no immediate likelihood of a change in terrorist tactics to embrace methods of mass destruction or mass disruption (the latter case including such things as destroying vital elements of the power grid, a communications network, an oil refinery, etc.).

On the whole, this assessment is probably correct. The question is, will this situation continue indefinitely? The answer would seem to be that the future is not so certain. Although it is easy to construct long and frightening lists of potential disruptive or destructive acts,[8] it is not so easy to see what advantage most terrorist groups could expect to gain by pursuing such tactics. There are, however, a number of reasons why the balance may be tipped in favour of more horrendous terrorist methods.

There can be little doubt, then, that it will soon be (if it is not already) possible to mount a credible terrorist threat involving nuclear, biological, or biochemical agents. The one factor which holds this eventuality in abeyance would appear to be a rational calculation concerning what would be achieved by such an act. It is generally conceded that terrorists make rational calculations and that these show the use of mass destruction weapons to be counter-productive. Will this be so in the future? A number of trends indicate that the answer may be a negative one. First, there is the emergence of groups without a national constituency. Broadly conceived organisations such as the Japanese Red Army whose vague goal is 'world revolution' do not have to make the calculations concerning the affections of an identified population which groups using terrorism as part of a national liberation campaign, for example, must make. As Russell, Banker, and Miller note:

Such a change could have a direct impact upon the nature and degree of terrorist violence, assuming that a constituency (real or imagined) acts as a moderating influence on the type, targets, and level of violence in terrorist operations. Put another way, if the terrorist feels a need to avoid alienating certain groups of people or sectors of society (the masses, 'the little man', the proletariat, the innocent victims of exploitation, and so forth), then this factor must enter his deliberations on target selection and the type of operation to be conducted.[9]

The trend away from terrorist groups having or attempting to attain broad bases of support appears to go hand-in-hand with a drift towards a nihilistic philosophy. It could be argued that in the past, terrorists, regardless of the carnage they may have caused, have been essentially conservative preferring to choose their targets relatively carefully and rely on trusted methods. But this no longer is always the case. There is evidence suggestive of motivation based on the 'thrills' of terrorism and destruction for destruction's sake.

A further factor is that such groups as have so far demonstrated a nihilistic strand in their thought have tended to be those that are small and/or facing the despair of being eliminated. Small groups may lack the patience which, whatever their apparent haste as advertised by their rhetoric and their brutality, characterises the major terrorist groups. Such haste, particularly when combined with the pressure generated by possible extinction, could well produce an inclination away from current conservatism toward more violent and destructive terrorist action. The only comforting thought here is that such groups, while having the motivation to perform a terrorist *Gotterdamerung* may be the least likely to have access to the means to do so.

Some commentators also perceive a reduction in the number of terrorist groups whose motivation is based on systematic ideological schools of thought. When a lack of a coherent ideological basis for terrorist action interacts with the despair of being overwhelmed, the lack of a perceived and relatively well-defined constituency, and the trend towards nihilism it is likely that constraints such as are self-imposed by most groups will cease to operate on a larger number of groups.

Finally, there is the problem of public familiarity with violence and destruction. To quote Russell *et al.* again:

Accidental catastrophes, coupled with the continued increase of criminal violence within our society, would appear to be reducing the impact of calculated terrorism upon the spectators. Assuming familiarity breeds contempt, repetition conditions, and a degree of one-upmanship exists between and among terrorist groups, they then, it would seem, have two basic alternatives. They can lower the threshhold of violence and redirect their operations at those aspects of society upon which the entire populace depends – utilities, energy, food and water, transportation, communications, monetary and financial systems, and similar essential services. Or, conversely, they may attempt to increase the number and range of casualties (human targets) by mustering greater resources and proceed to mass destruction.[10]

When these trends are taken together they would seem to increase the probability of a terrorist group threatening to use a weapon of mass destruction. It is a possibility that cannot be ignored. While there is no present evidence of groups planning such acts, the indications are that the inhibitions which in the past have prevented them will slowly be weakened over the next few years.

In all probability these changes will be evolutionary rather than planned, and will represent the culmination of a series of incremental changes in the factors considered above. It seems likely that terrorism will be a more serious problem towards the end of the century than it is currently. This is so for a number of reasons.

First, the present author believes that the incremental changes in the nature of terrorism and terrorist organisations will eventually lead some group to attempt mass destruction terrorism. The real danger lies not in this first event, but in the probability that once this inhibition has gone terrorism of this kind will be much more likely to be attempted more frequently. Paradoxically, the successful development of hostage negotiation techniques may also contribute to recourse to more extreme situations.

Second, the changes in political socialisation which have occurred worldwide over the past few decades, together with the easier access to powerful weapons, indicate to us that terrorism may become to be seen by a wider range of groups as an acceptable way to stop governments operating in ways that group members see as inimical to their interests. Russell *et al.* capture this possibility when they remind us that

Many issues and conflicts . . . today have the potential for developing opposing views so resolutely held that terrorism appears a thinkable tactic in their furtherance. These include such areas as energy and its nuclear sector, the environment, ethnic conflicts and minority rights, labour disputes, inflation, and various types of shortages, to name a few. Again, consistent with the activist bent away from absolute rights and wrongs, the decision to engage in terrorism becomes one of weighing relative values. Is it more acceptable to endure the foreseen destruction of the ecological balance, for example, than to terrorise one segment of society in order to draw attention to a more costly possibility (morally and possibly financially)? In short, will ends that are essentially apolitical justify violent means?[11]

Thus, as well as the possibility of a slow slide towards mass destruction terrorism, we are also faced with the possibility (we would argue, the *probability*) that terrorism such as that which is currently experienced will be practised by a wider range of groups during (probably) short campaigns over specific and limited issues. As well, the longer term campaigns of such nationalist groups as the IRA, ETA, and PLO will continue until they either succeed or are suppressed.

As well as developments in terrorism itself, the preceding chapters indicate that some responses to terrorism also have important implications which need to be analysed. As well as the potential changes in such areas as army/police relations, the authority given to intelligence agencies, control of the media, and so forth, discussed in the foregoing chapters, terrorism will have other significant impacts on society in the next two decades. Most of these consequences flow from attempts to stem terrorist violence. One disturbing development, for example, has been the recent emergence of private counter-terrorist strike forces. The dimensions of this new field of private security operations have been documented by Nathan who reports that:

Approximately 40 counter-terrorist firms offer an impressive panoply of services. Some provide protection through chauffeur training and electronic perimeter defences. Firms may also supply information on specific terrorists and even negotiate with terrorists for the release of kidnapped company personnel. In addition, counter-terrorist businesses may assume a more aggressive role – assisting in the identification of terrorists, engaging in paramilitary operations to release kidnap victims, and ferreting out terrorists in pre-emptive missions.[12]

Few would object to private security firms offering courses in evasive driving techniques, advising on physical and procedural security, and providing guards. But it is a potentially dangerous organisation which sets itself up as a private intelligence service or counter-terrorist para-military force. Governments will have to act to regulate the collection, storage, and dissemination of information held about individuals. More importantly they will have to legislate to prohibit private organisations from subverting the legitimate police authorities by negotiating with terrorists directly and from usurping the State's role as the sole possessor of military power. The implications for foreign relations of a private military force violating national sovereignty and committing a belligerent act to rescue hostages, for example, could be unpredictable and damaging to the fabric of international relations. One instance of such an operation has already occurred. In 1978, a Texas industrialist, H. Ross Perot, backed a private commando raid on an Iranian prison which successfully released two of his employees. Perot's explanation to Richard Shenkman of the *Washington Post* was that:

The government wouldn't do anything for us . . . The State Department wasn't really interested . . . Protecting American citizens is a role that our government should perform. Private companies, private individuals shouldn't be involved in this sort of thing. But if your government is not willing to protect American citizens, and if you have people in your company imprisoned in a country, you have an obligation to get them out of there.

This example should serve notice of two important concerns. First, that because of the potential danger of private military or para-military operations, particularly on foreign territory, governments need to take steps to regulate the activities of private security firms. Second, Perot's justification for his actions rested upon the alleged lack of concern and action evidenced by his government (in this case the United States Government). This illustrates either that the government has not been successful in 'selling' its policy on handling such situations to its people or that it, indeed, is showing less concern than it might for the plight of its citizens in trouble. In either case it is an indication that government action is needed. Such action should involve either a re-appraisal of the adequacy of attempts made to assist its citizens or consideration of ways in which it might be possible to convince the populace of the 'rightness' of its stand on dealing with such issues. Any changes resulting from these considerations will not eliminate the desire for independent action against terrorism, but handled properly they should reduce the incidence of such action. In conjunction with legal controls on private operations these measures should make it very much less likely that private anti-terrorist strikes would be mounted and be successful.

Some other possible avenues for dealing with terrorism would, if pursued, have more direct impacts on the lives of the average citizen. If it is considered likely that terrorists will resort to mass destructive or mass disruptive acts (probably as a result of such an act having occurred for the first time) there will be pressure to increase security at vital points (power stations, computer centres, refineries, storage depots, etc.) to unprecedented levels. Such security would have to be very sophisticated to be effective and, being both sophisticated and applied to a large number of locales, would be extremely expensive. Obviously these costs would have to be borne eventually by the consumer, and the costs could be very significant ones. The pursuance of such security would also raise the level of fear in the community as the impression of being under siege would inevitably be intensified. Such fear would obviously motivate some people to change their lifestyles to avoid what they see as dangers and overall the quality of life would be adversely effected.

Accompanying a change to a security-conscious environment would almost certainly be changes to the law which would curtail some civil liberties. The threat of nuclear terrorism, in particular, could lead to the invoking of stringent restrictions and increase of police powers. These and other adverse effects of a climate of fear engendered by terrorism could lead to what Greisman has termed the 'closure of society'.[13] As Greisman also points out it is especially necessary that we be able to adequately judge the real threat posed by terrorism, because:

The fear of terrorism can prompt the closure of society as readily as an actual terrorist presence. Hence the mere threat of terrorism can trigger responses with wide ramifications. This threat can be used by terrorists, or by governments that wish to usurp democratic processes by frightening the electorate into accepting the 'protection' of a dictatorship.[14]

In Part One of this book other trends which have contributed to the rise of terrorism as an important threat to modern life were discussed. The centralisation of decision-making and consequent alienation of the people, the decreasing number of critical nodes (computers, power grids, airports, etc.) around which modern industrial societies function, the increasing levels of education and consequent rising, but unfulfilled expectations, and the decay of traditional controls and loyalties are just some of the major features of contemporary life. They are features which will tend to be exaggerated even further in the future and can only function to increase the conditions conducive to terrorism.

If the future seems gloomy, what measures are likely to be invoked to deal with terrorism? The great liberal hope is that the objective causes of terrorism will be attacked. Thus the focus might be on the redistribution of power and wealth, the provision of adequate social services and the settlement of just claims for ethnic, religious, and social rights, for example. These are all goals which should be pursued with vigour and the reduction of terrorism is only a relatively unimportant reason why we should do so. However, the reality is that these goals will not be achieved, probably ever and certainly not quickly enough to suit those who are disadvantaged by the fact that they are not attained. Carlton[15] points to the example of the Palestinian problem as a thorny issue whose apparent resolution would not necessarily reduce terrorism in that region. He suggests that the peaceful creation of a Palestinian state may produce more, not less, terrorism. For example, some Israelis may consider their own government traitorous for acceding to such a move and begin a terrorist campaign to reverse the decision. Some Palestinians may be similarly outraged by a settlement which gave them less than 'justice' demands. Such a group, smaller and more desperate than their forerunners, may adopt even more extreme terrorist tactics to further their cause. This and other examples allow us to: 'conclude, therefore, that it is impossible for states, particularly in the postcolonial era, to pursue policies that will, except in rare instances, remove many of the conditions and the grievances, real or imagined, that motivate terrorists.'[16]

The most obvious response to this conclusion is to introduce repressive counter-measures. Intrusive surveillance, increased powers for the police, a greater involvement of the armed forces in internal security, restrictions on the news media are some of the most widely discussed options which have been analysed in previous chapters. The grave danger in these measures, particularly when combined, is that they may destroy the very society we are attempting to defend. We are, however, in a position to consider at least some alternatives. First, although it has been claimed that we cannot eliminate terrorism by attacking injustice it is likely that there is a large amount of what Gordon Rattray Taylor calls 'avoidable terrorism'[17] which might be reduced in this way. Second there are a number of ways of attempting to affect the terrorist situation which do not require repressive measures. These options have largely been the topic of Part Two of this book and include voluntary restraint by the news media, carefully controlled and defined military aid to the civil power, bilateral and international anti-terrorist treaties, properly directed intelligence activities, and high-quality research efforts directed towards devising and refining such techniques as hostage negotiation procedures.

There simply is no way that the reader can be left with simple options. The future looks bleak as far as forms of political violence in general, and terrorism as a specific technique, are concerned. Many of the factors that have led to the elevation of terrorism as a serious threat to open societies will be exacerbated in the future. To fail to respond firmly to the threat would be to give up a cherished way of life without fighting for it. But in many ways we are our own worst enemies. It is all too easy to over-estimate the threat and over-react. That too would destroy our type of society which, deficient though it is in many respects, is better than other contemporary systems. We must tread a careful and reasonable path. It is hoped that the considerations outlined in the previous chapters may contribute towards an understanding of the sorts of policies which might allow us to do so.

Notes to the text

PART ONE. AN INTRODUCTION TO POLITICAL TERRORISM

1 The problem of defining terrorism

1 P.L. Berger and T. Luckman, *The Social Construction of Reality* (Harmondsworth: Penguin, 1971).
2 H.C. Greisman, 'Social meanings of terrorism: Reification, violence, and social control', *Contemporary Crises*, 1977, *1*, 304.
3 K. Burke, *A Rhetoric of Motives* (Berkley: University of California Press, 1969), 19–23.
4 Greisman, 306–7.
5 J. Fletcher, *International terrorism: The nature of the problem.* Keynote address to the Sixth National Symposium on the Forensic Sciences, Adelaide, South Australia, March 1979.
6 P. Wilkinson, *Terrorism and the Liberal State* (London: Macmillan, 1977).
7 T.P. Thornton, 'Terror as a weapon of political agitation' in H. Eckstein (ed.), *Internal War* (London: Collier-Macmillan, 1964), 73.
8 *Ibid.*, 74.
9 *Ibid.*, 77.
10 *Ibid.*, 72.
11 W.F. May, 'Terrorism as strategy and ecstasy', *Social Research,* 1974, *41,* 277–98.
12 *Ibid.*, 277.
13 A.J.R. Groom, 'Coming to terms with terrorism', *British Journal of International Studies*, 1978, *4*, 62.
14 E.V. Walter, *Terror and Resistance: A Study of Political Violence with Case Studies of Some Primitive African Communities* (New York: Oxford University Press, 1969).
15 *Ibid.*, 5.
16 *Ibid.*, 341–2.
17 *Ibid.*, 342–3.
18 Some examples are F.J. Hacker, *Crusaders, Criminals, Crazies* (New York: W.W. Norton, 1976). E.F. Mickolus, 'Statistical approaches to the study of terrorism', in Y. Alexander and S.M. Finger (eds.), *Terrorism: Interdisciplinary Perspectives* (New York: John Jay Press, 1977) 209–69. A. Merari, 'A classification of terrorist groups', *Terrorism: An International Journal*, 1978, *1*, 331–46.
19 P. Wilkinson, *Political Terrorism* (London: Macmillan, 1974). An interesting attempt to refine Wilkinson's typology and to select a set of variables that may

be operationalised may be found in R. Shultz, 'Conceptualizing political terrorism: A typology', *Journal of International Affairs*, 1978, *32*, 7–15. Nevertheless, for expository purposes Wilkinson's outline provides the clearest scheme for analysis.
20 Walter, 14.
21 Wilkinson, *Political Terrorism*, 17.
22 M.C. Hutchinson, 'The concept of revolutionary terrorism', *Journal of Conflict Resolution*, 1973, *6*, 384.
23 Wilkinson, *Political Terrorism*, 17–18.
24 *Ibid.*, 36.
25 See, for example, N. Smelser, *Theory of Collective Behaviour* (London: Routledge and Kegan Paul, 1962).
26 See, for example, E. Fromm, *The Fear of Freedom* (London: Routledge and Kegan Paul, 1942).
27 Hutchinson, 385.
28 Wilkinson, *Political Terrorism*, 38.
29 *Ibid.*, 38.
30 *Ibid.*, 40.
31 Walter, 341.
32 A. Parry, *Terrorism from Robespierre to Arafat* (New York: Vanguard Press, 1976), 59.
33 *Ibid.*, 57.
34 D. Greer, *The Incidence of Terror During the French Revolution* (Cambridge, Mass.: Harvard University Press, 1935).
35 D. Fromkin, 'The strategy of terrorism', *Foreign Affairs*, 1975, *53*, 684.
36 P. Wilkinson, *Terrorism and the Liberal State*, 49.
37 B.M. Jenkins, 'International terrorism: a new mode of conflict' in D. Carlton and C. Schaerf (eds.), *International Terrorism and World Security* (London: Croom Helm, 1975), 13–49.

2 Terrorism: a historical perspective

1 *Dictionnaire, Supplement* (Paris, an VII, 1798), 775.
2 W. Laqueur, *Terrorism* (Boston: Little, Brown, 1977), 6.
3 N. Morozov, *Terroristicheskaya Borba* (London, 1880).
4 Laqueur, 38.
5 *Ibid.*, 41.
6 G. Woodcock, *Anarchism: A History of Libertarian Ideas and Movements* (Harmondsworth: Penguin, 1962).
7 D. Stafford, *From Anarchism to Reformism. A Study of the Political Activities of Paul Brousse 1870–1890* (London, 1971 – cited by Laqueur, 239, fn. 86).
8 Laqueur, 50.
9 *Ibid.*, 14.
10 Z. Iviansky, 'Individual terror: concept and typology', *Journal of Contemporary History*, 1977, *12*, 52.
11 Cited by Iviansky.
12 Cited by Iviansky.
13 L.S. Feuer (ed.), *Marx and Engels: Basic Writings on Politics and Philosophy* (London: Fontana, 1969), 37.
14 E.S. Beesly, 'The capitalist as ruler', *The Positivist Review*, 1894, *14*, 44.
15 Feuer, 39.

3 The changing nature of terrorism

1 R. Kupperman, *Facing Tomorrow's Terrorist Incident Today* (Washington, DC: US Department of Justice, Law Enforcement Assistance Administration, 1977), 1.

2 B.M. Jenkins, 'International terrorism: A new mode of conflict' in D. Carlton and C. Schaerf (eds.), *International Terrorism and World Security* (London: Croom Helm, 1975), 28.

3 B.M. Jenkins, 'International terrorism: A balance sheet', *Survival*, 1975, *17*, 158.

4 B.M. Jenkins, *High Technology Terrorism and Surrogate War: The Impact of New Technology on Low-Level Violence.* The RAND Paper Series, No. P-5339. January 1975, 17.

5 A.J.R. Groom, 'Coming to terms with terrorism', *British Journal of International Studies*, 1978, *4*, 65.

6 Groom, *ibid.*, 65, defines 'structural violence' as existing when 'an actor is denied the possibility of fulfilling, or even knowledge of, roles and opportunities due to structural factors. . . . Such taboos are as effective as if they were dependent on violence for their maintenance, hence the term "structural violence". When challenged, as by Catholics in Northern Ireland, structural violence can give rise to overt violence.' The term is also used by other authors to refer to the concrete ill-effects of social organisation. Thus capitalism is claimed to perpetrate massive structural violence because 'In asbestos mines, in coal mines, and in factories, workers die because profit-conscious managers skimp on safety equipment to pare costs and boost profits. A system which requires mass consumption in order to maintain production also demands that advertising mould public taste and increase mass demand for products (e.g. tobacco, compound analgesics) widely recognised as major causes of illness and premature death. The state, which could legislate to prevent or at least minimize these sources of injury, does not do so' – and thereby perpetrates structural violence. A. Mack, 'Terrorism and the Left', *Arena*, 1978, No. 51, 19.

7 'Relative deprivation' is defined as 'actors' perceptions of discrepancy between their value expectations and their value capabilities. Value expectations are the goods and conditions of life to which people believe they are rightfully entitled. Value capabilities are the goods they think they are capable of getting and keeping . . . The emphasis of the hypothesis is on the perception of deprivation; people may be subjectively deprived with reference to their expectations even though an objective observer might not judge them to be in want. Similarly, the existence of what the observer judges to be abject poverty or "absolute deprivation" is not necessarily thought to be unjust or irremediable by those who experience it.' T.R. Gurr, *Why Men Rebel* (Princeton, NJ: Princeton University Press, 1970), 24.

8 Groom, 65.

9 W. Laqueur, *Terrorism* (Boston: Little, Brown, 1977), 132.

10 For example, Laqueur, *ibid.*, 116; Jenkins, *High Technology Terrorism and Surrogate War.*

11 See, for example, A.S. Redlick, 'The transnational flow of information as a cause of terrorism' in Y. Alexander, D. Carlton, and P. Wilkinson (eds.), *Terrorism: Theory and Practice* (Boulder, Colorado: Westview Press, 1979), 73–95.

12 *Ibid.*, 84–5.

13 Z. Iviansky, 'Individual terror: Concept and typology', *Journal of Contemporary History*, 1977, *12*, 53.
14 By using the term 'stability' we enter again the marshy grounds of semantics. I do not intend to equate stability with the status quo. It seems to me that there is indeed much that is seriously, if not terminally, wrong with many contemporary societies. It may well be that violence in one form or another will be necessary to right the wrongs inherent in such social structures. That is a question of ethics (as well as tactics). However, there are also situations in which groups advocate the use of terrorism to effect changes which are clearly not supported by the majority (or in the weaker case, are not clearly supported by the majority). In such cases, resort to terrorism to try to effect changes is, in my view, both unethical and dangerous. It is a challenge to stability. It is in our interests to understand the nature of terrorism in order to counter such a challenge. It could, of course, be argued that such knowledge can be as effectively applied to situations in which we might agree that terrorism has at least an arguable ethical foundation. However, I believe that different historical and structural forces are at work here that negate this proposition.

4 The purpose of terrorism

1 T.P. Thornton, 'Terror as a weapon of political agitation' in H. Eckstein (ed.), *Internal War* (London: Collier-Macmillan, 1964), 74.
2 *Ibid.*, 83.
3 *Ibid.*, 84.
4 I. Janis, *Air War and Emotional Stress* (New York: McGraw-Hill, 1951). For example, Janis reports (on p. 23) 'From clinical observations in the European war, it appears that experiencing a narrow escape from danger often has the effect of temporarily shattering the individual's psychological defenses – defenses which had formerly prevented the outbreak of anxiety in the face of environmental threats by maintaining feelings of personal invulnerability.'
5 The evidence comes from studies of concentration camp prisoners, for example, B. Bettelheim, *The Informed Heart* (New York: Free Press, 1960); H.O. Bluhm, 'How did they survive? Mechanisms of defense in Nazi concentration camps' in B. Rosenberg *et al.*, *Mass Society in Crisis* (New York: Macmillan, 1964).
6 M.C. Hutchinson, 'The concept of revolutionary terrorism', *Journal of Conflict Resolution*, 1973, *6*, 388.
7 P.E. Vernon, 'Psychological effects of air raids', *Journal of Abnormal and Social Psychology*, 1941, *36*, 457–76.
8 M. Schmideberg, 'Some observations on individual reactions to air raids', *International Journal of Psychoanalysis*, 1942, *23*, 146–76.
9 Hutchinson, 389.
10 *Ibid.*, 389.
11 Janis, 126–9.
12 T.R. Gurr, *Why Men Rebel* (Princeton, NJ: Princeton University Press, 1970), 213.
13 N. Leites and C. Wolf, *Rebellion and Authority* (Chicago: Markham, 1970) 10.
14 Thornton, 82.
15 Carlos Marighela, *Minimanual of the Urban Guerrilla* (Harmondsworth: Penguin, 1971) 95.

16 B.M. Jenkins, 'International terrorism: A new mode of conflict' in D. Carlton and C. Schaerf (eds.), *International Terrorism and World Security* (London: Croom Helm, 1975), 17.

17 P. Wilkinson, *Terrorism and the Liberal State* (London: Macmillan, 1977), 50–1.

18 A.J.R. Groom, 'Coming to terms with terrorism', *British Journal of International Studies*, 1978, *4*, 67.

19 F. Fanon, *The Wretched of the Earth* (Harmondsworth: Penguin, 1967) 67.

20 W. Laqueur, *Terrorism* (Boston: Little, Brown, 1977), 125.

21 J.P. Sartre, *Critique de la Raison Dialectique* (Paris: Gallimard, 1960).

22 Of course, Sartre is not alone in emphasising the presumed cathartic and cleansing nature of violence. The leader of the 1916 Easter Rising in Dublin, Patrick Pearse had written: 'Bloodshed is a cleansing and sanctifying thing, and the nation that regards it as the final horror has lost its manhood.' (Quoted in Laqueur, 206). The French novelist Andre Gide emphasised the importance of the *acte gratuit* in attaining authenticity, and in *Les Caves du' Vatican* (Paris: Gallimard, 1922) discusses violence, in this case murder, as a liberating gratuitous act.

23 The distinction between Marxism and aspects of Sartre's existentialism is very important because of Sartre's often ambiguous relationship with Marxism. Although he has criticised Marxism (see, for example, *Critique de la Raison Dialectique*, 30–1) he often seems to draw very close to it in many respects. Perhaps the best explanation that can be offered for this ambiguity is given by Jacques Salvan who writes:

> His view seems to be that Marxism raised the questions most relevant to the general situation of our modern society. Even though they were formulated according to a faulty method of knowledge and solved in the wrong way, so long as these questions are not practically solved Marxism will remain a most living force.

J. Salvan, *To Be and Not To Be: An Analysis of Jean-Paul Sartre's Ontology* (Detroit: Wayne State University Press, 1962) 148–9.

24 Current Soviet thinking also expresses considerable suspicion about the use of terrorism as is illustrated by the quotation below:

> Marxism-Leninism rejects individual terror as a method of revolutionary action since it weakens the revolutionary movement by diverting the working people away from the mass struggle. "The first and chief lesson," V.I. Lenin wrote, "is that only the revolutionary struggle of the masses is capable of achieving any serious improvements in the life of the workers . . ." International terrorism is radically different from the revolutionary movement of the people's masses, whose aim is to effect fundamental changes in society and which alone is capable of so doing. The terrorist act, however, even if its main point is to awaken public opinion and force it to pay attention to a particular political situation, can only have limited political consequences: say, lead to the release of a group of prisoners, increase the financial assets of an organisation.

V. Terekhov, 'International terrorism and the struggle against it', *Novoye Vremya*, March 15, 1974, 20–2. Of course, such a view does not prevent the Soviet Union and its proxies from supporting some terrorist movements because their destabilising effects may be useful to Soviet foreign policy.

25 Fanon, 74.

26 Hutchinson, 393.

27 A. Ouzegane, *Le Meilleur Combat* (Paris: Julliard, 1962) 257.

28 *Ibid.*, 261.

29 Evidence that terrorists do quite deliberately make such calculations is given by Eckstein. Based on an interview with M. Chanderli, FLN Observer to the United Nations, December 1961, he reports that 'calculations about popular loyalties normally play a role in the decision to resort to political violence. The calculations may be mistaken but they are almost always made, sometimes as in the case of the Algerian nationalist struggle, in ways approaching the survey research of social science.' H. Eckstein, 'On the etiology of internal wars', *History and Theory: Studies in the Philosophy of History*, 1965, *4*, 159.

5 The development of terrorism as a strategy

1 B.M. Jenkins, *High Technology Terrorism and Surrogate War: The Impact of New Technology on Low-Level Violence*. The RAND Paper Series, No. P5339, January 1975, 4.
2 F. Fanon, *The Wretched of the Earth* (Harmondsworth: Penguin, 1967), 48.
3 Jenkins, *High Technology Terrorism and Surrogate War*, 7.
4 Jenkins, *ibid.*, 8.
5 Quoted in P. Paret, *French Revolutionary Warfare from Indochina to Algeria* (New York: Praeger, 1964) 16.
6 Mao Tse-tung, *Selected Works of Mao Tse-tung*, vol. II (Peking: Foreign Languages Press, 1967) 113–83.
7 *Ibid.*, 136–7.
8 R. Shultz, 'The limits of terrorism in insurgency warfare: the case of the Viet Cong', *Polity*, 1978, *11*, 75.
9 Mao Tse-tung, *Selected Works of Mao Tse-tung*, vol. I (Peking: Foreign Languages Press, 1967) 29.
10 R. Stetler (ed.), *The Military Art of People's War: Selected Writings of General Vo Nguyen Giap* (New York: Monthly Review, 1970) 213.
11 C. Guevara, *Guerrilla Warfare* (Harmondsworth: Penguin, 1969) 26.
12 *Ibid.*, 26.
13 R. Debray, *Revolution in the Revolution* (New York: Grove Press, 1967) 74.
14 C. Marighela, *Minimanual of the Urban Guerrilla*, (Harmondsworth: Penguin, 1971).
15 *Ibid.*
16 P. Paret and J. Shy, *Guerrillas in the 1960's* (New York: Praeger, 1962) 35.
17 P. Paret and J. Shy, 'Guerrilla warfare and U.S. military policy: a study', in T.N. Green (ed.), *The Guerrilla – And How to Fight Him* (New York: Praeger, 1965) 44. See also J. Paget, *Counter-Insurgency Campaigning* (London: Faber, 1967) 43–81.
18 R. Shultz, 'A study of the selective use of political terrorism in the process of revolutionary warfare (The NLF of South Vietnam)', *International Behavioural Scientist*, 1976, *8*, 60.
19 *Ibid.* Shultz's work is of some particular interest because his conclusions run counter to those of all major advice given to the US Government during the Vietnam War. Official opinion held that NLF successes were attributable to the indiscriminate and primary use of terrorism. Shultz, on the other hand, using data from 2400 interviews with NLF and North Vietnamese prisoners and defectors and South Vietnamese who had contact with the NLF, supplemented by captured enemy documents and other secondary sources, reaches a quite different conclusion. He makes a most convincing case that the NLF closely

adhered to the theoretical propositions of revolutionary warfare theory and used political terrorism as a controlled, ancillary weapon. See also Shultz's, 'The limits of terrorism in insurgency warfare'.

20 See, for example, C.A. Russell, L.J. Banker, and B.H. Miller, 'Out-inventing the terrorist' in Y. Alexander, D. Carlton, and P. Wilkinson (eds.), *Terrorism: Theory and Practice* (Boulder, Colorado: Westview Press, 1979) 3–42.

6 Trends in terrorism

1 Ambassador Anthony C.E. Quainton, 'Terrorism: Do Something! But What?' *Department of State Bulletin*, 1979, September, 60.
2 CIA Report Adds Thousands of Incidents to Statistics on International Terrorism. *Washington Post*, 16 June 1981, 10.
3 See, for example, *Chronology 1968–1974* (Santa Monica: Rand Corporation, Rand Paper Series R-1597-DOS/ARPA, March 1975).
4 B.M. Jenkins, 'International terrorism: Trends and potentialities', *Journal of International Affairs*, 1978, *32*, 114–23.
5 *Ibid.*, 118.
6 C.A. Russell, L.J. Banker, and B.H. Miller, 'Out-inventing the terrorist' in Y. Alexander, D. Carlton, and P. Wilkinson (eds.), *Terrorism: Theory and Practice* (Boulder, Colorado: Westview Press, 1979), 19.
7 W. Laqueur, *Terrorism* (Boston: Little, Brown, 1977), 128.
8 W.F. May, 'Terrorism as strategy and ecstasy', *Social Research,* 1974, *41*, 277–98.
9 *Ibid.*, 292.
10 See, for example, Laqueur, 112–15.
11 Claire Sterling, *The Terror Network* (New York: Holt, Rinehart and Winston/ Reader's Digest Press, 1981).
12 Brian Jenkins, 'World terrorism – the truth and nothing but the truth?' *Manchester Guardian Weekly*, 24 May 1981.
13 Barry Rubin, 'Some errors on terror', *Washington Quarterly*, 1981, Summer, 166.
14 Central Intelligence Agency, *Patterns of International Terrorism: 1980* (Washington, DC, 1981).
15 Lt. Col. W.J. Breede III, 'Book Review: The Terror Network, by Claire Sterling', *Marine Corps Gazette*, 1981, August, 63.
16 B.M. Jenkins, 'International terrorism: A new mode of conflict' in D. Carlton and C. Schaerf (eds.), *International Terrorism and World Security* (London: Croom Helm, 1975), 13–49.
17 *Ibid.*, 31.
18 Jenkins, 'International terrorism: Trends and potentialities', 120.

7 The effects of terrorism

1 W.M. Landes, 'An economic study of US aircraft hijacking, 1961–1976', *Journal of Law and Economics*, 1978, *21*, 1–31.
2 B.M. Jenkins, 'International terrorism: Trends and potentialities', *Journal of International Affairs*, 1978, *32*, 122.
3 Which will be discussed in more detail in Chapter 11.
4 Source: P. Hain (ed.), *Policing the Police*, vol. 1 (London: John Calder, 1979).

5 Great Britain. Home Office. Statistical Bulletin 10/80 (22 July 1980). *Statistics on the Prevention of Terrorism (Temporary Provisions) Acts 1974 and 1976 – Second Quarter 1980.*

PART TWO. SOME SELECTED PROBLEMS IN THE RESPONSE TO TERRORISM

8 Counter-terrorist policies: fundamental choices

1 L.R. Beres, 'Terrorism and international security: The nuclear threat', *Chitty's Law Journal*, 1978, *26*(3), 90.
2 P. Wilkinson, *Terrorism and the Liberal State* (London: Macmillan, 1977) 121.
3 F.J. Hacker, *Crusaders, Criminals, Crazies: Terror and Terrorism in Our Time* (New York: W.W. Norton and Co., 1976).
4 Wilkinson, 124.
5 See *Final Report of the Select Committee to Study Governmental Operations with Respect to Intelligence Activities* (the 'Church Report') Report No. 94-755 (Washington, DC: US Government Printing Office, 1976).
6 See discussion of this issue in *Royal Commission on Intelligence and Security. Fourth Report* (vol. 1) (The 'Hope Report') (Canberra: Australian Government Publishing Service, 1977).
7 Wilkinson, 129.
8 A more detailed examination of the ERP and its successes may be found in R. Clutterbuck, *Living With Terrorism* (London: Faber and Faber, 1975).
9 For an analysis of sources of terrorist finance and the uses to which the money is put see C. Dobson and R. Payne, *The Weapons of Terror: International Terrorism at Work* (London: Macmillan, 1979).
10 B. Jenkins, J. Johnson, and D. Ronfeldt, 'Numbered lives: Some statistical observations from 77 international hostage episodes', *Conflict. An International Journal for Conflict and Policy Studies*, 1978, *1*(1/2), 71–111.
11 *Ibid.*, 99.
12 D.B. Bobrow, 'Preparing for unwanted events: Instances of international political terrorism,' *Terrorism: An International Journal*, 1978, *1*, 397–422.

9 Terrorism and the media: a symbiotic relationship?

1 H.H.A. Cooper, 'Terrorism and the media' in Y. Alexander and S.M. Finger (eds.), *Terrorism: Interdisciplinary Perspectives* (New York: John Jay Press, 1977) 143.
2 J. Bowyer, Bell. 'Terrorist scripts and live-action spectaculars', *Columbia Journalism Review*, 1978, *17*(1), 50.
3 There is a growing criminological literature which suggests that sensationalistic media coverage of crime *causes* more crimes by inspiring modelling and imitation. See, for example, D. Phillips, 'Suicide, motor vehicle fatalities, and the mass media: Evidence toward a theory of suggestion', *American Journal of Sociology*, 1979, *34*, 1150–74; D. Phillips, 'Airplane Accident Fatalities Increase Just After Newspaper Stories About Murder and Suicide', *Science*, 1978, *201*, 748–50; L. Lenke, 'Criminal policy and public opinion towards crimes of violence' in *Collected Studies in Criminological Research*, vol. XI (Strasbourg: Council of Europe, 1974); L. Berkowitz and J. Macaulay, 'The Contagion of Criminal Violence', *Sociometry*, 1971, *34*, 238–60.

4 C. Rootes, 'Living with terrorism', *Social Alternatives*, 1980, *1* (6/7), 46–9.
5 C. Fenyvesi, remarks quoted in *The Media and Terrorism*, proceedings of a seminar sponsored by the Chicago Sun-Times and the Chicago Daily News (Spring 1977).
6 S.D. Gladis, 'The hostage/terrorist situation and the media', *FBI Law Enforcement Bulletin*, 1979, *48*(9), 11–15.
7 R. Salant, Speech given at the Convention of Radio and Television News Directors Association (US) 1977.
8 W. Breed, 'Social control in the newsroom', in A. Kirschner and L. Kirschner (eds.), *Journalism: Readings in the Mass Media* (Indianapolis: Odyssey Press, 1971). S. Cohen and J. Young, *The Manufacture of News: Deviance, Social Problems, and the Mass Media* (London: Constable, 1973). E.J. Epstein, *Between Fact and Fiction: The Problem of Journalism* (New York: Random, 1975).
9 W.B. Jaehnig, 'Journalists and terrorism: Captives of the libertarian tradition', *Indiana Law Journal*, 1978, *53*(4), 743.
10 A.H. Miller, 'Terrorism and the media: A dilemma', *Terrorism: An Interdisciplinary Journal*, 1979, *2*(1/2), 79.
11 Anon., 'Taking terror's measure', *Columbia Journalism Review*, 1977, *16* (May/June), 6.
12 United States. Department of Justice. National Advisory Committee on Criminal Justice Standards and Goals. *Disorders and Terrorism* (Washington, DC: US Government Printing Office, 1976).
13 A widely published set of guidelines are those promulgated by CBS News in the United States. The guidelines are set out below as an example of existing thought on the matter.

CBS News Issues Guidelines for Coverage of Terrorists
Production guidelines to be followed by CBS News in its coverage:

'Coverage of Terrorists'
Because the facts and circumstances of each case vary, there can be no specific self-executing rules for the handling of terrorist/hostage stories. CBS News will continue to apply the normal test of news judgement and if, as so often they are, these stories are newsworthy, we must continue to give them coverage despite the dangers of 'contagion'. The disadvantages of suppression are, among things, (1) adversely affecting our credibility ('What else are the news people keeping from us?'); (2) giving free rein to sensationalized and erroneous word of mouth rumours; and (3) distorting our news judgements for some extraneous judgemental purpose. These disadvantages compel us to continue to provide coverage.

Nevertheless in providing for such coverage there must be thoughtful, conscientious care and restraint. Obviously, the story should not be sensationalized beyond the actual fact of its being sensational. We should exercise particular care in how we treat the terrorist/kidnapper.
More specifically:

(1) An essential component of the story is the demands of the terrorist/kidnapper and we must report those demands. But we should avoid providing an excessive platform for the terrorist/kidnapper. Thus, unless such demands are succinctly stated and free of rhetoric and propaganda, it may be better to paraphrase the demands instead of presenting them directly through the voice or picture of the terrorist/kidnapper.

(2) Except in the most compelling circumstances, and then only with the approval of the President of CBS News or in his absence, the Senior Vice President of News, there should be no live coverage of the terrorist/kidnapper since we may fall into the trap of providing an unedited platform for him. (This does *not* limit live on-the-spot reporting by CBS News reporters, but care should be exercised to assure restraint and context.)

(3) News personnel should be mindful of the probable need by the authorities who are dealing with the terrorist for communication by telephone and hence should endeavor to ascertain, wherever feasible, whether our own use of such lines would be likely to interfere with the authorities' communications.

(4) Responsible CBS News representatives should endeavor to contact experts dealing with the hostage situation to determine whether they have any guidance on such questions as phraseology to be avoided, what kinds of questions or reports might tend to exacerbate the situation, etc. Any such recommendations by established authorities on the scene should be carefully considered as guidance (but not as instruction) by CBS News personnel.

(5) Local authorities should also be given the name or names of CBS personnel whom they can contact should they have further guidance or wish to deal with such delicate questions as a newsman's call to the terrorists or other matters which might interfere with authorities dealing with the terrorists.

(6) Guidelines affecting our coverage of civil disturbances are also applicable here, especially those which relate to avoiding the use of inflammatory catchwords or phrases, the reporting of rumors, etc. As in the case of policy dealing with civil disturbances, in dealing with a hostage story reporters should obey all police instructions but report immediately to their superiors any such instructions that seem to be intended to manage or suppress the news.

(7) Coverage of this kind of story should be in such overall balance as to length, that it does not unduly crowd out other important news of the hour/day.

14 Jaehnig, 738.
15 *Ibid.*, 744.
16 Bell, 50.

10 The role of the army in counter-terrorist operations

1 In most of the following discussion the army will be the centre of focus. Although elements of the air force and the navy would be utilised in internal security operations it is the army that would be used most frequently, in greatest numbers and possibly in greatest contact with the public. It is the use of armed members of the army that raises the most contentious issues, not, for example, the use of air force helicopters or transport aircraft.

2 In particular, Major-General Anthony Deane-Drummond's *Riot Control* (London: Royal United Services Institute for Defence Studies, 1975); and Major-General Frank Kitson's *Low Intensity Operations: Subversion, Insurgency, Peace-Keeping* (London: Faber and Faber, 1971).

3 M. Edmonds, 'The role of the armed forces in the maintenance of law and order in Britain: A discussion' in C.H. Enloe and U. Semin-Panzer (eds.), *The Military, the Police and Domestic Order: British and Third World Experiences* (London: Richardson Institute for Conflict and Peace Research, 1976).

4 T. Parsons, 'Some reflections on the place of force in social process' in H. Eckstein (ed.), *Internal War* (New York: Free Press, 1964).

5 Edmonds, 26.

6 P. Wilkinson, *Terrorism and the Liberal State* (London: Macmillan, 1977), 43.

7 *Protective Security Review* (Canberra: Australian Government Publishing Service, 1979), paragraphs 7.19 and 10.57.

8 For example, G. Cohn-Bendit and D. Cohn-Bendit, *Obsolete Communism: The Left-Wing Alternative* (London: Penguin, 1969); Tariq Ali, *The Coming British Revolution* (London: Cape, 1971).

9 For example, R. Clutterbuck, *Protest and the Urban Guerrilla* (London: Cassell, 1973); F. Kitson, *Low Intensity Operations* (London: Faber, 1971); R. Thompson, *Revolutionary War and World Strategy* (London: Seaker, 1970).

10 *Reference under S48A of the Criminal Appeal (Northern Ireland) Act 1968 (No. 1 of 1975)*, (1976) 2 All E.R., 937 at 946.

11 For extended discussion of these issues see especially N.S. Raeburn, 'The legal implications in counter terrorist operations', *Pacific Defence Reporter*, 1978, 4(10), 34–6.

12 *Protective Security Review*, Appendix 18, 342–3.

13 *Ibid.*, 343.

14 Major N.J. Sutton, 'The requirement in the Australian Army for wheeled armoured vehicles' in *Fort Queenscliff Papers* (Fort Queenscliff, Vic.: Australian Staff College, 1978), 79–100.

15 R.M. Ogorkiewicz, 'Armoured vehicles for internal security', *International Defense Review*, 1974, No. 5, 621.

16 Edmonds, 31.

17 See R. Plehwe and R. Wettenhall, 'Reflections on the Salisbury Affair: police-government relations in Australia', *Australian Quarterly*, 1979, 51(1), 75–91 for a comprehensive analysis of the statutory provisions governing the relationships between Police Commissioners and State Governments.

18 Edmonds, 82.

19 Major C. Groves, 'Para-military forces', *Pacific Defence Reporter*, 1980, 6(10), 91–2, and 6, (11), 59–69.

20 Z. Dian, 'Police: Para-military arm of government', *Asian Defence Journal*, 5/1979, 17.

21 Deane-Drummond, 63.

22 T. Bowden, 'Guarding the State: The police response to crisis politics in Europe', *British Journal of Law and Society*, 1978, 5, 85.

23 T. Bowden, 'Men in the middle – the UK police', *Conflict Studies*, February 1976, No. 68, 13.

24 Bowden, *Guarding the State*, 71.

25 C.H. Enloe, *Police and military in Ulster: Peacekeeping or peace-subverting forces*. Paper presented at the Annual Meeting of the American Political Science Association, Washington, DC, 4 September 1977.

26 Zia, 18–19.

27 *Protective Security Review*, 162.

28 Major J.P. Stevens, 'Greater emphasis should be given to preparation of the army for operating to built-up areas', In *Fort Queenscliff Papers* (Fort Queenscliff, Vic.: Australian Staff College, 1978), 40–58.

29 R. Evelegh, *Peace-Keeping in a Democratic Society* (London: C. Hurst and Company, 1978).

30 *Report to the Minister for Administrative Services on the Organisation of Police Resources in the Commonwealth Area and other Related Matters* by Sir Robert Mark (Canberra: Australian Government Publishing Service, 1978). See especially paragraph 25–36 on Military Aid to the Civil Power, and Appendix F (Keeping the Peace in Great Britain: The Differing Roles of the Police and the Army).

11 The legal regulation of terrorism: international and national measures

1 The first Convention was signed by Albania, Argentine Republic, Belgium, Bulgaria, Cuba, Czechoslovakia, Dominican Republic, Ecuador, Egypt, Estonia, France, Greece, Haiti, India, Monaco, Netherlands, Norway, Peru, Romania, Spain, Turkey, Union of Soviet Socialist Republics, Venezuela and Yugoslavia. However, only India eventually ratified it. Not a single nation ratified the second Convention.

2 *British Year Book of International Law*, 1938, *29*, 215. See also statement by the British delegate to the 1937 Conference, in Proceedings of the International Conference on the Repression of Terrorism, League of Nations Document C.94.M47.1938 v (1938.V.3), at 52.

3 UN Document A/8791 (1972).

4 UN Document A/C.6/418 (1972), p. 5.

5 United Nations. General Assembly. Study prepared by the Secretariat in accordance with the decision taken by the Sixth Committee at its 1314th meeting on 27 September 1972. (UN Document A/C.6/418, 2 Nov 1972), paragraph 66.

6 Quoted by Seymour Finger, 'The United Nations response to terrorism', in Yonah Alexander and Robert A. Kilmarx (eds.), *Political Terrorism and Business. The Threat and Response* (New York: Praeger Publishers, 1979), 261.

7 The members of the Committee were: Algeria, Austria, Barbados, Canada, Congo, Czechoslovakia, Democratic Yemen, France, Greece, Guinea, Haiti, Hungary, India, Iran, Italy, Japan, Mauritania, Nicaragua, Nigeria, Panama, Sweden, Syrian Arab Republic, Tunisia, Turkey, Ukranian Soviet Socialist Republic, Union of Soviet Socialist Republics, United Kingdom of Great Britain and Northern Ireland, United Republic of Tanzania, United States of America, Uruguay, Venezuela, Yemen, Yugoslavia, Zaire, and Zambia. (General Assembly Resolution 3034, 27 UN GAOR SUPP., para. 9, 1972).

8 J. Dugard, 'Towards the definition of international terrorism', *Proceedings of the American Society for International Law,* 1973, *67*, 100.

9 Afghanistan, Algeria, Cameroon, Chad, the Congo, Equatorial Guinea, Guinea, Guyana, India, Kenya, Madagascar, Mali, Mauritania, the Sudan, Yugoslavia, and Zambia.

10 Finger, 264.

11 United Nations. Document A/AC./60/2) (22 June 1973).

12 *Ibid.*

13 United Nations. General Assembly. *Report of the Ad Hoc Committee on International Terrorism* (Supplement No. 28 [A/9028] 1973), paragraph 26.

14 Finger, 266.

15 L.C. Green, 'The legislation of terrorism' in Y. Alexander, D. Carlton and P. Wilkinson (eds.), *Terrorism: Theory and Practice* (Boulder, Colorado: Westview Press, 1979), 184–5.

16 United Nations. General Assembly. *Report of the Ad Hoc Committee on International Terrorism* (Supplement No. 37 [A/32/37], 1977).

17 United Nations. General Assembly. 28th Session. 1974. Resolution 3166.

18 Statement by the Chilean representative during the 4th meeting of the ad hoc committee (United Nations document, A/32/39, p. 18, paragraph 8).

19 United Nations document A/32/39, p. 23, paragraph 18.

20 Statement by the Algerian representative during the 8th meeting of the ad hoc committee (United Nations document, A/32/39, p. 30, paragraph 2).

21 United Nations document, A/32/39, p. 35, paragraph 28.

22 *Ibid.*, p. 104, paragraph 7.

23 Clive C. Aston, 'The United Nations convention against the taking of hostages: realistic or rhetoric?', *Terrorism: An International Journal*, 1981, 5, (1–2), 139–60.

24 An incident is considered to contain an international element if either the hostage-takers or the hostages are foreign nationals, the demands are focused on a foreign government, or the location of the incident involves a foreign embassy, consulate, or international organisation.

25 Aston, 156.

26 See for example, M. Smith and J. Sloane, 'International conventions on terrorism: A selected review' in National Criminal Justice Reference Service. *International Summaries. A Collection of Selected Translations in Law Enforcement and Criminal Justice, Volume 3* (Washington DC: US Department of Justice, Law Enforcement Assistance Administration, 1979), 165–72.

27 The full text of the Convention may be found in *European Convention on the Suppression of Terrorism*, European Treaty Series No. 90 (Strasbourg: Council of Europe, 1977). It is also reproduced in *The Human Rights Review*, 1977, 2(2), 178–82.

28 Paul Wilkinson, 'Proposals for government and international responses to terrorism', *Terrorism: An International Journal*, 1981, 5, (1–2), 183.

29 E. McWhinney, *The Illegal Diversion of Aircraft and International Law* (Leiden: Sijthoff, 1975).

30 R.G. Bell, 'The U.S. response to terrorism against international civil aviation', *Orbis*, 1976, 19(4), 1326–43.

31 The countries participating at the Bonn Economic Summit included Canada, France, Germany, Italy, Japan, United Kingdom, and the United States.

32 Wilkinson, 176.

33 Green, 194–5.

34 J.J. Paust, 'A survey of possible legal responses to international terrorism: Prevention, punishment, and cooperative action', *Georgia Journal of Comparative Law*, 1975, 5(2), 433.

35 Dugard, 98.

36 In re Meurnier [1894] 2 Q.B.D. 415 at 419.

37 T.M. Franck and B.B. Lockwood, Jr. 'Preliminary thoughts towards an international convention on terrorism', *The American Journal of International Law*, 1974, *68*, 89.

38 For example, Spain, *Penal Code*, Article 260, 'Offences of Terrorism and Possession of Explosives', and *Military Penal Code*, Chapter 'Terrorismo' (November 15, 1971); South Africa, *Terrorism Act 1967* (which is particularly interesting because it had a preamble stipulating that it would apply retroactively to any act provided for in the Act which occurred on or after 27 June 1962); Czechoslovakia, *Penal Code*, Article 94; Sweden, *Anti-Terrorist Act 1973*.

39 M. Oppenheimer, 'The criminalisation of political dissent in the Federal Republic of Germany', *Contemporary Crises*, 1978, 2(1), 97.

40 *United States Code*, paragraph 7311 (1976).

41 Oppenheimer, 98–101.

42 *Ibid.*, 103.

43 See, for example, J. Becker, *Hitler's Children: The Story of the Baader-Meinhof Gang* (London: Michael Joseph, 1977).

44 The significant amendments were as follows: First Law on the Reform of the Criminal Procedure of December 9, 1974, BGBl. I, p. 3393; Supplemental Act

to the First Law on the Reform of the Criminal Procedure of December 20, 1974. BGBl. I, p. 3693; 15th Law on Modification of the Criminal Code of May 18, 1976, BGBl. I, p. 1213; Law on Amendment of the Criminal Code, the Criminal Procedure Code, the Law on the Judiciary, the Law on Federal Administrative Regulations, and the Law on Execution of Sentences of August 18, 1976, BGBl. I. p. 2181; Introductory Law to the Law on the Judiciary of September 9, 1977, BGBl, I. p. 1877; Law on Modification of the Criminal Procedure of April 14, 1978, BGBl, I, p. 497. Source: M. Radvanyi, *Anti-Terrorist Legislation in the Federal Republic of Germany* (Washington, DC: Law Library, Library of Congress, 1979).

45 *German Criminal Code*, Section 88(a).

46 *German Criminal Procedure Code*, Section 231a, paragraph 1.

47 *German Criminal Procedure Code*, Section 138a, paragraph 2.

48 See the pamphlet *Kontaktsperre – Information uber ein Gesetz zur Bekampfung des Terrorismus* (Contact Ban Between Prisoners and the Outside World – Information About a Law to Fight Terrorism) issued by the West German Ministry of Justice in 1978 to explain the background and provisions of the Contact Ban Law. An interesting inclusion in the pamphlet is a summary of provisions in other European countries which allow limitations on defence lawyers' contact with clients. This survey shows that most European laws allow for some form of contact ban under specified circumstances.

49 For example, see Radvanyi.

50 P.H. Bakker-Schut, 'The Baader-Meinhof Laws' (In Dutch), *Advocaten Blad*, 1975, 67.

51 Reuters News Service, 18 December 1975.

52 Press Release, German Section of Amnesty International, 7 October 1975.

53 E.J.H. Moons, 'Approche politique et juridique de terrorisme et de la criminalite anarchisante en Republique federale allemarde', *Revue de Droit Penal et de Criminologie*, May 1978, n.5, 503–43.

54 C. Scorer, *The Prevention of Terrorism Acts 1974 and 1976. A Report on the Operation of the Law* (London: National Council for Civil Liberties, 1976).

55 *Review of the Operation of the Prevention of Terrorism (Temporary Provisions) Acts 1974 and 1976* Cmnd 7324 (London: Her Majesty's Stationery Office, 1978).

56 Editorial, 'Prevention of Terrorism', *Criminal Law Review*, 1978 (November), 650–1.

57 D.R. Lowry, 'Draconian powers: The new British approach to pretrial detention of suspected terrorists', *Columbia Human Rights Law Review*, 1977, 9(1), 199.

58 *Ibid.*, 201.

59 *Ibid.*, 222.

12 Counter-measures against terrorism: the intelligence function

1 US Department of the Army, Field Manual 100-5, *Operations of Armed Forces in the Field* (Washington, DC: US Government Printing Office, 1968), paragraph 5–10.

2 See A.C. Porzecanski, *Uruguay's Tupamaros, The Urban Guerilla* (New York: Praeger Publishers, 1973), 32–7.

3 See R. Trinquier, *Modern Warfare* (New York: Frederick A. Praeger, 1964), 10–15.

4 See N.A. La Charite, *Case Studies in Insurgency and Revolutionary Warfare, Cuba 1953–1959* (Washington, DC: Special Operations Research Office, American University, 1963), 77–117.

5 J.B. Wolf, 'Organisation and management practices of urban terrorist groups', *Terrorism: An International Journal*, 1978, *1*(2), 174.

6 P. Wilkinson, *Terrorism and the Liberal State* (London: Macmillan, 1977), 134.

7 Wolf, 181.

8 W.A. Kerstetter, 'Terrorism and intelligence', *Terrorism: An International Journal*, 1979, *3*(1–2), 109.

9 See, for example, the criticisms levelled by Frank Donner, director of the American Civil Liberties Union project on political surveillance in F. Donner, 'The terrorist as scapegoat', *The Nation*, 1978, *226*(19), 590–4.

10 United States, Senate Select Committee to Study Governmental Operations with Respect to Intelligence Activities, *Final Report*, Senate Report No. 755, 94th Congress, 2nd Session, 1976 (The Church Report).

11 *Special Branch Security Records.* Initial Report to the Premier of South Australia by the Honourable Mr Acting Justice White. (Adelaide: South Australia Government Printer, 1978).

12 The Canadian Royal Commission Into RCMP Wrongdoing, touches on these matters.

13 R.H. Kupperman, *Facing Tomorrow's Terrorist Incident Today* (Washington, DC: US Department of Justice, Law Enforcement Assistance Administration, 1977), 3.

14 For discussion of these issues generally see *Report of the Royal Commission on Intelligence and Security, Volume 1–4* (Canberra: Australian Government Publishing Service, 1977).

15 *Protective Security Review* (Canberra: Australian Government Publishing Service, 1979), paragraph 5–6.

16 Australia, *Joint Services Staff Manual Glossary* (Joint Service Publication 101, 1970), pt. 1, p. 121.

17 J.B. Wolf, 'Intelligence stupidity (Private enterprise, government agencies need more effective intelligence analysis)', *Terrorism, Violence, Insurgency Journal*, 1979, *1*(1), 10.

18 US Department of the Army, *Psychological Operations*, Field Manual 33–5 (Washington, DC: US Government Printing Office, 1969), 58.

19 Wolf, 'Intelligence stupidity', 10.

20 See, for example, D.A. Waterman and B.M. Jenkins, *Heuristic Modeling Using Rule-Based Computer Systems* (Santa Monica, Calif.: Rand Corporation, 1977), Paper P-5811.

21 See, for example, Kerstetter, 110–14.

22 R.W. Mengel, 'Terrorism and new technologies of destruction: An overview of the potential risk' in *Disorders and Terrorism*. Report of the Task Force on Disorders and Terrorism. US National Advisory Committee on Criminal Justice Standards and Goals. (Washington, DC: US Government Printing Office, 1977), 443–73.

23 *Ibid.*, 453.

24 *Ibid.*, 469–70.

25 J.B. Wolf, 'An analytical framework for the study and control of agitational terrorism', *The Police Journal*, 1976, *49*, 165–71.

26 C.A. Russell, L.J. Banker, and B.H. Miller, 'Out-inventing the terrorist' in Y.

Alexander, D. Carlton, and P. Wilkinson (eds.), *Terrorism: Theory and Practice* (Boulder, Colorado: Westview Press, 1979), 28.
27 M.S. Miron and J.E. Douglas, 'Threat analysis. The psycholinguistic approach', *FBI Law Enforcement Bulletin*, 1979, *48*(9), 5–9.

13 Handling hostage situations

1 For example, see R.D. Crelinsten and D. Szabo, *Hostage-Taking* (Lexington, Mass.: Lexington Books, 1979); I. Goldaber, 'A typology of hostage-takers', *The Police Chief*, 1979, *46*(6), 21–3.
2 J.G. Stratton. 'The terrorist act of hostage-taking: A view of violence and the perpetrators', *Journal of Police Science and Administration*, 1978, *6*(1), 1–9.
3 For example, see Goldaber; F.J. Hacker, *Crusaders, Criminals, Crazies: Terror and Terrorism in Our Time* (New York: W.W. Norton and Company, 1976), especially 12–17.
4 J.G. Stratton, 'The terrorist act of hostage-taking: Considerations for law enforcement', *Journal of Police Science and Administration*, 1978, *6*(2), 123–34.
5 *Ibid.*, 128.
6 L. Mann, *Social psychology of terrorism*. Paper delivered at the Sixth National Symposium on the Forensic Sciences, Adelaide, South Australia, March 1979.
7 For an excellent description of the reactions of the hostages in this incident see S.R. Jacobson, 'Individual and group responses to confinement in a skyjacked plane', *American Journal of Orthopsychiatry*, 1973, *43*(3), 459–69. The author, a social worker, was one of the hostages on the TWA plane hijacked to Dawson's Field.
8 *Ibid.*, 11–12.
9 Editorial, *Pacific Defence Reporter*, 1980, *6*(12), 3.
10 A.H. Miller, 'Hostage negotiations and the concept of transference' in Y. Alexander, D. Carlton, and P. Wilkinson (eds.), *Terrorism: Theory and Practice* (Boulder, Colorado: Westview Press, 1979), 156.

14 Counter measures against terrorism: the role of behavioural science research

1 There is a considerable tradition of this type of research, particularly in psychology and political science, which was briefly discussed in Part One of this book. But in comparison with other work in the terrorism field, such research is a relatively poor cousin. More resources need to be devoted to this particularly frustrating and complex research area.
2 R.D. Crelinsten, 'International political terrorism: A challenge for comparative research', *International Journal of Comparative and Applied Criminal Justice*, 1978, *2*(2), 107–26.
3 D.B. Bobrow, 'Preparing for unwanted events: Instances of international political terrorism', *Terrorism: An International Journal*, 1978, *1*(3/4), 397–422.
4 *Ibid.*, 415–16.
5 Crelinsten, 121.
6 For example, a 1970–71 sample drawn by the Federal Aviation Administration showed a prediction accuracy of 87 per cent with their profile (that is 87 per cent

of hijackers in that period fitted the profile). E. Pickrel, 'Federal Aviation Administration's behavioural research program for defence against hijacking' in J.J. Kramer (ed.), *The Role of Behavioural Science in Physical Security Proceedings of the First Annual Symposium, April 29–30, 1976* (Washington, DC: US Department of Commerce, National Bureau of Standards, 1977), 19–24.

7 Reported in *Sonntags Journal*, Zurich, 2 July 1972 and cited by P. Clyne, *An Anatomy of Skyjacking* (London: Abelard-Schuman, 1973).

8 E.D. Shaw, L. Hazlewood, R.E. Hayes, and D.R. Harris, 'Analysing threats from terrorism. A working paper' in J.J. Kramer (ed.), *The Role of Behavioural Science in Physical Security. Proceedings of the First Annual Symposium, April 29–30, 1976* (Washington DC: US Department of Commerce, National Bureau of Standards, 1977), 1–16.

9 A. Fine, 'Perpetrator attributes in threat analysis' in J.J. Kramer (ed.), *The Role of Behavioural Science in Physical Security. Proceedings of the First Annual Symposium, April 29–30, 1976* (Washington DC: US Department of Commerce, National Bureau of Standards, 1977), 27–34; and A. Fine, 'Attributes of potential adversaries to U.S. nuclear programs' in J.J. Kramer (ed.), *The Role of Behavioural Science in Physical Security, Proceedings of the Second Annual Symposium, 23–24 March, 1977* (Washington DC: US Department of Commerce, National Bureau of Standards, 1978), 27–33.

10 Shaw *et al.*, 9.

11 *Ibid.*, 15–16.

12 *Ibid.*, 16.

13 D.H. Harris, 'Link analysis of threats and physical safeguards' in J.J. Kramer (ed.), *The Role of Behavioural Science in Physical Security. Proceedings of the Third Annual Symposium, May 2–4, 1978* (Washington DC: US Department of Commerce, National Bureau of Standards, 1979), 17.

14 D.H. Harris, 'Development of a computer-based program for criminal intelligence', *Human Factors*, 1978, *20*, 47–56; and, W.R. Harper and D.H. Harris, 'The application of link analysis to police intelligence', *Human Factors*, 1975, *17*, 157–64.

15 P.A. Karber and R.W. Mengel, 'A behavioural analysis of the adversary threat to the commercial nuclear industry – A conceptual framework for realistically assessing threats' in J.J. Kramer (ed.), *The Role of Behavioural Science in Physical Security. Proceedings of the Second Annual Symposium, March 23–24, 1977* (Washington DC: US Department of Commerce, National Bureau of Standards, 1978), 7–19.

16 *Ibid.*, 7.

17 P.G. Meguire and J.J. Kramer, *Psychological Deterrents to Nuclear Theft: A Preliminary Literature Review and Bibliography* (Washington DC: US Department of Commerce, National Bureau of Standards, 1976).

18 *Ibid.*, 1.

19 *Ibid.*, 34.

20 P.G. Meguire, J.J. Kramer, and A. Stewart, *Security Lighting For Nuclear Weapons: A Literature Review and Bibliography* (Washington DC: US Department of Commerce, National Bureau of Standards, 1977).

21 R.E. Bailey and M.B. Bailey, 'Uses of animal sensory systems and response capabilities in security systems' in J.J. Kramer (ed.), *The Role of Behavioural Science in Physical Security. Proceedings of the Second Annual Symposium,*

March 23–24, 1977 (Washington DC: US Department of Commerce, National Bureau of Standards, 1978), 49–62.

22 *Ibid.*, 62.

23 R.E. Lubow, 'High-order concept formation in the pigeon', *Journal of the Experimental Analysis of Behaviour*, 1974, *21*, 475–83.

24 P. Watson, 'How the Israelis train pigeons to spy on the Arabs', *Psychology Today* (UK edition), 1975, vol. 1, no. 1, April. See also R.E. Lubow, *The War Animals* (New York: Doubleday, 1977).

25 S. Weinstein and C.D. Weinstein, *Development of Neurophysiological Processes for the Detection of Organic Contaminants in Water.* Final Report, Contract No. DAMD 17-77-C-7008, February 15, 1978. (Fort Detrick, Maryland, US Army Medical Research and Development Command).

26 S. Weinstein, C.D. Weinstein and R.V. Nolan, 'Neurophysiological operant and classical conditioning methods in rats in the detection of explosives' in J.J. Kramer (ed.), *The Role of Behavioural Science in Physical Security. Proceedings of the Third Annual Symposium, May 2–4, 1978* (Washington DC: US Department of Commerce, National Bureau of Standards, 1979), 7–16.

27 R.E. Lubow, *The Use of Biological Systems to Detect Explosives.* Progress Report, 1972–73, Israel Ministry of Police.

28 K. Montor and D. Afdahl, 'Brain wave and biochemical research findings' in J.J. Kramer (ed.), *The Role of Behavioural Science in Physical Security. Proceedings of the Third Annual Symposium, May 2–4, 1978* (Washington DC: US Department of Commerce, National Bureau of Standards, 1979), 75–80.

29 R. Mackie, 'Some human factors that influence reliability of signal detection and identification in surveillance systems' in J.J. Kramer (ed.), *The Role of Behavioural Science in Physical Security. Proceedings of the First Annual Symposium, April 29–30, 1976* (Washington DC: US Department of Commerce, National Bureau of Standards, 1977), 43–56.

30 R.A. Fite and S. Kilpatrick, 'Final report. Joint Services perimeter barrier penetration evaluation' in J.J. Kramer (ed.), *ibid.*, 75–106. And, J. Kramer and P. Meguire, 'Preliminary observations of complex fence and barrier assaults – Phase II' in *ibid.*, 107–13.

31 S.J. Andriole and J.A. Daly, 'Potential application of computer-based crisis management aids to problems of physical security' in J.J. Kramer (ed.), *The Role of Behavioural Science in Physical Security. Proceedings of the Third Annual Symposium, May 2–4, 1978* (Washington DC: US Department of Commerce, National Bureau of Standards, 1979), 47–73.

32 I.L. Janis and L. Mann, *Decision-Making: A Psychological Analysis of Conflict, Choice, and Commitment* (New York: Free Press, 1977).

33 M.S. Miron and J.E. Douglas, 'Threat analysis. The psycholinguistic approach', *FBI Law Enforcement Bulletin*, 1979, *48*(9), 6.

34 Learning the Arabs' silent language. Edward T. Hall interviewed by Kenneth Friedman. *Psychology Today*, August 1979, 45–54.

35 E.F. Loftus, 'Words that could save your life', *Psychology Today*, November 1979, 102–10, 136–7.

36 A.C.P. Sims, A.C. White, and T. Murphy, 'Aftermath neurosis: Psychological sequelae of the Birmingham bombings in victims not seriously injured', *Medicine, Science, and the Law*, 1979, *19*(2), 78–81.

15 The future of political terrorism

1 D. Carlton, 'The future of political substate violence' in Y. Alexander, D. Carlton, and P. Wilkinson (eds.), *Terrorism: Theory and Practice* (Boulder, Colorado: Westview Press, 1979), 202.

2 A similar case may be found in the *Princeton Alumni Weekly*, 25 October 1976, in which a 21-year-old undergraduate physics student, John Phillips, was reported to have designed an atomic bomb in four months on the basis of data available entirely from public sources. Phillips claimed that the point of the exercise 'was to show that any undergraduate with a physics background can do it, and therefore that it is reasonable to assume that terrorists could do it too.' (1976, p. 6).

3 M. Willrich and T. Taylor, *Nuclear Theft: Risks and Safeguards* (Cambridge, Mass.: Ballinger, 1974), 20–1.

4 B.M. Jenkins, 'Nuclear terrorism and its consequences', *Society*, 1980, July/August, 5–16.

5 *Ibid.*, 7.

6 *Ibid.*

7 Carlton, 210.

8 N.C. Livingstone, 'Low-level violence and future targets', *Conflict*, 1980, 2(4), 351–82 lists a number of examples.

9 C.A. Russell, L.J. Banker, and B.H. Miller, 'Out-inventing the terrorist', in Y. Alexander, D. Carlton, and P. Wilkinson (eds.), *Terrorism: Theory and Practice* (Boulder, Colorado: Westview Press, 1979), 12.

10 *Ibid.*, 14.

11 Russell *et al.*, 9.21.

12 J.A. Nathan, 'The new feudalism', *Foreign Policy*, 1981, No. 42 (Spring), 156–66, at 156.

13 H.C. Greisman, 'Terrorism and the closure of society: a social-impact projection', *Technological Forecasting and Social Change*, 1979, *14*(2), 135–46.

14 *Ibid.*, 145–6.

15 Carlton.

16 *Ibid.*, 215.

17 G.R. Taylor, 'Terrorism: How to avoid the future' in M.H. Livingston (ed.), *International Terrorism in the Contemporary World* (Westport, Connecticut: Greenwood Press, 1978), 462–8.

Select bibliography

(This bibliography is not intended to be an exhaustive one. Rather it serves to acquaint the reader with a wide range of material which the author found useful in writing this book. Many of the works listed themselves contain extensive bibliographies which would be helpful in the specialised study of terrorism.)

Adkins, L., and Niehous, W.F., 'One hostage's experiences', *Dun's Review*, 1980, *115*(3), 60–6.

Alcock, N., and Quittner, J., 'The prediction of civil violence to the year 2001', *Journal of Interdisciplinary Cycle Research*, 1978, *9* (4), 307–24.

Alexander, Y., 'Terrorism, the media and the police', *Police Studies*, 1978, *1*(2), 45–52.

Alexander, Y., Carlton, D., and Wilkinson, P., *Terrorism: Theory and Practice* (Boulder, Colorado: Westview Press, 1979).

Alexander. Y., and Finger, S.M. (eds.), *Terrorism: Interdisciplinary Perspectives* (New York: John Jay Press, 1977).

Alexander, Y., and Levine, H.M., 'Prepare for the next Entebbe', *Chitty's Law Journal*, 1977, *25*(7), 240–2.

Arendt, H., *On Violence* (New York: Harcourt, Brace and World, Inc., 1969).

Australia, *Protective Security Review* (Canberra: Australian Government Publishing Service, 1979).

Avery, J.K., 'The terrorist siege/hostage situation: negotiation or confrontation?', *Australian Police College Journal*, 1978, No. 4, 3–16.

Becker, J., *Hitler's Children – The Story of the Baader-Meinhof Gang* (London: Michael Joseph, 1977).

Bell, J.B., *Transnational Terror* (Washington, DC: American Enterprise Institute for Public Policy Research, 1975).

Bell, J.B., 'Assassination in international politics', *International Studies Quarterly*, March 1972, *16*(1), 59–82.

Bell, J.B., 'Trends on terror: the analysis of political violence', *World Politics*, 1977, *29*(3), 446–88.

Bell, J.B., 'Terrorist scripts and live-action spectaculars', *Columbia Journalism Review*, 1978, *17*(1), 47–50.

Bell, R.G., 'The U.S. response to terrorism against international civil aviation', *Orbis*, 1976, *19*(4), 1326–43.

Beres, L.R., 'Terrorism and international security: the nuclear threat', *Chitty's Law Journal*, 1978, *26*(3), 73–90.

Bienen, H., and Gilpen, R., 'Economic sanctions as a response to terrorism', *The Journal of Strategic Studies*, 1980, *3*(1), 89–98.

Bishop, J.W. Jr., 'Can democracy defend itself against terrorism?', *Commentary*, 1978, *65*(5), 55–62.

Blackshield, A.R., 'The siege of Bowral – the legal issues', *Pacific Defence Reporter*, 1978, *4*(9), 6–10.

Blair, B.G., and Brewer, G.D., 'The terrorist threat to world nuclear programs', *Journal of Conflict Resolution*, 1977, *21*(3), 379–403.

Bobrow, D.B., 'Preparing for unwanted events: Instances of international political terrorism', *Terrorism: An International Journal*, 1978, *1*(3/4), 397–422.

Bowden, T., *Beyond the Limits of the Law* (Harmondsworth: Penguin Books, 1978).

Bowden, T., 'Men in the middle – the U.K. police', *Conflict Studies*, No. 68, February 1976.

Bowden, T., 'Guarding the state: the police response to crisis politics in Europe', *British Journal of Law and Society*, 1978, 5, 69–88.

Bristow, A.P., 'Preliminary research on hostage situations', *Law and Order*, 1977, *25*(3), 73–7.

Brock, G., Lustig, R., Marks, L., Parker, R., and Seale, P., with Maureen McConville, *Siege – Six Days at the Iranian Embassy* (Melbourne: Sun Books, 1980).

Bunyan, T., *The History and Practices of the Political Police in Britain* (New York: St. Martin's Press, 1976).

Burton, A., *Urban Terrorism – Theory, Practice and Response* (New York: The Free Press, 1975).

Camus, A., *The Rebel* (Harmondsworth: Penguin Books, 1962).

Carlson, E.R., 'Hostage negotiation situations', *Law and Order*, 1977, *25*(7), 12–15, 59–60.

Carlton, D., and Schaerf, C. (eds.), *International Terrorism and World Security* (London: Croom Helm, 1975).

Carlton, D., and Schaerf, C. (eds.), *Arms Control and Technological Innovation* (London: Croom Helm, 1977).

Catton, W.R. Jr., 'Militants and the media: partners in terrorism?', *Indiana Law Journal*, 1978, *53*, 680–715.

Chapman, B., *Police State* (New York: Praeger, 1970).

Civiletti, B.R., 'Terrorism: the government's response policy', *FBI Law Enforcement Bulletin*, 1979, *48*(1), 19–22.

Clutterbuck, R., *Living with Terrorism* (London: Faber and Faber, 1975).

Clutterbuck, R., *Britain in Agony – The Growth of Political Violence* (London: Faber and Faber, 1978).

Clutterbuck, R., *Kidnap and Ransom – The Response* (London: Faber and Faber, 1978).

Clutterbuck, R., 'The police and urban terrorism', *The Police Journal*, 1975, *XLVIII*(3), 204–14 and 190.

Cockerham, W.C., and Cohen, L.E., 'Attitudes of U.S. army paratroopers toward participation in the quelling of civil disturbances', *Journal of Political and Military Sociology*, 1979, *7*(2), 257–69.

Cohen, E.A., *Commandos and Politicians: Elite Military Units in Modern Democracies* (Cambridge, Mass.: Harvard University Center for International Affairs, 1978).

Cohn-Bendit, G., and Cohn-Bendit, D., *Obsolete Communism: The Left-Wing Alternative* (Harmondsworth: Penguin Books, 1968).

Comay, M., 'Political terrorism', *Mental Health Society*, 1976, *3*, 249–61.

Cooper, H.H.A., 'The terrorist and the victim', *Victimology: An International Journal*, 1976, *1*(2), 229–39.

Cooper, H.H.A., 'Terrorism and the intelligence function', *Chitty's Law Journal*, 1976, *24*(3), 73–8.

Cooper, H.H.A., 'What is a terrorist: a psychological perspective', *Legal Medical Quarterly*, 1977, *1*(1), 16–32.

Cooper, H.H.A., 'Whither now? Terrorism on the brink', *Chitty's Law Journal*, 1977, *25*(6), 181–90.

Cooper, H.H.A., 'Terrorism: the problem of the problem of definition', *Chitty's Law Journal*, 1978, *26*(3), 105–8.

Cooper, H.H.A., 'Hostage rescue operations: denouement at Algeria and Mogadishu compared', *Chitty's Law Journal*, 1978, *26*(3), 91–103.

Cooper, H.H.A., 'Terroristic fads and fashions: the year of the assassin', *Chitty's Law Journal*, 1979, *27*(3), 92–7.

Crelinsten, R.D., Laberge-Altmesd, D., and Szabo, D., *Terrorism and Criminal Justice – An International Perspective* (Lexington, Mass.: Lexington Books, 1978).

Crelinsten, R.D., and Szabo, D., *Hostage-Taking* (Lexington, Mass.: Lexington Books, 1979).

Crelinsten, R.D., 'International political terrorism – a challenge for comparative research', *International Journal of Comparative and Applied Criminal Justice*, 1978, *2*(2), 107–26.

Cunningham, W.C., and Gross, P.J., *Prevention of Terrorism: Security Guidelines for Business and Other Organizations* (McLean, Virginia: Hallcrest Press, 1978).

Dawe, D., ' "Police problems of the future" terror: future trends in hostage taking and violence', *Canadian Police College Journal*, 1979, *3*(1), 44–54.

Deane-Drummond, A., *Riot Control* (London: Royal United Services Institute, 1975).

de Boer, C., 'The polls: Terrorism and hijacking', *Public Opinion Quarterly*, 1979, *43*(3), 410–18.

de Wit, J., and Ponsaers, P., 'On facts and how to use them', *Terrorism: An International Journal*, 1978, *1*(3/4), 363–75.

Dian, Z., 'Police: paramilitary arm of government', *Asian Defence Journal*, 1979, No. 5, 16–20.

Dixon, J., 'Britain may need special weapons and tactics teams to fight urban guerillas', *Police Review*, 1976, *84*, 644–8.

Dobson, C., and Payne, R., *The Weapons of Terror – International Terrorism at Work* (London: MacMillan 1979).

Donner, F., 'The terrorist as scapegoat', *The Nation*, 1978, *226*(19), 590–4.

Doyle, E.J., 'Propaganda by deed: the media response to terrorism', *The Police Chief*, 1979, *46*(6), 40–1.

Dugard, J., 'Towards the definition of international terrorism', *Proceedings of American Society for International Law*, July 1973, *67*, 94–101.

Eckstein, H., 'On the etiology of internal wars', *History and Theory*, 1965, *4*(2), 133–63.

Eckstein, H. (ed.), *Internal War – Problems and Approaches* (New York: The Free Press, 1964).

Edelhertz, H., and Walsh, M., *The White-Collar Challenge to Nuclear Safeguards* (Lexington, Mass.: Lexington Books, 1978).

Elliott, J.D., and Gibson, L.K. (eds.), *Contemporary Terrorism – Selected Readings* (Gaithersburg, Maryland: International Association of Chiefs of Police, 1978).

Elliott, R.J., 'Are urban guerrillas invincible?, *Commonwealth*, June–July 1980, 5–9.

Elwin, G., 'Swedish anti-terrorist legislation', *Contemporary Crises*, 1977, *1*(3), 289–302.

Enloe, C.H., *Ethnic Soldiers: State Security in a Divided Society* (Harmondsworth: Penguin Books, 1980).

Enloe, C.H., and Semin-Panzer, U. (eds.), *The Military, The Police and Domestic Order British and Third World Experiences* (London: Richardson Institute for Conflict and Peace Research, 1976).

Evans, A.E., and Murphy, J.F. (eds.), *Legal Aspects of International Terrorism* (Lexington, Mass.: Lexington Books, 1978).

Evelegh, R., *Peacekeeping in a Democratic Society* (London: C. Hurst and Company, 1979).

Fairbairn, G., 'Terrorism and defence', *World Review*, 1979, *18*(1), 48–53.

Fattah, E.A., 'Some reflections on the victimology of terrorism', *Terrorism: the International Journal*, 1979, *3*(1/2), 81–108.

Fitzgerald, B.D., 'The analytical foundations of extortionate terrorism', *Terrorism: An International Journal*, 1978, *1*(3/4), 347–62.

Franck, T.M., and Lockwood, B.B., 'Preliminary thoughts toward an international convention on terrorism', *The American Journal of International Law, 68*, 69–90.

Friedlander, R.A., 'Terrorism and international law: what is being done?', *Rutgers Camden Law Journal*, 1977, *8*(3), 383–92.

Fromkin, D., 'The strategy of terrorism', *Foreign Affairs*, July 1975, *53*(4), 683–98.

Fugua, P., and Wilson, J.V., *Terrorism: The Executive's Guide to Survival* (Houston, Texas: Gulf Publishing Company, 1978).

Gallagher, R., and Remsberg, C., *Hostage Negotiation for Police – Officer Reference Guide* (Schiller Park, Illinois: MTI Teleprograms Inc., 1977).

Gaynes, J.B., 'Bringing the terrorist to justice: a domestic law approach', *Cornell International Law Journal*, 1978, *11*, 71–84.

Gladis, S.D., 'The hostage/terrorist situation and the media', *FBI Law Enforcement Bulletin*, 1979, *48*(9), 11–15.

Goldaber, I., 'A typology of hostage-takers', *The Police Chief*, 1979, *46*(6), 21–2.

Great Britain, *Report of the Committee of Inquiry into Police Interrogation Procedures in Northern Ireland* (London: Her Majesty's Stationery Office, 1979).

Great Britain, *Report of the Commission to Consider Legal Procedures to Deal with Terrorist Activities in Northern Ireland* (London: Her Majesty's Stationery Office, 1972).

Greaves, A.E., and Pickover, D., 'Prevention of terrorism', *Police Review*, 31 August 1979, 1400–4.

Greisman, H.C., 'Social meanings of terrorism: reification, violence and social control', *Contemporary Crisis*, 1977, *1*(3), 303–18.

Griesman, H.C., 'Terrorism and the closure of society: a social-impact projection', *Technological Forecasting and Social Change*, 1979, *14*(2), 135–46.

Groom, A.J.R., 'Coming to terms with terrorism', *British Journal of International Studies*, 1978, *4*, 62–77.

Groves, C., 'Para-military forces', *Pacific Defence Reporter*, 1980, 6(10), 91–2; and 6(11), 59–69.

Gutmann, D., 'Killers and consumers: the terrorist and his audience', *Social Research*, 1979, 46(3), 517–26.

Hacker, F.J., *Crusaders, Criminals, Crazies – Terror and Terrorism in Our Time* (New York: W.W. Norton and Company, 1976).

Hamilton, C.M.P., 'Terrorism: its ethical implication for the future', *The Futurist*, 1977, 11(6), 351–4.

Hart, W., 'Ulster's prison guards', *Corrections Magazine*, 1980, 6(3), 20–7.

Hassell, C.V., 'The hostage situation: exploring the motivation and the cause', *The Police Chief*, 1975, 42(9), 55–8.

Hayes, B., 'The effects of terrorism in society: an analysis, with particular reference to the United Kingdom and the European economic community', *Police Studies*, 1979, 2(3), 4–10.

Hoffman, C.M., and Byall, E.B., 'Identification of explosive residues in bomb scene investigations', *Journal of Forensic Sciences*, 1974, 19(1), 54–63.

Horner, C., 'The facts about terrorism', *Commentary* (USA), 1980, 69(6), 40–5.

Horowitz, I.L. (ed.), *The Anarchists* (New York: Dell Publishing Co., Inc., 1964).

Horowitz, I.L., 'Political terrorism and the state', *Journal of Political and Military Sociology*, 1973, 1(1), 147–57.

Hughes, G.L., 'The law in Australia relating to the unlawful seizure of aircraft', *University of Tasmania Law Review*, 1968, 6(1), 39–59.

Hutchinson, M.C., 'The concept of revolutionary terrorism', *Journal of Conflict Resolution*, 1973, 6(3), 383–96.

Ingram, T.B. Jr., 'Are airport searches still reasonable?', *Journal of Air Law and Commerce*, 1978, 44(1), 131–75.

Iviansky, Z., 'Individual terror: concept and typology', *Journal of Contemporary History*, 1977, 12, 43–63.

Jacobson, S.R., 'Individual and group responses to confinement in a skyjacked plane', *American Journal of Orthopsychiatry*, 1973, 43(3), 459–69.

Jaehnig, W.B., 'Journalists and terrorism: captives of the libertarian tradition', *Indiana Law Journal*, 1978, 53(4), 727–44.

Janis, I.L., and Mann, L., 'Coping with decisional conflict', *American Scientist*, 1976, 64, 657–67.

Jenkins, B.M., *High Technology Terrorism and Surrogate War: The Impact of New Technology on Low-Level Violence* (Santa-Monica, Calif.: Rand Corporation, 1975).

Jenkins, B.M., *Hostage Survival: Some Preliminary Observations* (Santa Monica, Calif.: Rand Corporation, 1976).

Jenkins, B.M., 'International terrorism: trends and potentialities', *Journal of International Affairs*, 1978, 32(1), 115–23.

Jenkins, B.M., 'Nuclear terrorism and its consequences', *Society*, 1980, 17(5), 5–15.

Kerstetter, W.A., 'Terrorism and intelligence', *Terrorism: An International Journal*, 1979, 3(1–2), 109–15.

Kitson, F., *Low Intensity Operations* (London: Faber and Faber, 1971).

Knutson, J.N., 'The terrorists' dilemmas: some implicit rules of the game', *Terrorism: An International Journal*, 1980, 4, 195–222.

Kobetz, R.W., 'Hostage incidents – the new police priority', *The Police Chief*, 1975, 42(5), 32–5.

Kobetz, R.W., and Cooper, H.H.A., 'Hostage rescue operations – teaching the unteachable', *The Police Chief,* 1979, *46*(6), 24–7.

Kramer, J.J. (ed.), *The Role of Behavioral Science in Physical Security – Proceedings of the First Annual Symposium, April 29–30, 1976* (Washington, DC: National Bureau of Standards, US Department of Commerce, 1977).

Kramer, J.J. (ed.), *The Role of Behavioral Science in Physical Security – Proceedings of the Second Annual Symposium, March 23–24, 1977* (Washington, DC: National Bureau of Standards, US Department of Commerce, 1978).

Kramer, J.J. (ed.), *The Role of Behavioral Science in Physical Security – Proceedings of the Third Annual Symposium, May 2–4, 1978* (Washington, DC: National Bureau of Standards, US Department of Commerce, 1979).

Kupperman, R.H., *Facing Tomorrow's Terrorist Incident Today* (Washington, DC: US Department of Justice, Law Enforcement Assistance Administration, 1977).

Kupperman, R.H., 'Treating the symptoms of terrorism: Some principles of good hygiene', *Terrorism: An International Journal,* 1977, *1*(1), 35–49.

Kupperman, R.H., and Trent, D.M., *Terrorism – Threat, Reality, Response* (Stanford, Calif.: Hoover Institution Press, 1979).

Kupperman, R.H., Wilcox, R.H., and Smith, H., 'Crisis management: some opportunities', *Science,* 1975, *187*, 404–10.

Kuriyama, Y., 'Terrorism at Tel Aviv Airport and a "new left" group in Japan', *Asian Survey,* 1973, *XIII*(3), 336–46.

Landes, W.M., 'An economic study of U.S. aircraft hijacking, 1961–1976', *Journal of Law and Economics,* 1978, *21*, 1–31.

Laqueur, W., *Guerrilla – A Historical and Critical Study* (Boston: Little, Brown and Company, 1976).

Laqueur, W., *Terrorism* (Boston: Little, Brown and Company, 1977).

Leaney, B.K., 'Terrorism – a summary', *The Australian Police Journal,* 1980, *34*(2), 100–4.

Liston, R., *Terrorism* (New York: Thomas Nelson Inc., 1977).

Livingston, M.H. (ed.), *International Terrorism in the Contemporary World* (Westport, Connecticut: Greenwood Press, 1978).

Lomas, O.G., 'The executive and the anti-terrorist legislation of 1939', *Public Law,* 1980 (Spring) 16–33.

Lowry, D.R., 'Terrorism and human rights: counter-insurgency and necessity at common law', *Notre Dame Lawyer,* 1977, *53*, 49–89.

Lowry, D.R., 'Draconian powers: the new British approach to pretrial detention of suspected terrorists', *Columbia Human Rights Law Review,* 1977, *9*(1), 185–222.

McGuire, E.P., 'The terrorist and the corporation', *Across the Board,* May 1977, *14*(5), 11–19.

Mack, A., 'Terrorism and the left', *Arena,* 1978, No. 51, 18–31.

Maher, G.F., *Hostage – A Police Approach to a Contemporary Crisis* (Springfield, Illinois: Charles C. Thomas, 1977).

Maher, G.F., 'Organizing a team for hostage negotiation', *The Police Chief,* 1976, *43*(6), 61–2.

Mallison, W.T. Jr., and Mallison, S.V., 'The concept of public purpose terror in international law: doctrines and sanctions to reduce the destruction of human and material values', *Howard Law Journal,* 1973, *18*, 12–28.

Mallison, W.T., and Mallison, S.V., 'The juridicial status of irregular combatants under the international humanitarian law of armed conflict', *Case Western Reserve Journal of International Law*, 1977, *9*, 39–78.

Marighela, C., *Urban Guerrilla Minimanual* (Vancouver. Pulp Press, 1974).

Mark, R., *Report to the Minister for Administrative Services on the Organisation of Police Resources in the Commonwealth Area and Other Related Matters* (Canberra: Australian Government Publishing Service, 1978).

May, W.F., 'Terrorism as strategy and ecstasy', *Social Research*, 1974, *41*, 277–98.

Meguire, P.G., and Kramer, J.J., *Psychological Deterrents to Nuclear Theft: A Preliminary Literature Review and Bibliography* (Washington, DC: National Bureau of Standards, US Department of Commerce, 1976).

Miller, A.H., 'Negotiations for hostages: implications from the police experience', *Terrorism*, 1978, *1*(2), 125–46.

Miller, A.H., 'Terrorism and government policy', *Chitty's Law Journal*, 1979, *27*(2), 44–9.

Miron, M.S., and Douglas, J.E., 'Threat analysis – the psycholinguistic approach', *FBI Law Enforcement Bulletin*, 1979, *48*(9), 5–9.

Miron, M.S., and Goldstein, A.P., *Hostage*, (Kalamazoo, Michigan: Behaviordelia, Inc., 1978).

Moore, K.C., *Airport, Aircraft and Airline Security* (Los Angeles: Security World Publishing Co., 1976).

O'Brien, W.V., 'The jus in bello in revolutionary war and counterinsurgency', *Virginia Journal of International Law*, 1978, *18*(2), 193–242.

Ochberg, F., 'The victim of terrorism: psychiatric considerations', *Terrorism: An International Journal*, 1978, *1*(2), 147–68.

Olin, W.R., 'An evaluation of the United States counter-terrorism response capability', *The Police Chief*, 1979, *46*(6), 34–8.

Oppenheimer, M., 'The criminalization of political dissent in the Federal Republic of Germany', *Contemporary Crisis*, 1978, *2*(1), 97–103.

Owen, C.C.L.O., 'The politics of futility', *RUSI*, 1978, *123*, 20–4.

Parry, A., *Terrorism from Robespierre to Arafat* (New York: The Vanguard Press, 1976).

Paust, J.J., 'International law and control of the media: terror, repression and the alternatives', *Indiana Law Journal*, 1978, *53*, 621–77.

Pedersen, F.C., 'Controlling international terrorism: an analysis of unilateral force and proposals for multilateral cooperation', *The University of Toledo Law Review*, 1976, *8*(1), 209–50.

Powitzky, R.J., 'The use and misuse of psychologists in a hostage situation', *The Police Chief*, 1979, *46*(6), 30–3.

Raeburn, N.S., 'The Mark Report', *Pacific Defence Reporter*, 1978, *4*(11), 6–10.

Raeburn, N.S., 'The legal implications in counter terrorist operations', *Pacific Defence Reporter*, 1978, *4*(10), 34–6.

Rasch, W., 'Psychological dimensions of political terrorism in the Federal Republic of Germany', *International Journal of Law and Psychiatry*, 1979, *2*, 79–85.

Reiner, R., 'Forces of disorder: How the police control "riots" ', *New Society*, 1980, *52*(914), 51–4.

Ronchey, A., 'Terror in Italy, between red and black', *Dissent*, 1978, *25*(2), 150–6.

Rootes, C., 'Living with terrorism', *Social Alternatives*, 1980, *1*(6/7)3, 46–9.

Royal United Services Institute for Defence Studies, *The Role of the Armed Forces in Peacekeeping in the 1970's* (London: Royal United Services Institute for Defence Studies, 1973).

Sargant, W., 'Stress: making friends of enemies', *International Journal of Offender Therapy and Comparative Criminology*, 1980, *24*(1), 84–5.

Schornhorst, F.T., 'The lawyer and the terrorist: another ethical dilemma', *Indiana Law Journal*, 1977–78, *53*(4), 679–702.

Scott, P.D., 'A psychiatrist's cooperation with the police', *The Police Journal*, 1977, *XLX*(1), 6–22.

Shaw, J., Gueritz, E.F., and Younger, A.E. (eds.), *Ten Years of Terrorism – Collected Views* (New York: Crane, Russak and Company, Inc., 1979).

Shultz, R., 'A study of the selective use of political terrorism in the process of revolutionary warfare, (The N.L.F. of South Vietnam)', *International Behavioral Scientist*, 1976, *8*, 43–77.

Shultz, R., 'The limits of terrorism in insurgency warfare: the case of the Viet Cong', *Polity*, 1978, *11*(1), 67–91.

Shultz, R., 'Conceptualizing political terrorism', *Journal of International Affairs*, 1978, *32*(1), 7–15.

Silverstein, M.E., 'Emergency medical preparedness', *Terrorism: An International Journal*, 1977, *1*(1), 51–69.

Sims, A.C.P., White, A.C., and Murphy, T., 'Aftermath neurosis: psychological sequelae of the Birmingham bombings in victims not seriously injured', *Medicine, Science and the Law*, 1979, *19*(2), 78–81.

Sigelman, L., and Simpson, M., 'A cross-national test of the linkage between economic inequality and political violence', *Journal of Conflict Resolution*, 1977, *21*(1), 105–28.

Sloan, S., 'International terrorism: academic quest, operational art and policy implications', *Journal of International Affairs*, 1978, *32*(1), 1–5.

Sloan, S. and Kearney, R., 'An analysis of a simulated terrorist incident', *The Police Chief*, 1977, *44*(6), 57–9.

Sloan, S., Kearney, R., and Wise, C., 'Learning about terrorism: analysis, simulations and future directions', *Terrorism: An International Journal*, 1978, *1*(3/4), 315–29.

Smiaklek, J.E., and Spitz, W.U., 'Short-range ammunition – a possible anti-hijacking device', *Journal of Forensic Sciences*, 1976, *21*(4), 856–61.

Snyder, D., 'Collective violence – a research agenda and some strategic considerations', *Journal of Conflict Resolution*, 1978, *22*(3), 499–534.

Stohl, M. (ed.), *The Politics of Terror: A Reader in Theory and Practice* (New York: Marcel Dekker, 1979).

Stratton, J.G., 'The terrorist act of hostage-taking: a view of violence and the perpetrators', *Journal of Police Science and Administration*, 1978, *6*(1), 1–9.

Stratton, J.G., 'The terrorist act of hostage-taking: considerations for law enforcement', *Journal of Police Science and Administration*, 1978, *6*(2), 123–34.

Street, H., 'The Prevention of Terrorism (Temporary Provisions) Act 1974', *The Criminal Law Review*, 1975, 192–9.

Strentz, T., 'Law enforcement policy and ego defenses of the hostage', *FBI Law Enforcement Bulletin*, 1979, *48*(4), 2–12.

Sunday Times Insight Team, *Siege!* (London: Hamlyn, 1980).

Suter, K., 'What is terrorism?', *British Society Review*, December 1977, 66–72.

Tafoya, W.L., 'Special weapons and tactics', *The Police Chief*, 1975, *42*(7), 70–4.

Terry, H.A., 'Television and terrorism: professionalism not quite the answer',

Indiana Law Journal, 53(4), 745–7.

Tittmar, H.G., 'Crowd control: a comparative viewpoint', *RUSI*, December 1979, 57–60.

Trent, D.M., 'A national policy to combat terrorism', *Policy Review*, 1979, *9*, Summer, 1–13.

United States. National Advisory Committee on Criminal Justice Standards and Goals. *Disorders and Terrorism* (Report of the Task Force on Disorders and Terrorism) (Washington, DC: US Department of Justice, 1976).

Wardlaw, G., 'Terrorism and para-military forces', *Pacific Defence Reporter*, 1980, *7*(1), 46–51.

Waterman, D.A., and Jenkins, B.M., *Heuristic Modelling Using Rule-Based Computer Systems* (Santa Monica, Calif.: Rand Corporation, 1977).

Watson, F.M., *Political Terrorism: The Threat and the Response* (New York: Robert B. Luce Co., Inc., 1976).

Weeks, A.L., 'Terrorism: the deadly tradition', *Freedom at Issue*, 1978, May–June No. 46, 3–11.

Wilkinson, P., *Political Terrorism* (London: Macmillan, 1974).

Wilkinson, P., *Terrorism and the Liberal State* (London: Macmillan, 1977).

Wilkinson, P., *The New Fascists* (London: Grant McIntyre, 1981).

Wilkinson, P., (ed.), *British Perspectives on Terrorism* (London: George Allen & Unwin, 1981).

Wilkinson, P., 'Terrorism: The international response', *The World Today*, 1978, *34*(1), 5–13.

Wilkinson, P., 'Terrorism: international dimensions – answering the challenge', *Conflict Studies*, No. 113, November 1979.

Wilkinson, P., 'After Tehran', *Conflict Quarterly,* 1981, *1*(4), 5–14.

Wilson, J.S., 'Modern siege warfare', *The Medico-Legal Journal*, 1977, *45*(4), 119–34.

Wise, C., and Sloan, S., 'Countering terrorism: the U.S. and Israeli approach', *Middle East Review*, 1977, *9*(3), 55–9.

Wohlstetter, R., 'Terror on a grand scale', *Survival*, 1976, *XVIII*(3), 98–104.

Wolf, J.B., 'Terrorist manipulation of the democratic process', *The Police Journal*, 1975, *XLVIII*(2), 102–12.

Wolf, J.B., 'Police intelligence: focus for counter-terrorist operations', *The Police Journal*, 1976, *XLIX*(1), 19–27.

Wolf, J.B., 'An analytical framework for the study and control of agitational terrorism', *The Police Journal*, 1976, *XLIX*(3), 165–71.

Wolf, J.B., 'Urban terrorist operations', *The Police Journal*, 1976, *XLIX*(4), 277–84.

Wolf, J.B., 'A global terrorist condition – its incipient stage', *The Police Journal*, 1977, *L*, 328–39.

Wolf, J.B., 'Prisons, courts and terrorism: the American and West German experience', *The Police Journal*, 1977, *LI*(3), 221–30.

Wolf, J.B., 'Organization and management practices of urban terrorist groups', *Terrorism: An International Journal*, 1978, *1*(2), 169–86.

Wolf, J.B., 'Anti-terrorism: operations and controls in a free society', *Police Studies*, 1978, *1*(3), 35–41.

Woods, C., 'Problems of international terrorism', *Australian Journal of Forensic Sciences*, 1979/1980, *12*(2/3), 67–74.

Young, R., 'Revolutionary terrorism, crime and morality', *Social Theory and Practice*, 1977, *4*(3), 287–302.

Index

218   *Index*